Hiking Iowa

Help Us Keep This Guide Up to Date

Every effort has been made by the author and editors to make this guide as accurate and use-ful as possible. However, many things can change after a guide is published—trails are rerouted, regulations change, techniques evolve, facilities come under new management, etc.

We would love to hear from you concerning your experiences with this guide and how you feel it could be improved and kept up to date. While we may not be able to respond to all comments and suggestions, we'll take them to heart, and we'll also make certain to share them with the author. Please send your comments and suggestions to the following address:

The Globe Pequot Press
Reader Response/Editorial Department
P.O. Box 480
Guilford, CT   06437

Or you may e-mail us at:

editorial@GlobePequot.com

Thanks for your input, and happy trails!

Hiking Iowa

A Guide to Iowa's Greatest Hiking Adventures

Elizabeth Corcoran Hill

FALCONGUIDES ®

GUILFORD, CONNECTICUT
HELENA, MONTANA
AN IMPRINT OF THE GLOBE PEQUOT PRESS

FALCONGUIDES®

Copyright © 2005 Morris Book Publishing, LLC

All interior photos by the author.
Maps by XNR Productions © Morris Book Publishing, LLC

Library of Congress Cataloging-in-Publication Data
Hill, Elizabeth, 1981-
   Hiking Iowa / Elizabeth Hill and Kate Corcoran.—
   1st ed.
      p. cm. — (A Falcon guide)
   ISBN 978-0-7627-2240-2
   1. Hiking—Iowa—Guidebooks. 2. Iowa—Guidebooks. I. Corcoran, Kate. II. Title. III. Series

GV191.42.I8H55 2005
796.51'09777—dc22   2005045968

Printed in the United States of America
First Edition/Fifth Printing

Contents

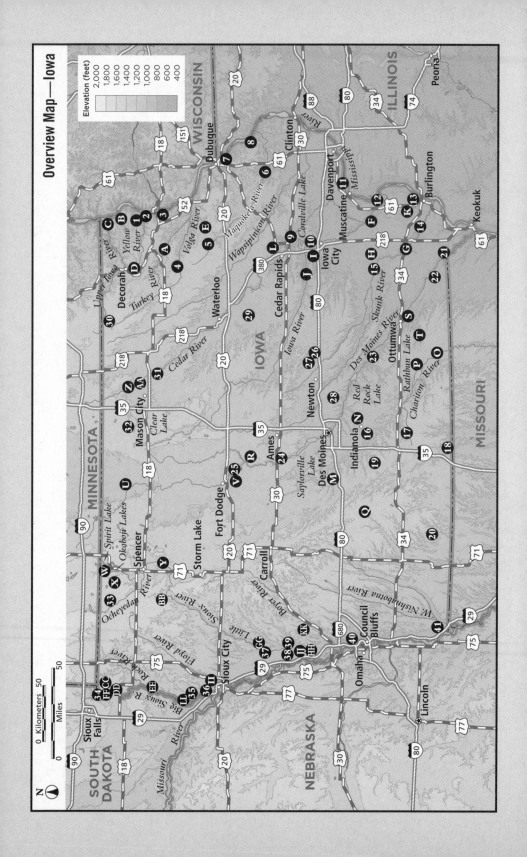

Overview Map—Iowa

Acknowledgments

First in order is a big thanks to the weather, which provided one of the coolest summers on record for my travels. Hiking around the state during one of the scorchers of my youth would have been an impossible feat for these legs.

My mother, Kate Corcoran, selflessly dedicated herself to editing the entire book. She, together with my father, Lars Hill, and my brother, Alexander Hill, supported me every step of the way. Through their friendship, inspiration, and many kindnesses, Joanna, Megan, and Tom Corcoran provided yet another familial base from which I could jump.

My now somewhat distant mentors, Dr. Steven G. Herman and Dr. Nalini Nadkarni, taught me to find the eyes with which to see the land and words with which to tell its stories. With wisdom endowed by her dear grandfather and some all her own, Jessica Herman, matriarch of the Tiger Family, taught me that to go outside is to play in the fields of the gods.

The staff of all ninety-nine county conservation boards, the Iowa Department of Natural Resources, the U.S. Fish and Wildlife Service, and the National Park Service made every attempt to answer all my questions. I don't suppose a place could ask for more earnestly dedicated people working to preserve remarkable places. Mark Edwards, Connie Mutel, John Pearson, Jean Prior, Tom Rosburg, and Larry Stone each took time out of their busy days to speak with me. Their generous willingness to share their knowledge was inspiring and made me look harder into the intricacies of this land I adore. Showing the highest levels of technical and technological expertise, Jodi, Dean, and Molly Langstaff, as well as Michael Close and Gary McGlumphry, each individually came to my rescue.

A loving shout-out to respected and appreciated friends who accompanied me on various travels of abundant fun and learning: Bryce, Billy, Seth, Adam, Alyson, and Bijou. The company of two very special dogs, Ruby and George, was also vital to days spent walking and running over hills and through valleys. Come to think of it, each person that I met during the six months of traveling back roads and hiking trails provided gifts of friendship and insight, a markedly Iowan trait. As well, the greater community of Iowa City friends and family has encouraged and helped me to develop as a person since I moved here nineteen years ago. I doubt that anyone could ever be raised by a more apt and gracious group of people. And, with whom else but dearest Shanti could I have spent countless hours exploring the Johnson County wilderness?

Thank you to Jeannie Hanson, and to my editors, Scott Adams, Mimi Egan, and Paulette Baker, for understanding the obstacles faced by an inexperienced, twenty-three-year-old writer who likes to walk around and learn about things that grow and fly.

Lastly, I thank the hills that I love. Wander I must, but to you, gorgeous hills of my Iowa home, I will always return.

About the Author

Elizabeth Hill wasn't born in Iowa, but she was raised here. Growing up in Iowa City, she learned to love the hills of southeast Iowa but like most Iowa kids, dreamed of far-away places. She spent summers climbing Colorado's Rocky Mountains; lived in rural northern Sweden, her father's birthplace; and traveled around the North American continent.

More recently Elizabeth attended the Evergreen State College in Olympia, Washington, for two years and studied temperate rain forests and shrub-steppe ecology. In the Pacific Northwest she found human and nonhuman mentors who helped her cultivate a deep love and commitment to learning about and preserving wild places. Amid the old-growth rain forest she realized what Iowa had taught her of subtle beauty and decided to come home to learn more about it. For as much as climbing tall trees, wandering amid sagebrush, and identifying nonvascular plants made her heart sing, she had to return to the prairies of her beloved Iowa.

Elizabeth spent the spring and summer of 2004 traveling the state and hiking more than 350 miles. She will finish her bachelor of science degree at Iowa's Drake University. *Hiking Iowa* is her first book, and she hopes it will encourage more people to go on more walks.

Introduction

"Let's go hiking in Iowa."

"Really . . . where?"

That's the reaction most people have to the suggestion they might enjoy walking around our presumably flat state. Their impression of Iowa is one founded on underestimation of its landscape. Taught to judge scenic beauty by the grandeur and enormity of landforms, they have no gauge to measure the subtle beauty of Iowa.

Granted, the state has no Rocky or Smoky Mountains, no raging coastlines or basalt-framed coulees, and frighteningly little of its native ecosystems. What it does have, though, are fragments of what once was, an ecological puzzle with a bunch of missing pieces. When still intact, the images captured in the puzzle must have been some of the most splendid scenes a person could conceive.

Pursuit of Iowa's missing pieces, or fragments of them, involves a change in attitude. It means adopting a new interpretation of seasons, another way to judge wilderness and beauty, and then using those new senses to seek out hidden treasures. The best way to explore any terrain is on foot, and the state's many parks, forests, preserves, and recreation areas virtually beg your legs to get busy.

In order to understand the visible landscape—all that appears above the crust of the earth, it's best to start by understanding what lies beneath. When referring to Iowa's general placement, geologists say it's part of the Stable Interior; laypeople often call it Flat as a Pancake. Both representations are revealing, for Stable Interior was derived from the relatively undisturbed sedimentary bedrock that lies horizontally across the region. Moreover, Iowa is anything but flat, with glacial till and loess atop its bedrock that have been sculpted into hills and valleys. Even though we see the impact of our state's glacial history every day, it tells only the last several million years of the story. It's best to start earlier, before the limestone pancakes were deposited.

What we know of Precambrian Iowa comes directly from core and well drilling, for our geologic basement is made up primarily of banded metamorphic and igneous rocks that lie several miles beneath the earth's surface. Beginning more than two billion years ago, the underlying metamorphic rocks were formed below a massive belt or belts of mountains, which were at some point leveled by erosion. Because the successive creation of mountains usually forms along active tectonic plate boundaries, it's thought that Iowa was once a hotbed of crustal movement.

Some of the igneous rocks, the basalts and granites, were deposited about 1.1 million years ago, when central North America's crust was spread apart by magma pushing to the surface. The Midcontinent Rift System once stretched from Lake Superior to Kansas, crossing through Iowa in a zone of volcanic activity. This gaping tear was later filled in by lakes similar to those in the Great Rift Valley of eastern Africa, followed by deposits of red-colored sand and mud known as red clastics.

From roughly 550 to 250 million years ago, Paleozoic Iowa was located close to the equator, as the coastline of a huge shallow sea migrated back and forth over the Midwest. Limestone, dolomite, shale, and sandstone were deposited either as mud on the seafloor or sand on coasts and river deltas; within these rocks are fossils of both marine and terrestrial organisms. Ordovician (475 to 430 million years ago) limestone has preserved fossils of brachiopods, bryozoa, crinoids, snails, and nautiloid cephalopods, with the most impressive outcrops found in northeast Iowa. Brachiopods, corals, crinoids, and early fish dominate exposures in the 375-million-year-old bedrock of the Devonian Fossil Gorge north of Iowa City.

As the oceans and inland seas advanced and retreated, Iowa was situated above sea level during several long periods. Within that span, 80 million years during the Mesozoic era (230 to 65 million years ago) are missing from our rock record. The Permian strata that make up the rim of the Grand Canyon and the Triassic exposures of the Petrified Forest in Arizona are all but missing from underneath us. Directly after the erosion of those layers, sandstone, shale, and lignite were deposited when Cretaceous inland seas covered the state. North of Sioux City in western Iowa, a gap of 1.5 billion years exists where Cretaceous rocks, our youngest, lie directly atop the state's oldest exposed rocks, Sioux quartzite.

During the nearly 600 million years of the marine invasion of Iowa, the continent was slowly inching northward, setting the stage for the advance of water once again, except this time in the form of the glaciers' icy grip. Beginning roughly 2.5 million years ago, because of the earth's wobbling axis or variations in the energy of the sun, an uncountable series of advances and retreats of ice sheets slowly began its tenure here. Three distinct periods of glaciation, the Pre-Illinoian (500,000 to 2,500,000 years ago), Illinoian (300,000 to 130,000 years ago), and Wisconsinan (30,000 to 10,500 years ago) gouged out and removed tremendous amounts of underlying bedrock, while the glacial till and loess that we walk on today were left behind. North-central Iowa was occupied by the Des Moines Lobe, the last ice sheet to retreat from Iowa some 10,000 years ago. Evidence of the landscape's veritable youth lies in its large glacial lakes—Spirit Lake, Lake Okoboji, and Clear Lake—and the pothole marshes that dot areas near them.

Rising global temperatures and the subsequent receding of glaciers brought enormous amounts of meltwater that thundered through our river valleys, widening and deepening them while also creating entirely new drainage networks. Loess was brought from the north by way of the rivers, deposited on the banks, and lifted by the wind to blanket most of Iowa. Along the Missouri River in western Iowa lie the deepest deposits of loess in the Western Hemisphere.

Because of the excessively long timeline behind and below us and the relatively short lives we live, our human eyes see very minute geologic changes: the flux of a shifting river channel, the leaching of minerals and nutrients from topsoil, erosion and gully creation from heavy rainfall, and the removal of groundwater from our ancient aquifers.

Weather

The four distinct seasons that annually grace Iowa are wonderfully individual expressions of its placement in the Upper Midwest. Many Iowans are concerned with weather because of their agricultural pursuits, as they try to forecast, bet, or conjure the dates of the first fall and final spring frosts, which delineate the growing season. Our winters and summers contrast starkly, and while spring and fall have their own eye-opening differences, they serve mainly as transitions between very cold and very hot temperatures. Prairie vegetation tends to "green up late," and though certain plants bloom in early spring, wildflower forays are best done during the heat of the summer, as long as you wear a large sunhat and carry a supply of water. The summer months, June to August, tend to be blisteringly hot and humid. Luckily, 70 percent of our annual precipitation falls between April and September. Once temperatures hit more than 100 degrees, your only hope is for a thunderstorm with its whipping winds and cooling rain. Normally you can't "get caught" unintentionally in these storms, for their thunderheads—dark rolling cumulonimbus clouds—are always visible as they approach. However, should the sky turn an eerie purplish-green cast, you'll want to find a basement to huddle in as soon as possible. Between twenty and a hundred tornadoes and countless funnel clouds historically roll through Iowa each year, sometimes accompanied by violent hailstorms. With wind speeds of 100 to 500 miles per hour, they can cause destruction of property, injury, and even death.

As summer comes to an end and the cool of autumn arrives, prairie grasses turn rich gold and auburn, and changing leaves swirl into a spectrum of orange, amber, russet, and garnet. Although fall is beautiful everywhere in the state, northeast Iowa's forested bluffs offer an especially gorgeous palette of autumnal splendor. Hiking trips during fall usually elicit a strong feeling of nostalgia, causing many to love autumn in a special way. When crisp fall breezes turn into icy northwesterly winds, winter has only begun. Snow constitutes only 10 percent of our annual precipitation but can blanket the state in a fluffy dreamland or fall on an ice-encrusted, subzero polarscape. Estherville's local newspaper, the *Northern Vindicator,* claims to have first used the term "blizzard" to describe one hellacious snowstorm that blew through Emmet County in March 1870. Many of us keep our fingers crossed for as much snow as the sky will give, for cross-country skiing along the trails you hike during summer is the best way to spend winter.

As is the case throughout most of the northern temperate zone, spring's arrival is welcomed when it rolls around. Warming temperatures bring an array of spring wildflowers that bloom in the forests from April to June. Migratory birds begin heading north during this time, and a May morning spent looking at trout lilies and wood warblers is a real treat. Hiking is at its best during this not-too-hot, not-too-cold interval and should be enjoyed to the maximum extent.

Flora and Fauna

Iowa's lowest point (480 feet) lies in its southeast corner, which consequently receives more rainfall than anywhere else in the state. In the rising plains of the northwest corner is our high point (1,670 feet), situated in the driest part of the state. It's no mystery, then, that forests dominate the southeast, while prairie once covered the northwest.

Iowa contains the westernmost extent of the deciduous forests of the East and the easternmost margin of the great plains of the West and before settlement was the heart of the tallgrass prairie. When Euro-American settlers arrived, three predominant ecotypes covered the state: about 80 percent prairie, 12 percent forest, and 8 to 11 percent wetland. The edges of these biomes were somewhat hard to define—wet hill prairies, marshy openings in forest, and oak savannas/grasslands were often interspersed.

The tallgrass prairies of Iowa are composed of three main plant families—*Poaceae* (grasses), *Asteraceae* (asters, or composites), and *Fabaceae* (legumes), with hundreds of others, from moonworts to orchids, filling in the dense maze of vegetation. Grassland birds and butterflies are entirely dependent on prairie grasses and wildflowers for food, nesting material, and breeding grounds. Goat prairies, which are forest openings or rock outcrops covered in prairie vegetation, are common in the eastern part of the state, as are sand prairies, which support prickly pear cactus, a surprising sight in Iowa to most people.

The deciduous forests of the Northeast begin to peter out in density as one crosses the Mississippi River into Iowa. Our woodlands, most widespread in the eastern part of the state, are for the most part undergoing a large-scale succession after having been logged entirely during the 1800s. Upland forests are dominated by oaks and hickories, while silver maple, basswood, and green ash grow in moist lowland sites. Twenty-one species of oaks live in Iowa and provide food and shelter for more than seventy forest-associated animals. Riparian corridors are framed by willows, cottonwoods, and sycamores, which provide nesting habitat for many bird species, from wood warblers to bald eagles and great blue herons.

Due to the karst topography of the northeast corner, many holdovers from colder, glacial times are present. The most remarkable is the Iowa Pleistocene snail, a smaller-than-a-shirt-button snail thought to have been extinct for 10,000 years—until it was found eating birch leaves in northeast Iowa 25 years ago. Spring-fed trout streams meander through canyons dominated by balsam fir, eastern white pine, and yellow birch trees that grow over bunchberry and twinflower, plants with typically northern affinities.

Iowa's Loess Hills provide habitat for plants and animals typically found in western states: yucca, cowboy's delight, ten-petaled mentzelia, blue grosbeak, black-billed magpie, prairie rattlesnake, and prairie skink. During the past 150 years, these once prairie-covered hills have succumbed to forest invasion, and expanding woodlands have pushed the ranges of some forest birds northward. In contrast, populations of many prairie and savanna species have declined sharply and in some cases have disappeared altogether.

During spring and fall, the Mississippi and Missouri Rivers serve as flyways for extraordinary numbers of migratory birds. Many of them—ducks and geese, shorebirds, and songbirds—stay to nest. The backwaters, sloughs, and islands in the Upper Mississippi River National Fish and Wildlife Refuge are veritable treasure troves of diverse freshwater and riparian organisms.

Recent glaciation of the north-central lobe left vast pothole marshes that serve as breeding grounds for countless thousands of waterfowl, as well as homes for amphibians and unusual aquatic plants. Bogs and fens also dot the state, and growing in their calcium-rich seepages are some curious plants: grass of Parnassus, bull sedge, upright sedge, swamp saxifrage, sensitive fern, and fringed gentian. In one spot near the Minnesota border, you can even find a fen that features the carniverous sundew plant and a sphagnum moss mat.

Somehow, a large number of organisms manage to make their homes in fragmented young forests and croplands within the state. The "edge effect" has provided habitat for coyotes, white-tailed deer, and wild turkeys, whose populations are all soaring. Many species of birds tend to congregate around edges as well, and you'll be surprised at the diversity to be found in something as simple as a fencerow.

Public Land

Iowa has a total of seventy state parks, four major state forests, 340 state wildlife management areas, ninety state preserves, six national wildlife refuges, one national monument, two national historic trails, and one national historic site, in addition to hundreds of County Conservation Board parks. However, with more than 97 percent of its 56,276 square miles in private ownership, the percentage of publicly owned land is one of the lowest among the fifty states.

The mission of the Department of Natural Resources was molded by the vision of some of the state's most intrepid conservationists. Iowa's "dean" of conservation, Professor Thomas MacBride, once said, "The park shall set us free." He and his colleagues Louis Pammel and Bohumil Shimek, as well as other academics and naturalists, created the Iowa Conservation Association (ICA) in 1917, and by 1920 Backbone and Lacey-Keosauqua State Parks had already been dedicated. During the 1920s, Iowa's park system was one of the most progressive in the nation, and by 1926 it included thirty-three sites managed by the ICA.

Completed in 1933, the state's twenty-five-year conservation plan was drafted by many conservationists. Some of the more famous were J. N. "Ding" Darling, Margo Frankel, Ada Hayden, and J. G. Wyeth. The plan called for action on a number of issues, including preservation of prairie remnants, cleanup of polluted waterways, and conservation and restoration of habitat for wildlife. Iowa's state agencies have seen significant change since that earlier time, but the spirit of those revolutionary conservationists lives on in today's DNR staff.

In 1955 the Iowa legislature enacted a law allowing voters to establish county conservation boards, which were meant to reduce the stress on state and federal agencies and to provide local residents with the option to preserve land. Today, each of Iowa's ninety-nine counties has its own conservation board. Some hold large tracts of land, support nature centers, and even manage state parks and preserves; others care for small remnants or undeveloped parcels. Many county parks aren't as heavily used as state-owned land and boast hiking trails and free camping. The Iowa Association of County Conservation Boards publishes a park directory that can be ordered from the Web site, http://george.ecity.net/iaccb, which includes links to individual county conservation boards.

Map Legend

Symbol	Description	Symbol	Description
80	Interstate	⚠	Campground
30	U.S. highway	▲	Primitive Campground
2	State highway	○	City
L44	Other road	—	Dam
= = = = =	Unimproved road	≈	Falls
▬▬▬▬▬	Featured trail	•—•	Gate
- - - - - -	Other trail	⚒	Mine
••••🚲••••	Biking trail	🅿	Parking
••••🐎••••	Equestrian trail	⟩⟨	Pass
Lake	Lake	▲	Peak/elevation
Intermittent lake	Intermittent lake	🅰	Picnic area
Marsh/swamp	Marsh/swamp	▪	Point of interest
——	Stream	▮	Ranger Station
—·—	Intermittent stream	▫	Ruin/other site
♨	Amphitheater	▮	School
▦▦▦▦	Boardwalk	⊏	Shelter
⇒	Boat ramp	19	Signpost/trail locator
⨝	Bridge	🚶	Trailhead
⋀	Cave entrance	❓	Visitor information
⬆	Lodge/Cabin	👁	View Point

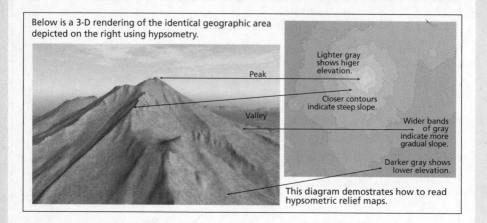

Below is a 3-D rendering of the identical geographic area depicted on the right using hypsometry.

Peak

Valley

Lighter gray shows higer elevation.

Closer contours indicate steep slope.

Wider bands of gray indicate more gradual slope.

Darker gray shows lower elevation.

This diagram demostrates how to read hypsometric relief maps.

A Note about the Maps A technique called hypsometric tinting has been used on the maps to separate terrain into elevation zones using varying shades of gray. Each gray tone represents an elevation range, which is shown on the scale bar that appears with every map. The darker tones are lower elevation, and the lighter grays are higher elevation. These maps will give you a good idea of elevation gain and loss for each hike and the slope of a terrain. For example, the narrower and more closely spaced the bands of grays, the steeper the terrain; wider bands of gray indicate areas of more gradual slope.

Paleozoic Plateau

n her book *Landforms of Iowa*, geologist Jean Prior observed that, "… if you had to divide Iowa into two different regions, one would be the extreme northeast corner and the other would be the rest of the state." The Paleozoic Plateau, as this area is known, is bound by the Minnesota state line to the north, the Mississippi River to the east, and a landform called the Silurian escarpment to the west and south. Whereas most of Iowa is covered by a thick blanket of loess and glacial till, northeast Iowa's bedrock is much closer to the surface, dominating the landscape. Spring-fed streams meander through narrow canyons framed by the towering blocky cliffs of Paleozoic strata—the limestones, dolomites, sandstones, and shales deposited 300 to 550 million years ago. Sinkholes, ice caves, and algific (cold-air) slopes can be found, characteristic of the karst topography of the area. This is the one truly rugged part of the state and the most densely forested. It's home to many boreal plant species on their southernmost margin and the only place in the state to find native populations of brook trout.

Until quite recently, the eastern part of Iowa's Paleozoic Plateau was once lumped with parts of southwestern Wisconsin, southeast Minnesota, and northwest Illinois known as the "Driftless Area." This name represents the area's position as a supposedly unglaciated island within the ice-scoured Midwest. Indeed, Iowa's section of the island was bypassed by the glaciers of recent times. However, 500,000-year-old Pre-Illinoian glacial drift has been found on isolated ridgetops. Although missed by recent glaciers, the Paleozoic Plateau was affected by their proximity. Ancient streams slowly eroded the narrow canyons, and glacial meltwater thundered through drainages, carving its way to the Mississippi River. Today the entrenched valleys of the Volga, Turkey, Yellow, and Upper Iowa Rivers are some of the most scenic and heavily canoed waterways in Iowa.

Almost all the parks in the Paleozoic Plateau are located within the labyrinth of hidden valleys. Pikes Peak State Park is located on the tallest bluff overlooking the entire length of the Mississippi River. Driving north on the Great River Road, you'll find Effigy Mounds National Monument, which harbors the largest congregation of bird- and bear-shaped mounds in Iowa, sculpted 1,400 to 750 years ago by hunter-gatherer peoples who lived along the Mississippi River and its major tributaries. Yellow River State Forest—Paint Creek Unit is home to the Backpack Trail, 25 miles of loop trails that wind through the valleys and bluffs overlooking the Big and Little Paint Creeks. The Maquoketa River's wanderings have carved a narrow 0.25-mile-long ridge from which Backbone State Park got its name. The dense forests and wide floodplains of Frog Hollow Creek and the Volga River are protected in the Volga River State Recreation Area, with 17 miles of multiuse trails. Maquoketa Caves State Park encompasses the most concentrated cave system in Iowa, a treat for spelunkers and a home to the endangered Indiana bat. Mines of Spain State Recreation Area, just south of Dubuque, encompasses the first white settlement in Iowa and the grave of Julien Dubuque, for whom the town was named. Bellevue State Park is located on bluffs overlooking the Mississippi and has the largest planted butterfly garden in the state.

Besides hiking the bluffs and canoeing the rivers, driving on the scenic byways of northeast Iowa is another great way to meet the landscape. The Great River Road, part of a ten-state scenic byway, follows the Mississippi River. The River Bluffs Scenic Byway traverses Clayton and Fayette Counties, and the Driftless Area Scenic Byway passes through Alamakee County.

1 Yellow River State Forest–Paint Creek Unit

When you tell Iowa outdoor-lovers you're going backpacking in the state, most assume your destination is Yellow River State Forest. With 25 miles of trails that wind through deep river valleys and over huge bluffs, happen upon overlooks with stunning vistas, and stop along the way at four "backcountry" campsites, it's truly the place for a wilderness experience in Iowa.

Distance: 25-mile trail system

Approximate hiking time: Day hike or long weekend

Total elevation gain: Varies with trails selected

Trail surface: Dirt paths and some road-hiking

Seasons: Year-round

Trail users: Hikers, mountain bikers, equestrians

Canine compatability: Dogs permitted on leash

Hazards: Poison ivy, ticks

Land status: State forest

Nearest towns: Harpers Ferry, Marquette

Fees and permits: Backcountry campsites are free; modern campsites are $9.00 per night during summer, $6.00 per night off-season.

Schedule: Heavily used by backpackers in spring and fall, by equestrians during summer. Cross-country skiing is allowed on many of the trails during winter.

Maps: USGS quad: Harpers Ferry; topo maps available at headquarters

Trail contact: Yellow River State Forest, 729 State Forest Road, Harpers Ferry, IA 52146; robert.honeywell@dnr.state.ia.us

Finding the trailhead: From junction of County Road X52 and County Road X42 in Harpers Ferry, drive 1.75 miles west on CR X42. Turn left (southeast) onto Forest Road B25 for 2 miles. The backpack trail trailhead is on the west end of the unit at Yellow River Headquarters. *DeLorme: Iowa Atlas and Gazetteer:* Page 23 F7–8

The Hike

The general view of Iowa is that it's a flat expanse of cornfield stretching as far as the eye can see. While agriculture does encompass many millions of acres of land in the state, Yellow River State Forest doesn't fit the stereotypical Iowan landscape (although you will encounter food plots in which corn is grown). The Paint Creek Unit, where the Backpack Trail is located, is dominated by rugged forest-covered bluffs that you can satisfyingly walk up, over, and around for days on end.

The best thing to come equipped with is an open mind. If you've spent time backpacking outside Iowa, you may be somewhat disappointed by our so-called wilderness area. You can hear cows mooing, farm dogs barking, and cars chugging from anywhere in the forest, but it's still worth it. Make up for the unwanted noise by catching a brown trout in Little Paint Creek (stocked weekly), collecting a handful of chanterelles (summer-fall fruiting), and whistling your way up to Heffern's Hill campsite, where you can cook your dinner over a fire.

THE BIG CHILL One common trait of the entire Driftless Area (glaciated or not) is the presence of algific (*al-ji-fick*) talus slopes, which provide habitat for some of the most curious organisms in Iowa's biotic community. In spring fractures and joints in the sedimentary bedrock are infiltrated by water, which freezes underground amid the cold rocks. Air is drawn down from the surface through sinkholes, flows over the ice-laden bedrock, and emerges from vents in the slopes. During summer average temperatures around these cold air vents hover from just above freezing to minus fifty-five degrees. In 1989 the Driftless Area National Wildlife Refuge was created to protect the algific slopes and two very special organisms. The Iowa Pleistocene snail (*Discus macclintocki*) was known only from fossil records. It was thought to be extinct for the past 10,000 years until a specimen was found in the collections of Bohumil Shimek, a professor at the University of Iowa from 1890 to 1937. In the late 1970s Shimek's collection sites were sought out, and live snails were found. The Iowa Pleistocene snail is listed as a federally endangered species. Thirty-seven colonies of the 0.25-inch snails have been found, and many are protected within the refuge. Northern wild monkshood (*Aconitum noveboracense*), a federally threatened member of the buttercup family, also grows on algific slopes, and 75 percent of the colonies in Iowa are protected. Other plants such as balsam fir, Canada yew, yellow birch, golden saxifrage, and a host of mosses are associated with these cool slopes and are not found anywhere else in Iowa.

In 1932 Civilian Conservation Corps (CCC) funds were used to purchase land at the mouth of the Yellow River on the Mississippi. In 1949 the land was transferred to the National Park Service to create Effigy Mounds National Monument. Land was bought along trout-bearing Big and Little Paint Creeks, and the CCC began planting and harvesting native and nonnative softwoods on the previously cultivated land in order to control soil erosion and provide lumber for projects on other state lands.

Though many plantations exist, native upland forests are anything but row crops: Dry south- and west-facing slopes are dominated by red, white, and bur oaks as well as shagbark hickory. North/east-facing slopes consist of sugar maple, basswood, white ash, and elm, with cottonwoods and willows surrounding the marshes and creeks. On the overlooks and rock outcrops, you'll find prairie plants like big and little bluestem, leadplant, Indian grass, and jeweled shooting star, an endangered species in Iowa.

Of the 25 miles of trail in the forest, 13 miles are also open to mountain bikers and equestrians, although I've frequently found bike tracks and horse scat on "hikers

◀ *Little Paint Creek is a trout angler's paradise.*

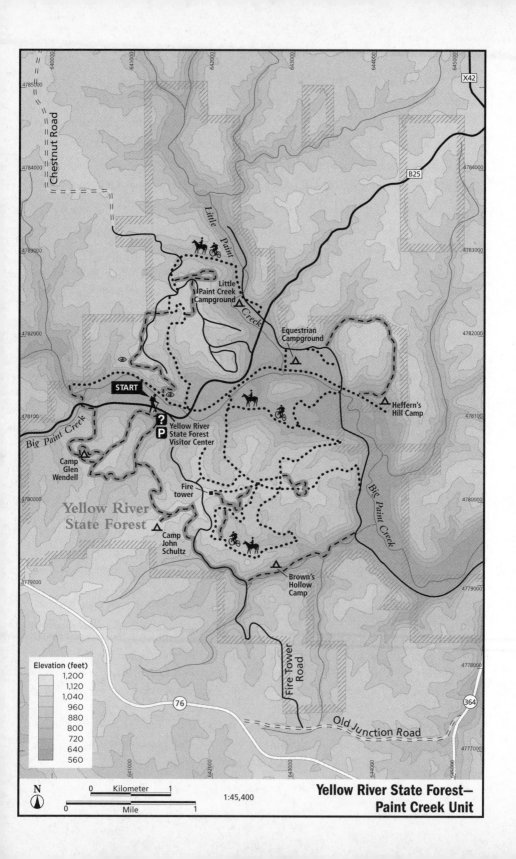

Yellow River State Forest—
Paint Creek Unit

only" trails. If you plan to spend several days at Yellow River, be prepared to do a little road-hiking—it'll be necessary to complete a full loop around the park. The quality of trails is varied because of their history and multiuse status. They've evolved from fire breaks built by the CCC in the 1930s and 1940s, and many have severe erosion problems caused by heavy horse and bicycle traffic. There are several steep sections, and some people gripe about the lack of switchbacks. I say, "What good is a backpacking trip without dramatic altitude fluctuations?"

Yellow River has four primitive campsites: Glen Wendell, John Shultz, Brown's Hollow, and Heffern's Hill. Each site is set in a spacious opening in the forest with at least one firepit, where ample wood has been cut and stacked for your modest usage. There are creeks near John Shultz and Brown's Hollow and a pond at Glen Wendell, but unless you have a pump filter, it's important to carry all the water you'll need for the trip. I always fill up at the spigot behind headquarters.

If you are planning a multiday trip within the forest, stop by the forest head-quarters on the west side of the unit before leaving. You'll be able to chat with the seasoned head forester and look at a larger map (or pick up one of their color-coded topographic maps). Day hikes at Yellow River State Forest are also quite satisfying, and the trail-running can be great as long as you avoid the heavily used equestrian trails. Ramble here for a few hours or a few days to fit your mood and your stamina.

Hike Information

Local Information
Waukon: www.waukon.com
Lansing: www.lansingiowa.com
Prairie du Chien, Wisconsin: (800) 732-1673, www.prairieduchien.org

Events/Attractions
Spook Cave, 13299 Spook Cave Road (between Monona and McGregor); (563) 873-2144
Museum of River History, 61 South Front Street, Lansing; (563) 538-4641
Seed Savers Exchange, 3094 North Winn Road, Decorah; (319) 382-5990, www.seedsavers.org
Laura Ingalls Wilder Park and Museum, 3603 236th Avenue, Burr Oak; (563) 735-5916, www.lauraingallswilder.us
Winneshiek Farmers' Market, City Park, Decorah; (319) 382-8123; May through October, Wednesday 3:00 to 6:00 P.M., Saturday 8:00 to 11:00 A.M.

Allamakee Farmers' Market, Allamakee County Fairgrounds, Waukon; (563) 568-6345; June through September, Monday 4:00 to 7:00 P.M.

Accommodations
Cedar Valley Lodge/Cabin, Harpers Ferry; (563) 586-2200
Houlihan House Bed & Breakfast, Harpers Ferry; (563) 586-2639 or (563) 586-2255
Ion Inn & The Natural Gait (camping and cabins at native seed nursery), Harpers Ferry; (800) 291-2143
Primitive and modern camping on-site at Yellow River State Forest

Restaurants
Mulligan Brothers Grill Pub, 610 Rossville Road, Waukon; (563) 568-5118
Gus and Tony's Pizza and Steak House, 508 West Main Street, Waukon; (563) 568-6015

2 Effigy Mounds National Monument—North and South Units

Traversing the bluffs that overlook the confluence of the Mississippi and Yellow Rivers provides one of the best cultural history lessons to be found in Iowa. After a day spent wandering among the earthen sculptures of bird and bear, you'll undoubtedly return. Of 10,000 mounds thought once to have existed in northeastern Iowa, 191 known mounds lie within the monument, 29 of which are shaped like animals. Two units include 13 miles of trails that navigate the forested bluffs, pass through prairie remnants and reconstructions, and pause at the overlooks where the remarkable mounds rest.

Distance: North Unit: 7.0 miles out and back; South Unit: 5.5 miles out and back
Approximate hiking time: 5 to 6 hours
Total elevation gain: North Unit: 1,781 feet; South Unit: 949 feet
Trail surface: North Unit: mulched forested footpath; South Unit: several sections of graveled roadbed
Seasons: Year-round
Trail users: Hikers
Canine compatability: Dogs permitted on leash

Hazards: Poison ivy, ticks, steep bluff edges
Land status: National monument, owned by National Park Service
Nearest towns: Marquette, McGregor
Fees and permits: $3.00 day-use fee; free tours led by NPS staff
Schedule: Open year-round during daylight hours
Map: USGS quad: Prairie du Chien
Trail contact: Effigy Mounds National Monument, 151 Highway 76, Harpers Ferry; (563) 873-3491; www.nps.gov/efmo

Finding the trailhead: From the junction of U.S. Highway 18 and Highway 76 in Marquette, take Highway 76 north. You'll see a DAY USE sign (South Unit) just before the road curves westward. Just after the curve you'll see the visitor center on the north side of the road. *DeLorme: Iowa Atlas and Gazetteer:* Page 23 G8

The Hike

The Effigy Moundbuilders inhabited the Upper Mississippi River Valley in Iowa, Illinois, Minnesota, and much of Wisconsin 750 to 1,400 years ago. This complex culture lived in campsites along river valleys in summer and in rock shelters on uplands during the harsh winters. They made lightweight, cord-impressed pottery; harvested a bounty of wild edibles; and hunted with bows and arrows. What they're best known for, though, are their complex religious ceremonies and burial traditions, expressed through the earthen effigy mounds they sculpted.

The first recorded evidence of the mounds was produced by Major Stephen Long's expedition to the Upper Mississippi River in 1817. Excavation of the

An old and gnarled eastern redcedar clings to Hanging Rock.

mounds began soon after, and many ideas surfaced as to their origin. A popular myth was that they had been built by the Lost Tribe of Israel, whose early, civilized society had been annihilated by migrating Indians. During Iowa's settlement that belief was used to justify extermination of the Indians, theft of their ceremonial objects, and destruction of the mounds.

Present-day understanding of Effigy Moundbuilder culture developed from the work of archaeologists and surveyors during the late 1800s and early 1900s. It is now

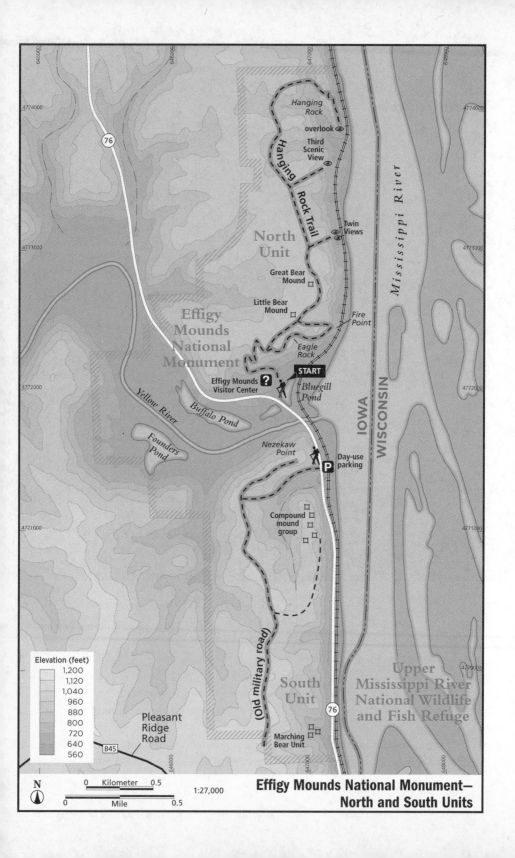

Effigy Mounds National Monument—
North and South Units

believed that the effigy mounds were constructed to honor the land's sustaining benevolence, as well as to venerate the Moundbuilders' relation to the cycles of life.

In 1949, in accordance with the American Antiquities Act of 1906, President Harry S Truman declared Iowa's Effigy Mounds a national monument. Because they constitute an ancient burial ground and are considered sacred by many, these lands must be treated with utmost respect and honor. *It is a federal criminal offense to alter a mound or to take any organic material from within the boundaries of the monument.*

In the North Unit, the Hanging Rock Trail departs from behind the visitor center, passes three 2,000-year-old conical mounds at the base of the bluff, and ascends in a series of switchbacks. At 0.5 mile, take a right onto the trail toward Fire Point. You'll pass Eagle Rock, where in winter bald eagles fly around their roosts at the mouth of the Yellow River. During summer look for leadplant, spiderwort, and blue-eyed grass on this sunny opening, or "goat prairie."

A half mile later you'll arrive at Fire Point, named for charred clay found during excavation of the mounds that sit atop this overlook. Follow the series of mounds west to 80-foot-long Little Bear Mound and 137-foot-long Great Bear Mound, the monument's largest.

On the way to Hanging Rock, you'll pass through prairie just before two eastbound trails lead to Twin Views and Third Scenic View. These overlook the backwaters of the 260-mile-long Upper Mississippi National Wildlife and Fish Refuge, a migratory corridor for birds and critical habitat for fish, mammals, and aquatic plants.

The trail drops steeply into several forested valleys and heads east toward the Mississippi River. At 3.5 miles, six conical mounds and several old bur oaks fringe the bluff's edge, a perfect spot for lunch. Continue 400 feet up and onto Hanging Rock, where you can catch your breath as you gaze across the Mississippi before returning to the visitor center.

Hike to the South Unit's Marching Bear Group and Nazekaw Point overlook by carefully walking 0.6 mile south along Highway 76 from the visitor center to the marked gate on the west side of the highway. For drivers, a parking lot is located across the highway. Step around the gate and walk up the steep road to the top of the bluff, where a 0.25-mile trail branches to the right (north) toward Nazekaw Point. Backtrack south and follow the old military road south along the ridge, passing through forests last logged in the 1940s.

At 1.25 miles you'll walk through a prairie remnant that erupts in color when cup plants, butterfly milkweed, blazing star, and several types of coneflowers are in bloom. A trail branches to the left toward an extraordinary feature: a 470-foot compound mound, and, with its 212-foot wingspan, the monument's largest bird effigy. Head back to the prairie remnant and walk south another 0.6 mile to the Marching Bear Group, also known as Walking Bear. This group of effigies—an astounding ten bears and three birds—is the largest group in the monument.

Miles and Directions

North Unit

0.0 Begin on the boardwalk that leaves from the north side of the visitor center.

0.2 Take a right onto the Eagle Rock–Fire Point Trail.

0.4 From Eagle Rock look down onto the Yellow River marshlands and Buffalo and Bluegill Ponds.

0.5 Fire Point's top layer is burned clay, which was carried to the ridgetop from the banks of the Mississippi. Here you can see Pikes Peak State Park to the south and Prairie du Chien across the river.

0.65 Pass trail to the right to view Little Bear mound, which has been outlined with rock for viewing purposes. Turn around and continue north.

0.75 Arrive at Great Bear just before passing through reconstructed prairie.

1.0 Turn off to Twin Views to the east, where an interpretive sign explains the bedrock that formed the bluff you're standing on.

1.3 Turn right (north) back onto the trail to Hanging Rock.

1.6 Turn off to Third Scenic View.

1.8 Third Scenic View; from here you have a perfect view of Hanging Rock to the north.

2.0 Turn right, back onto Hanging Rock Trail.

3.5 Arrive at Hanging Rock Mound Group and the outcrop itself. Turn around and walk back the way that you came, staying straight at the turnoff to Fire Point and Eagle Rock.

7.0 Arrive back at the visitor center.

NOTE: Be sure to stop in at the visitor center, where there is a museum with artifacts collected from excavations that stopped in the late 1970s. A large array of books for sale about the Mississippi River, American Indians, and traveling in Iowa.

South Unit

0.0 Start at the gate; walk through the gate and up the steep hill on dirt road.

0.6 At the top of the hill, turn right (south) onto the trail to Nezekaw Point.

1.0 Arrive at Nezekaw Point, overlooking the mouth of the Yellow River, and then backtrack to the top of the hill.

1.4 Arrive back at the road and continue straight (south) along the ridgetop's old military road.

2.1 Turn right (east) onto the trail that leads to the Compound Mound Group.

2.8 Arrive at the Compound Mound Group, and then backtrack to the old military road.

3.5 Arrive at the old military road and turn left (south).

4.2 Arrive at the Marching Bear Group; once you've explored, backtrack on the old military road northward.

4.9 Arrive at the top of the hill; turn right (east) and walk down the steep hill.

5.5 Arrive back at the gate and parking area.

Hike Information

Local Information

McGregor-Marquette Chamber of Commerce, (800) 896-0910, www.mcgreg-marq.org
Waukon: www.waukon.com
Prairie du Chien, (800) 732-1673, www.prairieduchien.org

Events/Attractions

HawkWatch Celebration (at Effigy Mounds National Monument), September; (563) 873-3491, www.npw.gov.efmo
Allamakee Farmers' Market, Allamakee County Fairgrounds, Waukon; (563) 568-6345; June through September, Monday 4:00 to 7:00 P.M.

Accommodations

Eagles Landing B&B, 82 North Street, Marquette, (563) 873-2509

Pike's Peak State Park; (563) 873-2341 Primitive camping available at several Clayton County Conservation Board Parks; (563) 245-1516

Restaurants

66 Cafe, 609 Rossville Road, Waukon; (563) 568-5019
Wildflour Bakery and Confectionary, 208 North Street, Marquette; (563) 873-3100
Marquette Bar and Cafe, 87 First Street, Marquette; (563) 873-9663

Other Resources

A Guide to Effigy Mounds National Monument, Dennis Lenzendorf (Eastern National)
Iowa's Archeological Past, Lynn Alex (Bur Oak Books Series, University of Iowa Press)

3 Pikes Peak State Park

Though Iowa's Pikes Peak shares its name with the better known 14,110-foot peak in Colorado, Lieutenant Zebulon Pike encountered the grand bluffs rising above the Mississippi River long before he came to know the Rocky Mountains. In comparison, our Pikes Peak rises a meager 500 feet above the floodplain. However, the view of the Upper Mississippi River National Wildlife and Fish Refuge and the mouth of the Wisconsin River is almost as majestic as its western counterpart. Trails begin at Pikes Peak and travel up and down several forested ravines to Point Ann at the park's northern tip.

Distance: 10.1 miles round-trip
Approximate hiking time: 3 to 5 hours
Total elevation gain: 2,147 feet
Trail surface: Forested footpath
Seasons: Year-round
Trail users: Hikers, mountain bikers
Canine compatability: Dogs permitted on leash
Hazards: Poison ivy, ticks, steep bluff faces
Land status: State park

Nearest towns: McGregor; Prairie du Chien, Wisconsin
Fees and permits: No fees or permits required unless you are camping
Schedule: Open year-round 4:00 A.M. to 10:30 P.M.
Map: USGS quad: Clayton
Trail contact: Pikes Peak State Park, 15316 Great River Road, McGregor; (563) 873-2341; www.iowadnr.com/parks/state_park_list/pikes_peak.html

Finding the trailhead: From the junction of U.S. Highways 18 and 52 west of McGregor, take US 18 east. Turn east onto Highway 76 toward McGregor and then south onto Highway 340 (which becomes County Road X56 and is also known as the Great River Road). Look for signs to Pikes Peak State Park and turn east toward the campground and overlook parking area.
DeLorme: Iowa Atlas and Gazetteer: Page 23 H8

The Hike

In 1673 Jacques Marquette and Louis Joliet left northern Michigan on an expedition in search of the "big river in the hidden valley," which they hoped might flow into the Pacific Ocean. From Green Bay, Wisconsin, they came up the Fox River, portaged overland to the Wisconsin River, and floated down to its mouth on the Mississippi at present-day Prairie du Chien. Astounded by the sight of the tall bluffs (present-day Pikes Peak State Park) over the Mississippi, Marquette referred to them as mountains in his journal.

Zebulon Pike explored the Upper Mississippi River in 1805, recommending to the U.S. Army that a fort be built at the top of Pikes Peak. Luckily, one was built in Prairie du Chien instead, and Iowa's bluffs were left undeveloped. In 1837 Alexander McGregor established a ferry across the Mississippi and used the bluffs above the ferry landing as a family picnic ground. The land was passed down through his family until 1928, when it was donated to the federal government and then to the State of Iowa to serve as Point Ann and Pikes Peak State Parks.

Begin the hike at the main overlook platform above the massive girth of the Mississippi where the Wisconsin River enters from the northeast. As you follow the boardwalk toward Crow's Nest, stop at the Bear Mound, an effigy built by people of the Late Woodland Culture between A.D. 600 and 1100, one of many mounds within the park

The boardwalk takes you past Crow's Nest, a semiopen ridge that's home to prairie grasses and wildflowers nestled between old eastern red cedars and chinquapin oaks. Signs lead toward Bridal Veil Falls, where an unnamed creek tumbles over a dolomite shelf on its way down to the Mississippi several hundred feet below. An extremely precipitous trail leads down the creek to Sand Cave, one of the most beautiful sandstone outcrops in Iowa. Striking red, yellow, brown, and orange bands formed by iron oxide precipitates appear in the creamy St. Peter sandstone. The small footpath is slippery, steep, and fragile and should not be attempted unless you are a very strong hiker.

The boardwalk ends at Bridal Veil Falls, and the rest of the trails in the park are wide paths that can get quite muddy when wet. Heading north toward Point Ann, you'll hike in and out of the park's three major ravines, all steeply dissected by small spring-fed streams. There are several ways to loop around to shorten or lengthen

*The view from the Crow's Nest, 500 feet
above the Mississippi River.* ▶

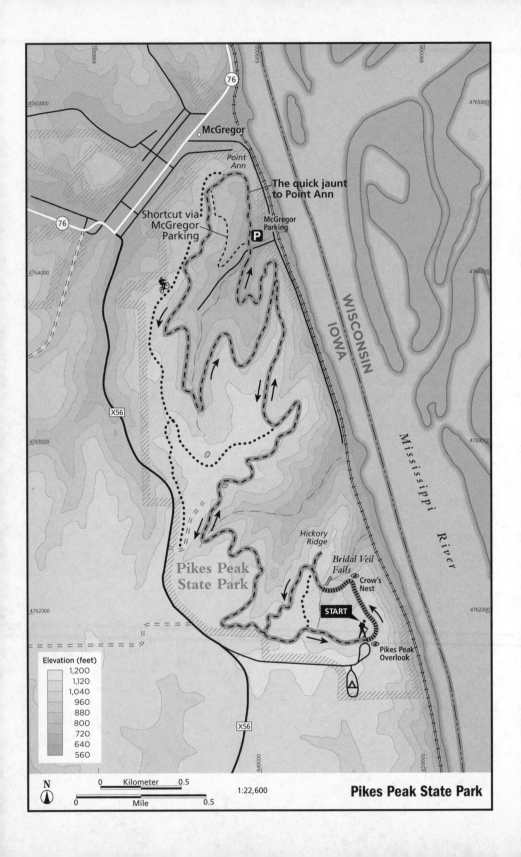

Pikes Peak State Park

Elevation (feet)
1,200
1,120
1,040
960
880
800
720
640
560

1:22,600

N

0   Kilometer   0.5

0   Mile   0.5

your trip. (The westernmost trail in the park, from Homestead parking to McGregor parking via Point Ann, is the only trail in the park open to mountain bikers.) The oldest exposed bedrock in the area, Jordan sandstone is exposed at Point Ann and was deposited near the end of the Cambrian period, about 505 million years ago. This sandstone is a very important aquifer for southeast Iowa and provides water to wells for surrounding communities, as well as the state park itself.

General Land Office surveys taken between 1837 and 1849 deemed Clayton County the most forested county in Iowa, with 70 percent "timber" coverage. Since those surveys, extensive logging has taken place surrounding the park, but the island of Pikes Peak remained relatively untouched because of previous owners' insight and its transfer to public land status in the early 1900s.

The mature upland forests are dominated by white and red oaks, shagbark hickory, sugar maple, and basswood, with small stands of eastern white pine scattered throughout. Because the Mississippi functions as a major flyway for migratory birds, forests in Pikes Peak along this corridor serve as perfect breeding areas for nesters or stopover sites for birds headed farther north to raise families. Look for cerulean, Kentucky, and blue-winged warblers; Bell's vireos; yellow-billed cuckoos; and scarlet tanagers, among many others.

The most special features of this place are the many spring-fed streams that tumble down steep gullies toward the Mississippi, many of them forming waterfalls. The water is somewhat cold, and although it's definitely not suitable for drinking, a splash on the face or back of the head will do you well on a hot day.

Miles and Directions

0.0 Start at the Overlook parking area.

0.2 Pikes Peak Overlook. Most people don't go much farther than here. Good thing you have your hiking boots on today! Continue north on the boardwalk past the Crow's Nest toward Bridal Veil Falls.

0.5 Arrive at Bridal Veil Falls; continue toward Hickory Ridge.

0.6 Atop Hickory Ridge you will see burial mounds extending toward the river.

2.0 At fork, turn right (east). Going the other way will take you to the Homestead parking area and the shortcut to Point Ann.

3.3 At fork, go right (north).

4.5 Arrive at McGregor parking area. Turn left (west) on the road to connect to the Point Ann Trail.

5.3 At both forks, turn right (east) for a quick jaunt out to Point Ann. When you return, take the first right fork for a shortcut or the second right fork for the long return. The mileage from here on out is via the long route.

7.0 Arrive back at main trail, and take a right (south). At each of the two successive forks, stay left for the best route to the trailhead. At the third fork go right to return to the parking lot or left to revisit Bridal Veil Falls and the Crow's Nest.

10.1 Arrive back at the trailhead.

Hike Information

Local Information

McGregor-Marquette Chamber of Commerce; (800) 896-0910, www.mcgreg-marq.org **Prairie du Chien;** (800) 732-1673, www.prairieduchien.org

Events/Attractions

Eagle Watch Weekend; January, Lock and Dam #10, Wyalusing State Park (10 miles south of Prairie du Chien, Wisconsin); (608) 996-2261 **Kickapoo Indian Caverns and Native American Museum,** Wauzeka, Wisconsin (15 miles east of Prairie du Chien); (608) 875-7723, www.kickapooindiancaverns.com **Allamakee Farmers' Market,** Allamakee County Fairgrounds, Waukon; (563) 568-6345; June through September, Monday 4:00 to 7:00 P.M.

Accommodations

Old Brewery Bed and Breakfast, 402 South Bluff Street, Guttenberg; (563) 252-2094

The Landing, A River Front Inn,701 South River Park Drive, Guttenberg; (563) 252-1615 **Grumpster's Log Cabin Getaway,** 535 Ash Street, McGregor; (563) 873-3767 **Little Switzerland Inn,** 126 Main Street, McGregor; (563) 873-2057, www.littleswitzerlandinn.com **Hickory Ridge Bed, Breakfast, and Bridle,** 17156 Great River Road, McGregor; (563) 873-1758

Restaurants

Guttenberg Bakery & Cafe, 408 River Park Drive; (563) 252-2225 **Breitbach Country Dining,** 563 Balltown Road, Balltown; (888) 266-1560 **The Stadium,** 1014 North Second Street, Guttenberg; (563) 252-2448

Other Resources

Paper Moon Books, 206 A Street, McGregor; (563) 873-3357

4 Volga River State Recreation Area

In the 1960s the Iowa Department of Natural Resources bought land around Frog Hollow Creek, a tributary of the Volga River, to create a large lake for recreational purposes. Because of cracks in the underlying bedrock, the lake never came to be. Instead the Volga River State Recreation Area was established, offering 25 miles of multiuse trails and canoe access to the Volga River. Trails take you through weathered bluffs, along the floodplains of the creek and river, and past several recovering grasslands and savannas. With room to roam and loop trails to choose among, the area offers hikes of varying length and difficulty.

Distance: 10.4-mile loop; longer loop available
Approximate hiking time: 4 to 6 hours
Total elevation gain: 224 feet
Trail surface: Gravel roads, mowed swaths
Seasons: Year-round
Trail users: Hikers, equestrians, snowmobilers, hunters
Canine compatability: Dogs permitted
Hazards: Poison ivy, ticks

Land status: State recreation area
Nearest town: Fayette
Fees and permits: No fees or permits required unless you are camping
Schedule: Open year-round 4:00 A.M. to 10:30 P.M.
Map: USGS quad: Baldwin
Trail contact: Volga River State Recreation Area; (563) 425–4161, www.state.ia.us/dnr/organiza/ppd/volga.htm

Finding the trailhead: From the junction of U.S. Highway 18 and Highway 150 in West Union, drive south on Highway 150. North of Fayette turn left (east) onto Ivy Road. Within the park, at the T-intersection turn left (north) onto I Avenue; follow to Frog Hollow Lake and the trailhead. *Delorme: Iowa Atlas and Gazetteer:* Page 32 83

The Hike

The State Conservation Commission (now the Iowa Department of Natural Resources) selected the then Big Rock Wildlife Area for part of its 1960s-era new "large lakes program." With rugged bluffs overlooking picturesque Volga River Canyon, it seemed a perfect place. However, the idea for a large lake was dropped after discovery that the underlying bedrock was fractured and wouldn't hold water. The state had already acquired more than 5,000 acres of highly cultivated, grazed, and logged land. In the end a recreation area was created, complete with 135-acre Frog Hollow Lake, food plots, brome fields, forested bluffs, and a number of multiuse trails. In its northern two-thirds there are 25 miles of trails consisting of old gravel and dirt farm roads and large mowed firebreaks.

The area is split down the middle by the floodplains of Frog Hollow Creek and the Volga River; hills and bluffs are mainly located in the western and southern portions. The prairie and savanna ecosystems that probably once dominated the area are

all but gone. Several small prairie glades along the creeks and a wet meadow near the eastern entrance are the only places where native grasses and prairie wildflowers still can be found. The DNR is carrying out an extensive management plan to use fire, logging, and planting to rehabilitate the native forest, prairie, and savanna.

The Lima Trail traverses the eastern half of the park, following a small creek toward the northeast corner and then heading south up and over several ridges. Though rarely seen, the two species of shrews that live in the area both like wet forests, characteristic of the habitat along the Lima Trail. Masked shrews consume their weight in food each day, and the northern short-tailed shrew produces a poison in its saliva that can paralyze small prey and leave humans with a nasty wound.

The Albany, Ridge, and Frog Hollow Trails ascend the bluffs on the west side of the park, following steep gravel roads and mowed paths through dense forests. The woodlands consist of bur, red, and white oaks, shagbark and bitternut hickories, white ash, basswood, elm, and sugar maple. You'll stumble upon several old homestead sites, evident because of the nonnative evergreen trees planted years ago as windbreaks. Though most homesites are situated on the floodplains, you'll find corn and alfalfa plantings scattered throughout the uplands, which now serve as food plots for wildlife.

Because of the area's fragmented landscape, it's a good place to observe birds that prefer woodland edge habitat. The usually secretive American woodcock puts on a marvelous early-spring territorial display, described eloquently in *A Sand County Almanac* by native Iowan and naturalist Aldo Leopold. Populations of northern bobwhite, also known as quail, have fluctuated dramatically because of habitat change and harsh weather, but the birds enjoy the hedgerows, food plots, and forest cover of the area. Look for the white belly, black cap, and gray wings of the eastern kingbird, which you'll see sitting on a fencepost and then swooping up to catch an insect.

The Volga is an exciting river to canoe, winding through canyons framed by towering Silurian dolomite cliffs. For the perfect float-hike trip, put in at Fayette, just southwest of the park. Take the 6.5-mile float down to the Albany Campground and take a long hike to stretch your legs. Continue down the 49 miles to Garber, where the Turkey and Volga Rivers meet.

The trails in the area are perfect for cross-country skiing during winter, but many are also open to snowmobiling, so be careful!

Miles and Directions

The loops can be explored separately or in one long day. You could even make a weekend backpacking trip and camp at Albany Primitive Camping Area. Described below is a decent-size day hike. Park at Frog Hollow Lake and walk south along the road to the trailhead.

◀ *Michigan lilies thrive in the wet prairie remnant of Volga River State Recreation Area.*

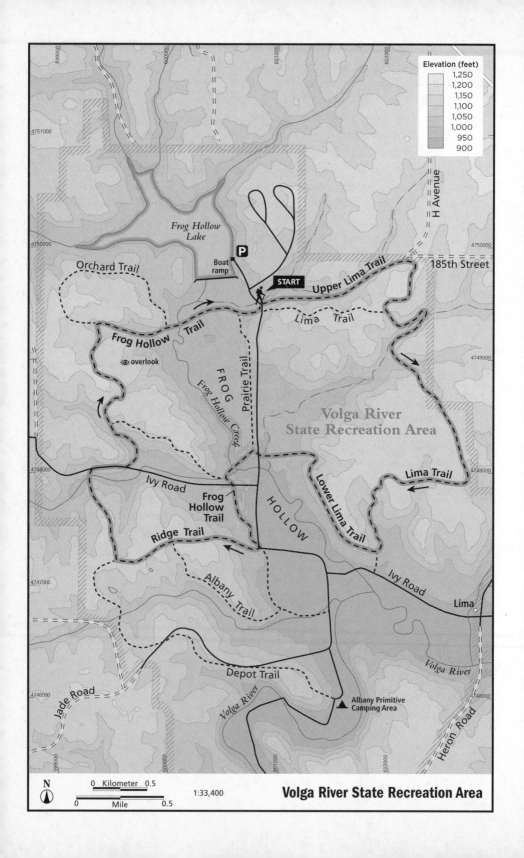

Volga River State Recreation Area

0.0 Start at the Upper Lima trailhead, walk east along the creek until you turn south, cross another creek, and climb a steep hill.

2.7 The trail turns west and descends to the floodplain. Stay right at two successive forks to remain on the Lower Lima Trail. **Option:** Turning left at either fork will take you to the Albany Day Use Area.

4.6 Cross Ivy Road.

5.0 Arrive at the junction of the Prairie and Lower Lima Trails. Turn left (southwest), crossing the creek and continuing to the Frog Hollow Trail. Turn left (southeast) onto Frog Hollow Trail.

5.6 At the fork turn right (west) onto the Ridge Trail.

6.6 At the fork turn right (north), continuing on the Ridge Trail.

7.2 Cross Ivy Road.

8.0 At the fork turn left (northwest) onto the Frog Hollow Trail. Follow this back to the trail-head.

10.4 Arrive back at the road, just west of the Upper Lima trailhead.

Hike Information

Local Information

Fayette: www.fayetteia.com

Events/Attractions

Watermelon Days, Fayette, September; www.fayetteia.com
Heritage Days, October, Elkader; (563) 245-1516
Big Springs Fish Hatchery, Elkader; (563) 245-2446
Fort Atkinson State Preserve, Fayette; (563) 425-4161
Osborne Conservation and Welcome Center; (563) 245-1516; e-mail: cccb@alpinecom.net

Accommodations

Glidden House Bed & Breakfast, 1901 Ford Drive, Fayette; (563) 425-4418
Goshawk Farm Bed & Breakfast, 27596 Ironwood Road, Elkader; (563) 964-9321, www.goshawkfarm.com

Restaurants

Scottie's Pizza, 104 South Main Street, Fayette; (563) 425-3322
Sugar Bowl Bakery, 152 South Main Street, Fayette; (563) 425-4012

5 Backbone State Park

When E. R. Harlan spoke during the 1920 ceremonies dedicating Iowa's first state park, he quoted Shakespeare to convey the importance of the sanctuary: ". . . those who 'find tongues in trees, books in the running brooks, sermons in stones, and good in everything' will find here an exalted interest." Indeed, the Backbone, a narrow ridge sculpted by the Maquoketa River, towers above Backbone Lake and offers a breathtaking view of the gorge below. In the park's large tract of forest—untouched for the past eighty years—you'll find diverse migratory bird visitors and more than 600 species of plants.

Distance: 8.0-mile loop
Approximate hiking time: 3 to 5 hours
Total elevation gain: 132 feet
Trail surface: Mowed footpaths, some road hiking, Backbone Trail is a skinny ridgeline trail.
Seasons: West Lake–East Lake Loop is very wet and muddy in spring. The park's roads close during winter and are open for cross-country skiing and snowmobiling.
Trail users: West Lake–East Lake Loop: hikers, equestrians, mountain bikers, snowmobilers; Backbone Trail: hikers only
Canine compatability: Dogs permitted on leash

Hazards: Poison ivy, ticks, very steep rock faces
Land status: State park
Nearest towns: Strawberry Point, Manchester
Fees and permits: No fees or permits required unless you're camping
Schedule: Open year-round 4:00 A.M. to 10:30 P.M.
Map: USGS quad: Dundee
Trail contact: Backbone State Park; (563) 924-2527; www.state.ia.us/dnr/organiza/ppd/backbone.htm

Finding the trailhead: From the junction of Highway 13 and Highway 3 in Strawberry Point, take Highway 13 south. After 1 mile, instead of following the big curve to the east, go straight (south) and then right (west) onto Highway 410. This will take you in through the north side of the park, past Richmond Springs and the cave, until you get to the Backbone. *DeLorme: Iowa Atlas Gazetteer:* Page 32 E5

The Hike

Iowa's first Board of Conservation was appointed in 1918. The same year, locals from Manchester, Strawberry Point, and Lamont formed the Travel Club and met several members of the board at the Backbone in an attempt to persuade them to preserve the area. It took several years to purchase the land, but at the dedication of Iowa's first state park on May 28, 1920, the statewide vision of a park system became a reality.

To fully appreciate the sculpted terrain of Backbone State Park, hike the 8.0-mile West Lake–East Lake Loop around Backbone Lake, formed by damming the

Take a break atop the Backbone to view the park's forest-covered hills.

Maquoketa River. In 1996 the lake was drained and dredged to remove 200,000 tons of silt, which had clogged the lake. Start by following the West Lake Trail, which winds through forested ravines dominated by red, black, and white oaks as well as basswood, sugar maple, shagbark hickory, and a scattering of eastern white pine. The understory is quite diverse here in the upland forest, with wild geranium, mayapple, Virginia creeper, tick-trefoil, and several species of ferns (lady, maindenhair, and interrupted). The large continuous tract of forest offers habitat for red fox, gray squirrel, skunk, and white-tailed deer, as well as diverse avifauna. In spring and summer look for American redstart, black- and yellow-billed cuckoos, great crested flycatcher, scarlet tanager, and eastern wood pewee. Winter residents include ruffed grouse, black-capped chickadee, northern cardinal, and tufted titmouse.

Once you cross the dam you'll have to navigate the more heavily developed area of the park, but the easily found East Lake Trail will lead you along the base of 30-to-50-foot bluffs. Diverge east off the main trail to walk the Bluebird Trail (forks after you've passed the last of the cabins) or to stand atop the Overlook Platform, which you'll see 0.2 mile before you reach the Backbone trailhead. Return to the

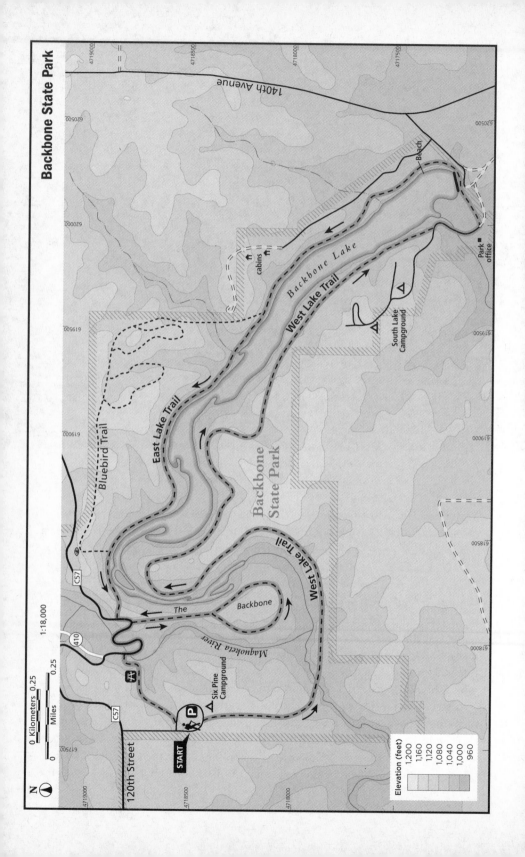

Backbone State Park

N

1:18,000

0 Kilometers 0.25

0 Miles 0.25

120th Street

START

Six Pine Campground

Maquoketa River

The

Backbone

Bluebird Trail

East Lake Trail

West Lake Trail

Backbone State Park

Backbone Lake

cabins

Beach

West Lake Trail

South Lake Campground

Park office

140th Avenue

Elevation (feet)

1,200
1,160
1,120
1,080
1,040
1,000
960

trailhead by road hiking and catching a connector trail from the picnic area south-west of the Backbone.

The Backbone, for which the park is named, is a narrow ridge of bedrock carved by the meandering Maquoketa River. The entrenchment of the river, or downcutting into the valley walls, has formed the steep-sided canyon framed by Silurian dolomite cliffs, deposited as lime roughly 430 million years ago. The tallest section of the Backbone rises almost 200 feet above the water and then tapers to as narrow as several yards across. The ridge then descends to the floodplain in a series of slump blocks.

Traverse the Backbone via the 1.0-mile loop trail. The ridge is an inhospitable place for most woodland plant species because of its sun exposure and thin soils. Here you'll find eastern red cedar, chinquapin oak, and quaking aspen overstory with interestingly diverse prairie and cliff species understory. Look for bastard toad-flax, columbine, golden alexander, porcupine grass, little bluestem, lousewort, Indian paintbrush, smooth cliff brake, and creeping fragile fern. Check the sky above for turkey vultures and red-tailed hawks riding the wind currents or for the occasional flyover by a pileated woodpecker or great blue heron.

Many small trails diverge from the main path, following crevices down to the water's edge. With so many hidden spots to find, you could spend an entire day exploring the various gullies formed by blocks of the Backbone splitting away. The trails that follow the cliff base wind through riparian wetlands, willow groves, and tall cottonwoods and can be impassable if the river is high.

Although they are not along hiking trails, there are several other pretty cool features within the park. The Backbone Cave necessitates some serious spelunking, crawling, etc., to navigate to its end. Hanging Rock, a massive boulder, is supported by a very small base. Richmond Springs, on the north end of the park, flows 2,000 gallons per minute, bubbling up through the porous limestone. It flows into the Maquoketa River within the park and is stocked with native trout, a place to do a little fishing or just cool your feet in the forty-eight-degree water. Refreshing water-cress grows along the edges of the spring. Backbone State Forest, just to the north of the park, contains several equestrian trails through the eastern white pine planta-tion. A Civilian Conservation Corps (CCC) museum is located just before you exit through the west gate of the park. Here you can view pictures of various projects in Iowa that were completed by the CCC, including all the structures in Backbone except the park office and residence.

Miles and Directions

To complete the entire loop, start at the Six Pines Campground, where it's also very nice to spend a night and start out hiking in the morning.

0.0 Start at Six Pines Campground; the West Lake trailhead is on the southwest side of the loop around the campground.

3.3 Arrive at the boat ramp, and follow the trail to the dam.

4.0 Walk past the beach, continuing along the side of the lake onto the East Lake Trail.

4.9 At the fork take the left (west) trail. **Option:** The Bluebird Trail will add another 1.5 miles to your total and explores the uplands.

5.8 A small trail forks to the east and goes up the hill to the Overlook Platform, which you can see from the main trail.

6.0 Arrive at County Road C57; turn left (west) and walk around the curve to get to the Backbone Trail.

6.1 Arrive at Backbone trailhead; walk south along the ridge.

7.2 Arrive back at Backbone trailhead. Turn left (west) onto the road and follow the curve down to the picnic area. Just after you pass the huge rock outcrop on the west side of the road, turn left (west) onto a small trail leading up the gully. This will take you back towards Six Pines Campground.

8.0 Arrive back at the north side of Six Pines Campground.

Hike Information

Local Information
Strawberry Point: www.strawberrypt.com
Manchester: www.manchesteriowa.org

Events/Attractions
Backbone Bluegrass Festival, July, Strawberry Point; (563) 427-5386, www.strawberry pt.com/Bluegrass/bluegrass.htm
Manchester Fish Hatchery, 22693 205th Avenue, Manchester; (563) 927-3276, www.iowadnr.com/fish/programs/hatchery/manchest.html
Osborne Conservation Center, 5 miles south of Elkader; (563) 245-1516
Strawberry Days, Strawberry Point, June; www.strawberrypt.com/Days/poster.htm
Strawberry Point Farmers' Market, parking lot of Joe's Pizza, Strawberry Point; (563) 933-4052; June through September; Wednesday 3:00 to 5:00 P.M.

Accommodations
Ivy Rose Inn, 624 Commercial, Strawberry Point; (563) 933-4485
Osborne Conservation Center Campground; (563) 245-1516
Twin Bridges Park and Wildlife Area (Delaware County Conservation Board); (563) 927-3410
Jakway Forest Area (Buchanan County Conservation Board); (563) 636-2617

Restaurants
Country Cafe, 1622 220th Street, Manchester; (563) 927-2562
Hazel's Cafe, 211 North Franklin Street, Manchester; (563) 927-5534
Cornerstone Pizza, 102 Main Street, Elkader; (563) 245-2800

Other Resources
Backbone Lake Friends Organization; e-mail: econdev@strawberrypt.com

6 Maquoketa Caves State Park

The 323-acre Maquoketa Caves State Park offers 6 miles of hiking trails and spelunking for varying levels of curiosity and ability. Situated in the Raccoon Creek Valley and one of the most geologically interesting sites in the state, the park is home to Iowa's largest cavern system, a 60-foot natural bridge spanning Raccoon Creek, and a seventeen-ton balanced rock.

Distance: 6.0 miles of loops
Approximate hiking time: 3 to 5 hours, including cave exploration
Trail surface: Dirt path with wooden boardwalk or concrete path in tricky places
Seasons: Year-round beauty
Trail users: Hikers only
Canine compatability: Dogs permitted on leash
Hazards: Ticks, poison ivy, spelunking scrapes and bumps
Land status: State park
Nearest town: Maquoketa

Fees and permits: No fees or permits required unless you are camping
Schedule: Open year-round, 4:00 A.M. to 10:30 P.M. Visitor center open Friday through Sunday between Memorial Day and Labor Day. Located at the intersection of Highway 428 and County Road Y-31
Map: USGS quad: Maquoketa
Trail contact: Maquoketa Caves State Park, 10970 98th Street, Maquoketa; (563) 652-5833; www.state.ia.us/dnr/organiza/ppd/maqucav.htm

Finding the trailhead: From the west end of Maquoketa and the junction of Highways 61 and 64, head north on Highway 61 for 1.5 miles. Turn west (left) onto Caves Road and drive until STATE PARK signs point west into the park. Follow the road past the visitor center to the two parking lots. *DeLorme: Iowa Atlas and Gazetteer:* Page 45 C6-7

The Hike

The Cave Trail begins at the lower of the two parking lots. Wooden staircases lead to the upper and middle entrances of the 1,100-foot-long Dancehall Cave, the most awe-inspiring and accessible cave in the park because of its sheer enormity and the electrically lit, paved walkway through its entirety. The park's two most complex caverns to explore, Steel Gate Passage and Bat Passage, are accessed from between the upper and middle entrances to Dancehall Cave. Exiting from the lower entrance of Dancehall Cave, look upslope for a glimpse of seventeen-ton Balanced Rock.

Walking south into Rainy Day Cave, pass through the first room and into the second, where you'll find the source of Raccoon Creek, which enters the Maquoketa River several miles south of the park. Here the lowlands are dominated by cottonwood, elm, and ash trees. Wild geranium, Virginia waterleaf, and woodland

Looking out from inside Dancehall Cave.

phlox form a dense undergrowth. Keep an eye out for white-breasted nuthatch, red-eyed vireo, common yellowthroat, American redstart, northern oriole, and indigo bunting.

Follow the trails to the blufftop overlooks on either side of the valley to see tree, northern rough-winged, barn, bank, and cliff swallows perched in the upper canopy or foraging above. Eastern redcedar, Canada yew, columbine, and walking fern all grow precariously from the upper rock ledges, while Virginia creeper vines hang down almost to the valley floor. Along the edge of the bluffs, small prairie openings, or "glades," support big bluestem, sideoats grama, and bastard toadflax. More than 350 plant species have been counted throughout the small park, a high diversity reflecting numerous habitats.

To access the natural bridge and eight caves north of Dancehall Cave, retrace your steps through the large cavern. Photographs taken in 1920 of Dancehall Cave's interior show a scene much different from today's: Milky white stalactites and flow-stones once covered the walls and ceiling. However, a century of thievery has left us to wait another several thousand years to replace the geologic wonders once housed inside this cave.

The Maquoketa Caves are a prime example of the karst topography typical of northeast Iowa. This configuration is characterized by shallow carbonate bedrock (such as the park's limestone and dolomite) dissected by fissures, sinkholes, and cavern systems. All but two of the caves are "dissolution caves," formed when surface water drained into the soil and combined with carbonic acid to dissolve the limestone bedrock.

Many historic cultures used the caves as dwellings and meeting places and for ceremonies. Explorers and archaeologists have discovered thousands of artifacts from the past 6,500 years. The name "Maquoketa" is derived from the Mesquakie words "maqua" (medicine) and "keto" (place). A second meaning from the Fox words "mako" (bear) and "keta" (river) refers to the historically high density of bears along the Maquoketa River.

Although no bears remain, another, although much smaller, mammal still inhabits the caves. Each fall, up to 3,000 little brown bats fly into the cave housing their hibernaculum; months later, they emerge together as a group. When they aren't hibernating, the bats spend their days roosting upside-down in the caves, exiting at dusk to forage for insects.

In 1834 Joshua Bear and David Scott, early Jackson County settlers, discovered Dancehall Cave when they tracked a herd of deer inside. In 1868 a dance pavilion was constructed south of the natural bridge. Designated as a state park in October 1933, Maquoketa Caves have since been a favorite place for Iowans to explore.

Miles and Directions

Hikers should read about the various caves and decide how intense a spelunking experience they want. Always travel in pairs and take extra flashlights or headlamps. Be ready to get muddy and wet and possibly a little scraped up. Explorations of Bat and Steel Gate Passages should not be attempted without headlamps and water. Also, claustrophobia must be conquered or at least dealt with if hikers are going to make it to the back of most caves. Be extremely careful of the stalactites and other speleothems, since even a small amount of oil from human skin can halt their growth.

The Department of Natural Resources map and most booklets on Maquoketa number the caves in the following sequence:

1. Wide Mouth Cave—A large gash in the bluff that leads back 100 feet to three rooms.

2. Dug Out Cave—Little more than a shelter dug out of the natural bridge, accessed by climbing up the rocks. A little difficult to get to if you're afraid of heights, this is a nice spot for lunch nonetheless.

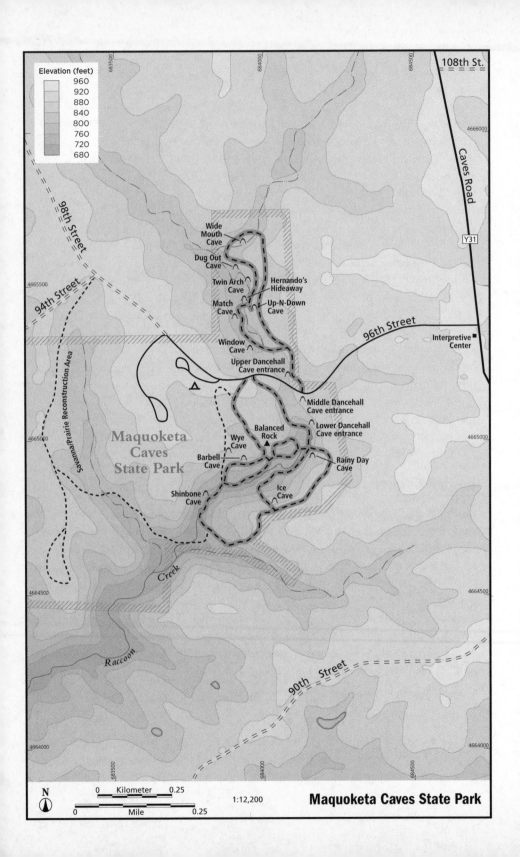

Maquoketa Caves State Park

3. Twin Arch Cave—A rock shelter within the limestone bluff that looks like a huge nose with two flaring nostrils coming out of the hillside. Crinoid and brachiopod fossils can be seen in the 20-foot-diameter domed roof; seating is provided by large boulders within the cave.

4. Hernando's Hideaway—A fairly good climb from the path to the entrance; belly crawling and slithering necessary to get to the back.

5. Up-N-Down Cave—A gnarled opening several feet off the ground that's tough to get up into, after which you will head down into the 27-foot-long cave.

6. Window Cave—A small crevice in the limestone bluff.

7. Match Cave—Good for beginners. Two passages lie within the cave; the largest is about 30 feet long. Belly crawling is necessary, but the cave is dry.

8. Barbell Cave—Two visible openings; however, the left entrance is impassable. Boost yourself inside the hole on the right and shimmy to the back of the cave, where it opens up to offer enough room for two persons to lie down. Excellent speleothems.

9. Shinbone Cave—From a distance, the apparent opening is quite visible; however, the actual access lies to the right of the big hole. Crawl 75 feet back into the inter-connected space between boulders—and watch your shins.

10. Wye Cave—Begins in the debris of an enormous sinkhole, much higher in the park than other caves. Enter by dropping down 6 feet into the small hole in the right corner of its cavern face. The route plummets in depth and divides, with the left passage becoming the main one. Farther along, there is more passage to explore, but it's very tight and easy to get stuck in. One of the most interesting caves in the park, Wye is nearly 500 feet long. Don't enter unless you are very sure of your athletic capability!

11. Balanced Rock—A seventeen-ton boulder balances precariously on a small rock platform.

12–14. Dancehall Cave—The biggest, most developed of the Maquoketa Caves is 1,100 feet long. Raccoon Creek flows through its entirety. Other than a short distance at the north entrance, you can walk upright throughout the cave on a lighted concrete walkway. Because Raccoon Creek flows through the cave, it's always wet and muddy.

15. Rainy Day Cave—One of its two rooms is enormous and easy to find. Listen for gurgling, and find the source of Raccoon Creek in the dark depths of the cave's other room. Nearly constant fifty-five-degree temperature.

MAQUOKETA CAVES ARCHAEOLOGY

Prior to any work done by the state, several Jackson County natives took it upon themselves to investigate the archaeological history of the Maquoketa Caves area. Paul Sagers's excavations just north of the park yielded materials used by Late Woodland through Middle Archaic peoples, a span of more than 6,500 years. In 1980 an Iowa State Conservation Commission study unearthed a basin-shaped fire pit, pottery shards, animal-bone tools, and spear points in Dancehall, Rainy Day, and Ice Caves. The artifacts suggested a Late Woodland occupation, sometime between A.D. 300 and 1000. The 1980 excavations were only to a depth of 172 centimeters. Sagers's surveys were much more invasive and conclusive, lasting ten years and yielding thousands of artifacts.

16. Ice Cave—Two rooms approximately 20 feet above the stream, with cold air being funneled down into them; perfect on a hot day.

Steel Gate Passage—Accessible from upper Dancehall Cave, it's the most difficult of the Maquoketa Caves to explore. It will take about forty-five minutes to an hour to explore the 800 feet of tunnel. Jagged stones will cut up your knees and elbows, but you'll see some of the best speleothems in the park.

Bat Passage—Located inside Dancehall Cave close to the upper entrance. The access hole is several feet above the ground, and the first several yards are cut by a channel a foot wide and deep. Stooping and crawling are occasionally required. As you reach the end of the cave, through a large hole you'll be able to see the paved walkway of Dancehall Cave below. However, unless you want to jump 10 feet down, retrace your steps and leave the way you came. If you're claustrophobic or have broad shoulders, think twice before entering Bat Passage. You don't want to get stuck.

Hike Information

Local Information

City of Maquoketa: www.maquoketaia.com
Maquoketa Chamber of Commerce: (563) 652-4602, www.maquoketachamber.com
Jackson County: www.jacksoncountyiowa.com

Events/Attractions

Timber City Adventure Race, fourth Saturday in June, Canton to Maquoketa; canoe 8 miles, bike 14 miles, and run 5K; (800) 989-4602; www.maquoketachamber.com/html/adventurerace.htm
Dark Hollow Bison Ranch, Maquoketa; (563) 322-7181

Hurstville Interpretive Center, 18670 Sixty-third Street, Maquoketa; (563) 652-3783
Maquoketa Farmers' Market, West Platt Street and South Second Street, Maquoketa; (563) 652-6097; June through September, Saturday 7:30 A.M. to noon

Accommodations

Squiers Manor Bed and Breakfast, 418 West Pleasant Street, Maquoketa; (563) 652-6961, www.squiersmanor.com
Whispering Meadows Resort (cabins), 110 East Main Street, Springbrook; (563) 872-4430

Bellevue State Park; (563) 872–4019

Buzzard Ridge Wildlife Area (Jackson County Conservation Board), primitive campsites; (563) 652–3783

Restaurants

Flapjacks Family Restaurant, 101 McKinsey Drive, Maquoketa; (563) 652–6779

Main Street Cafe, 136 Main Street, Maquoketa; (563) 652–6679

Hov's Pub, 110 South Olive Street, Maquoketa; (563) 652–9084

Other Resources

Book Depot, 147 South Main Street, Maquoketa; (563) 652–5112

Iowa Underground: A Guide to the State's Sub-terranean Treasures by Greg Brick (Trail Books)

A Guide to Maquoketa Caves State Park by Thomas Henry

7 Mines of Spain State Recreation Area

Mines of Spain State Recreation Area, located on the bluffs overlooking Catfish Creek and the Mississippi River, encompasses Catfish Creek State Preserve and the Julien Dubuque Monument (on the National Register of Historic Places). Steeped in cultural history, Mines of Spain SRA is situated in an area that has been inhabited for at least the past 8,000 years. It was also the site of the first Euro–American settlement in Iowa and the beginning of river town Dubuque. A short jaunt around the E. B. Lyons Interpretive Center's trails or a 15-mile day, over bluff and down valley can be enjoyed within the gorgeous park.

Distance: 7.5 miles out and back with loops

Approximate hiking time: 2 to 5 hours

Total elevation gain: 1,472 feet

Trail surface: Mowed footpaths, dirt trails; Julien Dubuque trail paved to the overlook

Seasons: Year-round; the southern trails are geared mainly to cross-country skiing

Trail users: Hikers, hunters, cross-country skiers

Canine compatability: Dogs permitted on leash

Hazards: Poison ivy, ticks

Land status: State preserve located within a state recreation area

Nearest town: Dubuque

Fees and permits: No fees or permits required

Schedule: Open year-round 4:00 A.M. to 10:30 P.M.

Map: USGS quad: Dubuque South

Trail contact: E. B. Lyons Interpretive Center, 8999 Bellevue Heights, Dubuque; (319) 556–0620; www.state.ia.us/dnr/organiza/ppd/minesof.htm

Finding the trailhead: To get to Mines of Spain State Recreation Area (main park area), where U.S. Highway 61/151 and U.S. Highway 52 merge south of Dubuque, take US 61/151/52 north. Take the Grandview exit. Turn right (east) onto Grandview and then an immediate right (south) onto Julien Dubuque Drive. Turn right (east) onto Marjo Hills Quarry Road and then right (south) onto Mines of Spain Road.

To get to E. B. Lyons Interpretive Center, where US 61/151 and US 52 merge, take US 52 south. Take an immediate exit onto Bellevue Heights Road and look for the signs to the parking area. *DeLorme: Iowa Atlas and Gazetteer:* Page 34 G3

The Hike

Julien Dubuque, a French fur trader, was one of the first Europeans to settle in Iowa, and his namesake city lies just north of where he first settled. In 1788 the Mesquakie, who had controlled the nearby lead mines since the mid-1700s, permitted Dubuque to begin mining. Near their village at the mouth of Catfish Creek, he built a small settlement with trading post, sawmill, blacksmith shop, forge, and smelting furnace. It's said he became very close with the tribe and that he married Potosa, daughter of chief Peosta. In 1796 Dubuque petitioned the governor of Louisiana, Baron Hector de Carondelet, to cede him a tract of land surrounding the mines 3 by 7 leagues (or 9 by 21 miles), which he named the "Mines of Spain," apparently to oblige the Spanish government. When Dubuque died in 1810, he was buried on a bluff overlooking the Mississippi River where the Julien Dubuque Monument, built in 1897, stands today.

From the nature center trails, take the 1.0-mile Mesquakie Trail east across Granger Creek to its intersection with Calcite Trail. Take the left fork, following Catfish Creek down to the Canoe Access point, and cross the bridge. Turn west onto the 2.0-mile Catfish Creek Trail, which follows the creek upstream on its north side. You'll ascend the bluffs and pass several conical burial mounds, just a few of the documented thirty-eight mounds within the recreation area.

On your return to the Canoe Access parking area, you'll see stairs on the east side of the road that lead up to the hill, steep but short. When you arrive at the edge of the bluff, you'll see the Julien Dubuque Monument, a 25-foot-tall tower built from limestone quarried from the hill on which it stands.

From the blufftop overlook, look south for the mouth of Catfish Creek below, with Horseshoe Bluff rising in the distance. To the north is the city of Dubuque; across the river in Wisconsin rises Sinsinewa Mound, an erosional outlier of the Silurian escarpment.

Return to the Catfish Creek Canoe Access parking area, cross the creek, and backtrack on Calcite Trail. Instead of continuing on Mesquakie Trail back to the nature center, walk to Calcite trailhead (look for huge calcite rock and pit mines at the trailhead). At the southern tip of the parking area, a short trail will take you along prairie edge to Horseshoe Bluff parking area and continue the southbound trail. Take a detour on the floating boardwalk over the wetland before entering Horseshoe Bluff Quarry.

◀ *The dug-out quarry of Horseshoe Bluff, with the Mississippi River visible in the background.*

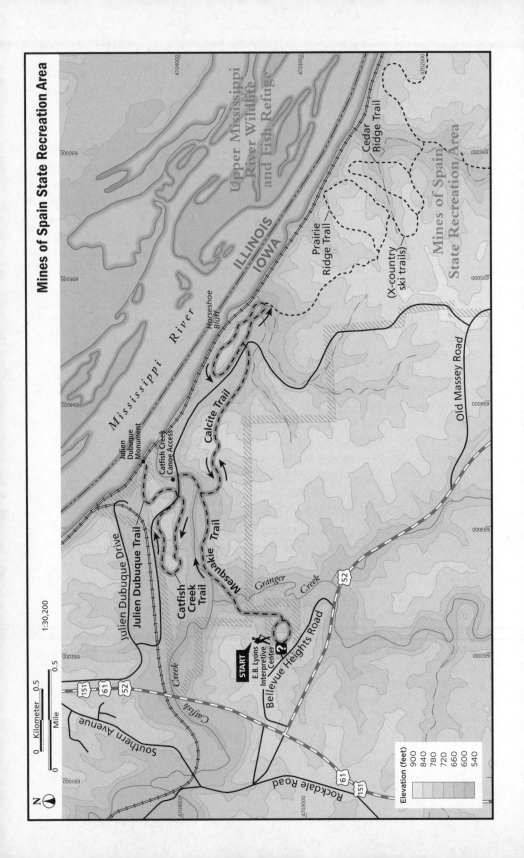

Mines of Spain State Recreation Area

1:30,200

Horseshoe Bluff was once a hill overlooking the Mississippi, but intensive quarrying carved out its center, forming the U-shaped canyon. The trail through the canyon has interpretive signs describing the rock exposures and the quarrying that took place and a prime example of "stream piracy" where you're standing. Both Catfish and Granger Creeks once occupied different streambeds, and Horseshoe Bluff was once an island in the Mississippi. Large amounts of glacial meltwater surging down the river and the two creeks repositioned the channels and the mouths of the creeks, leaving several valleys in Mines of Spain without the waterways they once housed.

Time your hike to visit the E. B. Lyons Nature Center, open year-round Monday through Friday, 9:00 A.M. to 4:00 P.M., and on weekends from April 15 through October 15, noon to 4:00 P.M. Exhibits include bird and mammal mounts, projectile points and pottery shards found on-site, tools once used by miners, and several pieces of the lead ore they searched for.

Trails wind around an old homestead and chapel built by the Junkermann family in the 1860s; two cellars excavated from rock outcrops for storage of wine and food; a sinkhole formed by a mine-shaft collapse; and small depressions of the pit mines from earlier days.

In the southern half of the park, the Prairie Ridge, Cedar Ridge, Eagle Scout, and Catesse Hollow Trails traverse upland prairie reconstructions and dive into heavily forested, cool ravines. These trails are wide, mowed swaths used mainly for cross-country skiing, but they're worth the energy if you're looking for a long hike.

Miles and Directions

0.0 Start at E. B. Lyons Interpretive Center; walk south on the Nature Center Trail, passing the lead mine shaft and mine pit. Turn left onto the Meadow Trail and then left onto the Mesquakie Trail.

1.0 Arrive at the road, on the south side of Catfish Creek. Turn left on the road and cross the creek. On your left (west) is the Catfish Creek Trail.

2.35 Back at the Catfish Creek trailhead, cross the road to the parking lot. From here a staircase to the north leads up the side of the bluff and connects to the Julien Dubuque Monument Trail.

2.75 Arrive at the Julien Dubuque Monument (FYI: How much has the view changed since Julien Dubuque stood atop here? The city that bears his name, adaptation of the Mississippi River, quarrying of Horseshoe Bluff, and much more. What remains the same? An entirely humbling view over that big ol' river.) Backtrack down to the Catfish Creek Canoe Access and onto the Mesquakie Trail.

3.4 At the fork, instead of continuing back up to the trailhead, take a left onto the Calcite Trail.

4.0 Arrive at the Calcite Trailhead. Look for the remnants of the pit mines as well as a huge block of calcite at the trailhead. Walk to the southeast tip of the parking lot and onto the trail that fringes the edge between forest and a prairie planting.

4.4 Arrive at the Horseshoe Bluff trailhead and parking area. Take the trail that heads south. **Option:** Take the boardwalk over the wetland area before heading up into the quarry.

4.7 At the southern mouth of Horseshoe Bluff, follow the interpretive signs to the northern tip, where the trail loops around back to the parking area. **Option:** Scramble up the south side of the ridge separating the old quarry from the Mississippi to a fine ridgewalk. There's a small trail on the southern tip, but you can access the ridge easier from the north side of the Horseshoe, at the overlook.

5.5 Back at the Horseshoe Bluff trailhead, backtrack to E. B. Lyons Interpretive Center the way you came, via the Prairie, Calcite, Mesquakie, and Nature Center Trails.

7.5 Arrive back at the trailhead and E. B. Lyons Interpretive Center. Don't forget to check out the great collection of natural and cultural history items inside.

Hike Information

Local Information

Dubuque Chamber of Commerce; (563) 557-9200, www.dubuquechamber.com

Events/Attractions

National Mississippi River Museum and Aquarium, 350 East Third Street, Port of Dubuque; (563) 557-9545, www.mississippiriver museum.com

Crystal Lake Cave, south of Dubuque on US 52; (563) 556-6451, www.crystallakecave.com

Dubuque Arboretum/Botanical Gardens, 3800 Arboretum Drive, Dubuque; (563) 556-2100, www.dbq.com/arboretum

Dubuque River Rides, Port of Dubuque; (563) 583-8093, www.dubuqueriverrides.com

Fenelon Place Elevator, world's shortest, steepest scenic railroad, 512 Fenelon Place, Dubuque; (563) 582-6496, www.dbq .com/fenplco

Sundown Mountain Ski and Snowboard Resort, 16991 Asbury Road, Dubuque; (563) 556-6676, www.sundownmtn.com

Dubuque Main Street Farmers' Market, Central and Iowa Streets, Dubuque; (563) 588-4400; May through October, Saturday 7:00 A.M. to noon

Accommodations

The Mandolin Inn, 199 Loras Boulevard, Dubuque; (563) 556-0069, www .mandolininn.com

The Richards House B&B Inn, 1492 Locust Street, Dubuque; (563) 557-1492, www .therichardshouse.com

Swiss Valley Campground, 13606 Swiss Valley Road, Peosta, and Finley's Landing, 24500 Finley's Landing Road, Sherrill (both owned by Dubuque County Conservation Board); (563) 556-6745, www.dubuquecounty.com

Restaurants

Bricktown Brewery & The Blackwater Grill, 299 Main Street, Dubuque; (563) 582-0608

Cafe Manna Java, 69 Main Street, Dubuque; (563) 588-3105

Other Resources

River Lights Bookstore, 806 Wacker Drive, Dubuque; (563) 556-4391

Dubuque Audubon: www.audubondubuque.org

Iowa Underground: A Guide to the State's Subterranean Treasures by Greg A. Brick (Trails Books)

Up on the River: An Upper Mississippi Chronicle by John Madson (Nick Lyons Books)

The Guide to Iowa's State Preserves by Ruth Herzberg and John Pearson (Bur Oaks Books Series, University of Iowa Press)

TWO SCRAMBLES AT MINES OF SPAIN

For two extra adventures check out Catfish Cave and the Horeshoe Bluff Ridgewalk. Catfish Cave is located at the base of the bluff housing the Julien Dubuque Monument. From the Catfish Creek Canoe Access, follow the north side of the creek toward the Misssissippi River. You'll have to wade a little in the water or scramble over the rocks to get to the small cave, which you'll find almost at the mouth of the creek.

The Horseshoe Bluff Ridgewalk is located on the east side of the Horseshoe Bluff area. A small footpath leads from the northern overlook along the precipitous ridge. It's best to double back, because the trail down the southern end of the bluff is quite hairy—very steep and very slick.

8 Bellevue State Park—Nelson and Dyas Units

Located on 300-foot bluffs overlooking the Mississippi River, Bellevue State Park was named for the town on the Mississippi to its north. The park is divided into two tracts: Nelson Unit to the north and Dyas Unit to the south. The park is a perfect place to camp out and explore with children. Several short trails, a butterfly garden, and three Woodland Period Indian mounds offer valuable glimpses into the area's natural history.

Distance: Nelson Unit, 1.85-mile figure eight; Dyas Unit: 3.9 miles out and back
Approximate hiking time: 1 to 2 hours at each unit
Total elevation gain: Nelson Unit: 383 feet; Dyas Unit: 808 feet
Trail surface: Forested footpaths
Seasons: May through September is best to visit butterfly garden
Trail users: Hikers, snowmobilers
Canine compatability: Dogs permitted on leash

Hazards: Poison ivy, ticks
Land status: State park
Nearest town: Bellevue
Fees and permits: No fees or permits required unless you are camping
Schedule: Open year-round, 4:00 A.M. to 10:30 P.M.
Map: USGS quad: Springbrook
Trail contact: South Bluff Nature Center, 21466 429th Avenue, Bellevue; (563) 872-4019; www.iowadnr.com/parks/state_park_list/bellevue.html

Finding the trailhead: From the junction of U.S. Highway 52 and Highway 62 in Bellevue, drive south on US 52. The Nelson Unit's entrance is just south of town; the Dyas Unit is 2 miles farther south. *DeLorme: Iowa Atlas and Gazetteer:* Page 45 9A

The Garden Sanctuary for Butterflies is nestled within the Nelson Unit of Bellevue State Park.

The Hike

Within the Nelson Unit, five named trails offer a total of 2.5 miles of walking paths. The Overlook and Indian Mound Trails leave from the eastern parking area. The Overlook Trail is a 0.1-mile jaunt down to an overlook from which you can view the town of Bellevue and a wide swath of the Mississippi River. During winter, congregations of bald eagles in the open waters below Lock and Dam #12 scavenge fish that have gone through the turbines. The Indian Mound Trail takes you 0.25 mile to the south to three conical burial mounds perched atop the bluff.

The Meadow, Quarry, and Nature Trails all start at South Bluff Nature Center. Follow the Meadow Trail 0.15 mile through reconstructed prairie and into the Garden Sanctuary for Butterflies. Volunteers from neighboring towns first helped create the garden in 1985 and now donate time and money to plant, weed, and water individual plots. Cottonwood, wild cherry, willow, and hackberry trees enclose the garden, which is planted with flowering trees and plants that serve as hosts and food for butterflies.

Sixty species of *Lepidoptera* have been sighted feeding on black-eyed susan, borage, cosmos, coneflower, dianthus, heliotrope, lupine, oxeye daisy, phlox, zinnia, and countless other native and nonnative plants, many of which are labeled. On a hot summer day, look for such butterflies as tiger and giant swallowtails, clouded and fiery skippers, large wood nymph, red admiral, eastern tailed blue, red-spotted purple, and tawny emperor, among many others. During the fall migration, you might see larger numbers of monarchs as well. Interpretive signs in the garden include pictures of many butterflies and an explanation of their life cycle.

Continuing on the Meadow Trail, take a left onto the Quarry Trail to complete a 1.2-mile loop, passing the quarry from which stone was taken to build the park's shelters in the 1920s. The forest here is early-successional, recovering from extensive logging that probably took place when the quarry was active. Garlic mustard, an invasive species, is prevalent throughout, forming almost uniform stands in some areas and displacing the native woodland wildflowers.

The Nature Trail is a 0.1-mile loop through native forest where spring wildflowers bloom in profusion. South Bluff Nature Center is open 1:00 to 4:00 P.M. Saturday and Sunday, as well as federal holidays and by appointment. Inside are several interpretive displays on the park's geology, plants, and animals. Seasonal programs such as a butterfly-tagging seminar in the fall are worth the trip; check with nature center staff for program information.

If you spend the afternoon in the Nelson Unit, head down to camp in the Dyas Unit. You can explore the Bluff, Duck Creek, and Deer Trails in the morning. Bypass the Campground Trail, which should be renamed the "Stinky Sewage Lagoon Trail."

Instead, head over to the northernmost parking area where the Bluff Trail starts. Head east 0.2 mile to the ridge, where you can loop back to the parking area or turn onto Duck Creek Trail to the left. This trail descends the ridge, paralleling first US 52 and then Duck Creek just before its entrance into the Mississippi.

Willow thickets and stinging nettles surround the trail, which can get quite muddy and buggy during rainy periods. The trail ascends the bluff to the west in a 0.9-mile loop before returning to the lowlands, onto Bluff Trail, and finally to the parking lot. From here you can follow the 0.25-mile Deer Trail through dense woodlands to the shelter to enjoy the overlook and have a snack.

Miles and Directions

Nelson Unit

0.0 Start at the trailhead, located at the South Bluff Nature Center parking lot.

0.15 Arrive at the Garden Sanctuary for Butterflies. Check out the sanctuary and then continue southwest on the Meadow Trail.

0.6 At fork, turn left (west) onto the Quarry Trail.

1.5 At fork, turn left (south) back onto the Meadow Trail.

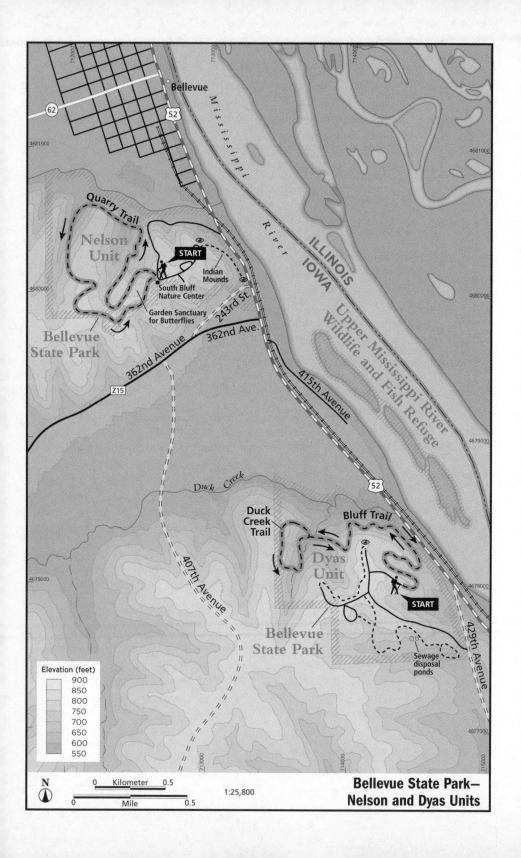

Bellevue
Mississippi
River
ILLINOIS
IOWA
Upper Mississippi River
Wildlife and Fish Refuge

Quarry Trail
Nelson
Unit
START
Indian
Mounds
South Bluff
Nature Center
Garden Sanctuary
for Butterflies
Bellevue
State Park
243rd St.
362nd Ave.
362nd Avenue
415th Avenue
Z15

Duck Creek

Duck
Creek
Trail
Bluff Trail
Dyas
Unit
407th Avenue
START
Bellevue
State Park
429th Avenue
Sewage
disposal
ponds

Elevation (feet)
900
850
800
750
700
650
600
550

N

0   Kilometer   0.5
0   Mile   0.5

1:25,800

**Bellevue State Park—
Nelson and Dyas Units**

1.7 Arrive back at the Garden Sanctuary for Butterflies, the perfect lunch spot. Follow the main trail back toward the trailhead.

1.85 Arrive back at South Bluff Nature Center and trailhead.

Dyas Unit

0.0 Start at eastern parking loop; walk east on the Bluff Trail.

0.6 At fork, turn right (southeast) onto Duck Creek Trail.

0.75 At fork, turn left (north) to hike down the bluff toward Duck Creek. (FYI: If you walk 40 feet down the right fork, you'll find a tiny opening dominated by prairie plants.)

1.7 Cross over a tributary of Duck Creek and ascend the ridge. You'll reach the "top" and quickly turn south, following the loop back down to the tributary.

2.2 Arrive back at the trail; backtrack the way you came to return to the trailhead.

3.9 Arrive back at the trailhead.

Hike Information

Local Information

Bellevue; (563) 872-5830, www.bellevueia.com

Jackson County Welcome Center, Sabula; (563) 687-2237

Events/Attractions

Dyas Farm and Hexagonal Barn, located just south of the Nelson Unit on 362nd Avenue, Bellevue

Bellevue Farmers' Market, Gazebo on Riverview Street, Bellevue; (563) 872-4173; May through September, Saturday 7:00 to 11:00 A.M.

Potters Mill, 300 Potter Drive, Bellevue; (563) 872-3838

Accommodations

Spruce Creek Park (Jackson County Conservation Board), Bellevue; (563) 652-3783

Pleasant Creek Recreation Area (U.S. Army Corps of Engineers), Bellevue; (319) 872-5782

Potter's Mill Restaurant Bed & Breakfast, 300 Potter Drive, Bellevue; (563) 872-4142

South Sabula Lake Park, Sabula (Jackson County Conservation Board); (563) 652-3783

Bounded by Water Bed & Breakfast, 601 Pearl Street, Sabula; (815) 541-4919

Castle Bed & Breakfast, 616 River Street, Sabula; (563) 687-2714

Restaurants

Second Street Station, 116 South Second Street, Bellevue; (563) 872-5410

Woody's, 407 Pearl Street, Sabula; (563) 687-2245

Other Resources

Bookworm, 110 South Riverside, Bellevue; (563) 872-4802

Up on the River: An Upper Mississippi Chronicle by John Madson (Nick Lyons Books)

National Audubon Society Field Guide to North American Butterflies by Robert Michael Pyle (Knopf; A Chanticleer Press Edition)

Honorable Mentions

A. Gilbertson Conservation Education Area

Five miles of loop trails leave from an access road behind the nature center. Take a 2.0-mile trail that leads down to the campground, or walk up through forests of oak, shagbark hickory, and black walnut to a trail-easement on private land. Brome grass dominates here, and you will most likely see white-tailed deer munching. Other trails lead down through wetland and around several buildings filled with home and farm antiques. The nature center has numerous animal mounts and live turtles and snakes. From the junction of County Roads B64 and W55 in Elgin, take CR B64 east to the entrance road to the park. For information: Fayette County Conservation Board; (319) 426–5740, www.westunion.com/county.htm.

B. Mount Hosmer

This Lansing city park, set atop Mount Hosmer (elevation 1,060 feet), is open from 7:00 A.M. to 9:00 P.M. In 1851, while waiting on a layover on a steamboat trip up the Mississippi River, famous sculptress Harriet Hosmer won a footrace to the top of the bluff. Today a steep climb up the forested bluff will yield a 50-mile view of Minnesota, Wisconsin, and the Upper Mississsppi National Wildlife and Fish Refuge. From the junction of Highways 26 and 9 in Lansing, drive 4 blocks west on Highway 9, and turn right (north) onto North Sixth Street to access the park. For information: www.lansingiowa.com/.

C. Fish Farm Mounds State Preserve and Wildlife Area

Seven miles north of Lansing on Highway 26, Fish Farm Mounds State Preserve is a three-acre preserve is located within the larger Fish Farm Mounds Wildlife Area. The cluster of thirty Middle-Late Woodland burial mounds were constructed 1,350 to 2,100 years ago. The terrace that the mounds were built upon rests beneath 300-foot-tall Cambrian sandstone bluffs deposited 500 million years ago. A short trail leads from the parking area to the mound group within the state preserve, and several other trails traverse the wildlife area. For information: www.state.ia.us/dnr/organiza/ppd/fishfarm.htm.

D. Decorah Area Trails

The trail system surrounding the town of Decorah is one of the most extensive in the state and traverses an area dense with natural wonders. Fourteen miles of multi-use and singletrack trails on the north side of town connect Dunning's Spring, Ice

Cave Hill, Barbara Barnhart Van Peenen Memorial, and Palisades Parks. You'll find huge waterfalls, densely forested bluffs, and the biggest ice cave in the state. Malanaphy Springs State Preserve and the Upper Iowa River Access Area lie northwest of town and require your attention. Show up in April for the Decorah Time Trials, the highest attended mountain biking competition in Iowa, or at the end of July for Nordic Fest, a celebration of Scandinavian heritage, and explore the many incredible facets of this small town. For information: www.decorah-iowa.com or www.state.ia.us/dnr/organiza/ppd/preslist.htm.

E. Bixby State Park and Preserve

From the intersection of Highway 3 and North Franklin Street in Edgewood, take North Franklin north out of town. North Franklin Street becomes Fortune Avenue, which will take you to the parking area. Spring-fed Bear Creek, a trout stream, transects this state park and preserve east-west. Characteristic of its location on the Silurian Escarpment, 184-acre Bixby State Park and Preserve contains algific slopes, sinkholes, seeps, and an ice cave. Stand in front of the cave (located across the creek from the shelter) on a warm summer's day—the fifty-two-degree breeze will cool you off. Small trails will take you along the creek, but the upper slopes, especially those north facing, are extremely sensitive; keep your wandering to the narrow floodplain. For information: www.state.ia.us/dnr/organiza/ppd/bixby.htm.

Bluffs over Rivers

owa is known as "The Land Between Two Rivers," and its eastern and western boundaries—the Mississippi and Missouri Rivers—usually receive the most notice. Little attention is paid to their countless tributaries, from which these mighty waterways draw their size and power. Just as arteries, capillaries, and veins course through our bodies, transporting oxygen-filled lifeblood, so branch the waterways of our state. The undulating hills that sweep across the southeast Iowa landscape were created and are defined by the rills, creeks, streams, and rivers that drain them. And the Mississippi River doesn't just absorb its tributaries, it swallows them.

Though each of southeast Iowa's rivers is distinct, as the waterways near their short-term destination (a mouth into the Mississippi River), they share several common traits. They all possess wide and deep valleys and, in some places, exposed bedrock in the form of bluffs, or Palisades, for which the state park on the Cedar River was named. A short 11,000 years ago, the Cedar, Iowa, and Skunk Rivers all had glaciers in their headwaters, and as the vast Des Moines Lobe ice sheet eroded, meltwater found various paths to the sea. Valley walls were eroded down to the underlying bedrock and widened considerably. The bluffs that now preside over and frame our rivers are a testament to the sheer velocity of erosion caused by waters melting off glaciers.

The first people in Iowa lived along the floodplains of streams and rivers, hunting and gathering and later growing corn, squash, beans, tobacco, sunflowers, and goosefoot. They used the rivers as networked trade routes and quarried flint and chert from banks and bluffs for tools. Euro-American steamships brought the first loads up the Cedar and Iowa Rivers in the 1830s and 1840s. Saw and gristmills stood along the bulk of the larger streams and rivers, providing energy to mill the forests that were being logged and process the grain that was being grown, fueling the infant Iowan economy.

Southeast Iowa houses a plethora of river towns. The biggest are the Quad Cities (Bettendorf and Davenport in Iowa and in Moline and Rock Island in Illinois) sitting alongside the Mississippi River, Iowa City and Cedar Rapids (their names indicating the associated rivers) are two cities rapidly sprawling into one megalopolis. The corridor for development is broken only by the Coralville Reservoir and Lake MacBride, two lakes created by damming the Iowa River and several small tributaries, respectively. During the 1993 floods, the Devonian Fossil Gorge, located next to Coralville Dam, was scoured out by water flowing over the spillway, exposing 375-million-year-old coral, brachiopod, crinoid, and armored fish fossils.

Wildcat Den State Park, located east of the Mississippi River town of Muscatine, boasts an entrenched, sandstone-framed canyon just upstream of Pine Creek's mouth. In his book *Life on the Mississippi,* river-rat-turned-author Mark Twain wrote, "I remember Muscatine—still more pleasantly—for its summer sunsets. I have never seen any, on either side of the ocean, that equaled them. They used the broad smooth river as a canvas, and painted on it every imaginable dream of color."

The Mark Twain National Wildlife and Fish Refuge encompasses 45,000 acres divided between units spanning 345 river miles along the Mississippi, as well as the Iowa River Corridor, a 10,000-acre greenbelt located in Tama, Benton, and Iowa Counties. Iowa's portion of the Mark Twain NWRF, Port Louisa National Wildlife Refuge (and adjacent state-owned Lake Odessa Wildlife Management Area), is located just south of Muscatine. Between the bluffs and the levee along the river are nearly 4 square miles of wetlands and floodplain forests teeming with wildlife.

Between hikes at Geode State Park and Starr's Cave Park and Preserve, you can check out Snake Alley in Burlington, known as the "crookedest street in the world." Aldo Leopold, a seasoned conservationist, forester, wildlife biologist, and writer of several books, including *A Sand County Almanac,* was born and raised in Burlington, and his legacy lives on through the work of many. From Geode State Park, if you travel up the Skunk River, you'll pass the town of Mount Pleasant on your way to Brinton Timber, a park in Washington County just next door to Lake Darling State Park.

Standing atop a bluff and peering down onto any of our rivers, you can't help but look to the water for reflection. Rivers that course through our Iowa valleys are monuments to change. Harbingers of transformation, they bring the promise of a healthy crop of corn, a new family of wood ducks, or a hatch of russet-tipped clubtail dragonflies. Our rivers do not always reflect such beauty as Mark Twain wrote of; instead, their health is evidence of grave injury. The Cedar, Iowa, Mississippi, and Skunk Rivers, as well as Lake MacBride and the Coraville Reservoir, are all on the Environmental Protection Agency's "Impaired Waters List" due to high levels of nitrates, siltation, fecal matter, and pesticides. Restoration and cleanup work that state and federal agency staff, local volunteers, and organizations like Living Lands & Waters do each year is crucial to the health of our rivers—and help is always welcomed.

9 Palisades-Kepler State Park

"The valley of the red cedar is in eastern Iowa, a long strip of fertile land sprawling out besides the river whose name it bears." So said native Iowan Bess Streeter Aldrich of the Cedar River Valley in her book *Song of Years*. The palisades for which the park was named are sheer 60-foot-high cliffs that loom over the valley of the red cedar. Hiking trails traverse the palisade crests and the forested hills of the park, which doubles as a rock-climber's paradise.

Distance: 3.8 miles round-trip
Approximate hiking time: 1 to 2 hours
Total elevation gain: 602 feet
Trail surface: Forested footpaths, rock stairs
Seasons: Year-round
Trail users: Hikers
Canine compatability: Dogs permitted on leash
Hazards: Poison ivy, ticks, steep rock faces over fast-flowing river

Land status: State park
Nearest towns: Cedar Rapids, Mt. Vernon
Fees and permits: No fees or permits required unless you are camping here
Schedule: Year-round, 4:00 A.M. to 10:30 P.M.
Map: USGS quad: Bertram
Trail contact: Palisades-Kepler State Park, 700 Kepler Drive; (319) 895-6039, www .state.ia.us/dnr/organiza/ppd/palikepl.htm

Finding the trailhead: From the junction of U.S. Highway 30 and Highway 1 in Mt. Vernon, drive west on US 30. Before you cross over the Cedar River, turn left (south) onto Kepler Drive, which will take you into the park. *DeLorme: Iowa Atlas and Gazetteer:* Page 43 10F

The Hike

To stand above an eastern Iowa river, whose downward action has cut a wide chasm in the surrounding forested hills, is to see that river not only for what it is but for what it once was.

The resistant dolomite cliffs towering above the Cedar River at Palisades–Kepler were deposited 420 to 440 million years ago, when they were muddy tropical reef–like masses on the Silurian Sea floor. Colonial coral, crinoid beds, and brachiopod fossils found in the mounds of the exposed Scotch Grove and Gower Formations paint a picture of a sea that was very different from those of today. Organisms that once inhabited shallow marine shelves are now deepwater dwelling, their old niches having been commandeered during the last 400–plus million years. Also, the coral reefs of today are composed mainly of piled-up coral cemented together by calcifying algae, whereas the carbonate "mounds" of the Silurian age were made of various fossils held in a carbonate mud matrix.

Because of the resistance to erosion of the dolomite bedrock, the ridgelike Silurian Escarpment is a major landscape feature in northeast Iowa and can also be seen at Backbone, Maquoketa Caves, and Bellevue State Parks.

Also found within Palisade-Kepler's bluffs are nodules of chert, a hard rock composed of silicon dioxide. Because of its sharp, glasslike edges, many native peoples used chert to make tools. Archaeological excavations from rock shelters in Palisades-Dows State Preserve across the river have yielded extensive caches of animal bones and pottery shards, evidence of occupation over the past 2,500 years.

From the parking lot walk north onto the Cedar Cliff Trail, which passes along the river and then climbs up on the ridge overlooking it. The sugar maple–basswood forest is quite dense, but as you ascend the rocks to the blufftop, the world opens up. Oak-hickory forest covers the dry uplands, while prairie glades command the exposed ridgetops. The oldest known tree in Iowa, an eastern red cedar approaching 500 years old, lives here on the bluffs, hanging fast to its rock base over the river that bears its name.

Continue up the trail and you'll ascend stairs to the overlook gazebo, built by the Civilian Conservation Corps (CCC) in the 1930s and recently restored. Eastern Iowa rock climbers flock to the palisades below for some of the best top-roping and traditional routes around. The climbing is free, but you must register with the ranger, and because of the fast flowing river below, *don't attempt anything if you're unsure of yourself.* Whether you're climbing or just exploring, be careful not to disturb the diverse communities of moss, liverwort, lichen, and fern growing on the rocks.

The Cedar Cliff Trail continues to the northern boundary of the park, where you'll have to turn around and loop back. The trail follows just below the ridge, above several steep ravines. You'll find yourself at canopy height of the trees growing on the sides of the steep drainages, the perfect place to look for birds. Look for scarlet tanager and American redstart flitting along.

Turn left onto the first trail you encounter, which will take you up to several Indian mounds. From the mounds, cross the road onto the aptly named Cool Hollow Trail, which will take you in and out of a large ravine on your way back down to the river road and parking lot. By walking south on the road instead of north, you can add another 1.4 miles to your hike. Complete the figure–eight circuit by walking east up the big ravine just southeast of the low head dam. This will bring you up and over the road and back into Cool Hollow, where you can retrace your steps back down to the trailhead.

Miles and Directions

0.0 Start at the Cedar Cliff trailhead. Hike to the top of the bluff and walk above the Cedar River. Continue due north; save the forks for later. (FYI: Try to figure out which eastern red cedar is the oldest, but don't lean too far over the edge. If the sides of the river freeze in winter, you can get views of all the trees from the ice below.)

0.4 Climb the stairs up to the small shelter; take a moment to gaze at the Cedar River.

Climb the rock staircases built by the Civilian Conservation Corps (CCC) to wander the palisades.

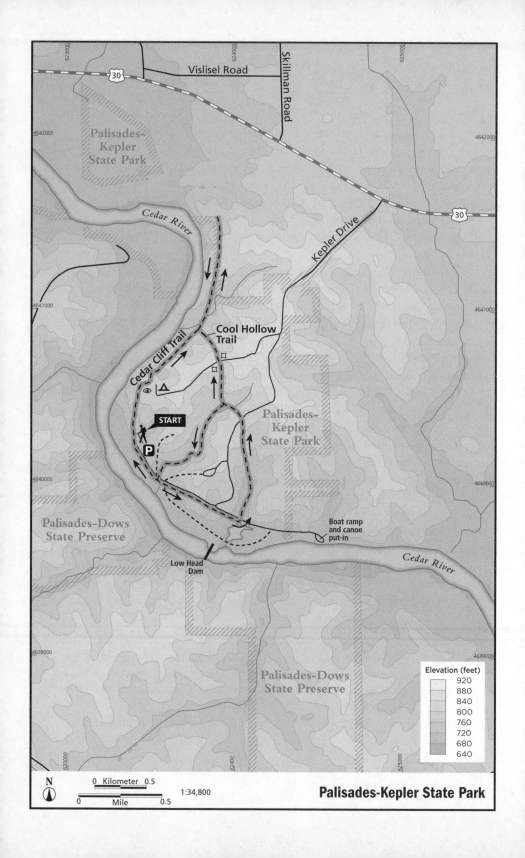

Vislisel Road

Skillman Road

30

Palisades-
Kepler
State Park

4642000

4642000

Cedar River

Kepler Drive

30

4641000

4641000

Cool Hollow
Trail

Cedar Cliff Trail

START

P

Palisades-
Kepler
State Park

4640000

4640000

Palisades-Dows
State Preserve

Boat ramp
and canoe
put-in

Cedar River

Low Head
Dam

4639000

4639000

Palisades-Dows
State Preserve

Elevation (feet)
920
880
840
800
760
720
680
640

N

0   Kilometer   0.5

0   Mile   0.5

1:34,800

Palisades-Kepler State Park

1.1 Arrive at the northern boundary of the park; turn around and backtrack.

1.5 At the fork turn left (southeast). Ascend the ridge toward the road.

1.7 Arrive at the road and the conical burial mounds, some of the many that probably once stood on these bluffs above the Cedar River. Cross the road and continue on the Cool Hollow Trail.

1.8 At the bottom of the ravine, turn right (south) after you've crossed the bridge, and follow the creek down to the trailhead.

2.3 Arrive at the road; turn right (north) to get back to the trailhead. To continue hiking, albeit on less defined trails, turn left (south) and follow the road past the low head dam and the shelter.

2.7 When you see the large ravine to the northeast, turn left (west) onto the small footpath at the base of the ravine.

2.9 Climb up the second or third finger ridge to the north, whichever suits you, toward the road.

3.1 Cross the road and continue straight northwest down the finger ridge into Cool Hollow.

3.2 Arrive back at the bridge you crossed before, and follow your same path back down to the road/trailhead.

3.7 Arrive at the road, and turn right (northwest) to get back to the trailhead.

3.8 Arrive back at the trailhead.

Hike Information

Local Information
Cedar Rapids; www.cedar-rapids.org

Events/Attractions
Cedar Rapids Museum of Art, 410 Third Avenue, Cedar Rapids; (319) 366-7503, www.crma.org

African American Historical Museum & Cultural Center of Iowa, 55 Twelfth Street SE, Cedar Rapids; (319) 862-2101

Indian Creek Nature Center, 6665 Otis Road SE, Cedar Rapids; (319) 362-0664

Curtis Hill Indian Museum, Iowa's largest private collection of artifacts; (319) 848-4323

Cedar Rapids City Market, 1350 A Street SW, Cedar Rapids; (319) 286-5731; April through October, Tuesday and Thursday 3:30 to 5:30 P.M., Saturday 6:30 to 11:30 A.M.

Accommodations
Joy in the Morning B&B, 1809 Second Avenue SE, Cedar Rapids; (319) 363-9731

Linn County Conservation Board Parks, extensive campgrounds; (319) 892-6450, www.linncountyparks.com

Restaurants
Thai Moon Restaurant 4362 Sixteenth Avenue SW, Cedar Rapids; (319) 390-7747

The Greek Place, 2663 Mt. Vernon Road SE, Cedar Rapids; (319) 366-7817

Taj Mahal Cuisine of Indian, 5454 Blairs Forest Way NE, Cedar Rapids; (319) 393-4500

Lincoln Cafe, 117 First Street West, Mt. Vernon; (319) 895-4041

Other Resources
The Cedar Amateur Astronomers; www.cedar-astronomers.org

CSPS, music venue/art museum, 1103 Third Street SE; (319) 364-8591

Basically Books, 212 Edgewood Road NW, Cedar Rapids; (319) 396-8420

Cedar Rapids Audubon Society; www.iowabirds.org/birdingiowa/clubs.asp

10 Coralville Reservoir–Linder and Squire Points

One of the many developed trail systems around the Coralville Reservoir–Lake MacBride complex, the connecting loops of Linder and Squire Points Trails have long served as a haven for dog walkers and trail runners. A few loops on the trails here combined with a nice bike ride around the reservoir make for a great day. Add in a jump off the cliffs into the reservoir during the hot summer, and you've got a perfect day.

Distance: 4.4 miles of connecting loops
Approximate hiking time: 1 to 3 hours
Total elevation gain: 908 feet
Trail surface: Forested footpath, connecting trails
Seasons: Year-round
Trail users: Hikers and cross-country skiers
Canine compatability: Dogs permitted
Hazards: Poison ivy, ticks
Land status: U.S. Army Corps of Engineers property

Nearest towns: Iowa City, North Liberty
Fees and permits: No fees or permits necessary
Schedule: Open year-round, dawn to dusk
Map: USGS quad: Iowa City West
Trail contact: U.S. Army Corps of Engineers Rock Island District, Coralville Lake Project, 2850 Prairie Du Chien Road NE, Iowa City, IA 52240; (319) 338-3543; www.coralvillelake.org

Finding the trailhead: From Interstate 80, take exit 244, and follow Dubuque Street north 2.6 miles. Turn right (east) onto West Overlook Road; you'll see a sign for Linder Point and Woodpecker Trail parking area. Follow West Overlook Road down the hill; just before ascending to cross the dam, you'll find the Devonian Fossil Gorge entrance on the right. Continue over the dam and follow the signs to the visitor center on the north side of the road. Drive 0.3 mile farther to play the eighteen-hole disc-golf course. *DeLorme: Iowa Atlas and Gazetteer:* Page 43 I10

The Hike

Floods in the 1930s prompted Congress to establish the Flood Control Act of 1938, which authorized the U.S. Army Corps of Engineers (USACE) to build dams on tributaries of the Mississippi. The Iowa River was one of the first to be dammed. The Coralville Dam, 100 feet high and 1,400 feet long, was completed in 1958. Land bordering the newly created Coralville Reservoir was left fallow after decades of agricultural use had decimated the native flora. The Woodpecker Trail interpretive loop connects the Squire and Linder Point Trail networks on the southern end of the Coralville Reservoir. Loops of various lengths and elevation gains allow hikers to choose desired distances and difficulty. Deep ravines cut the hilly terrain, and

Limestone and dolomite outcrops form steps down to the waters of Coralville Reservoir.

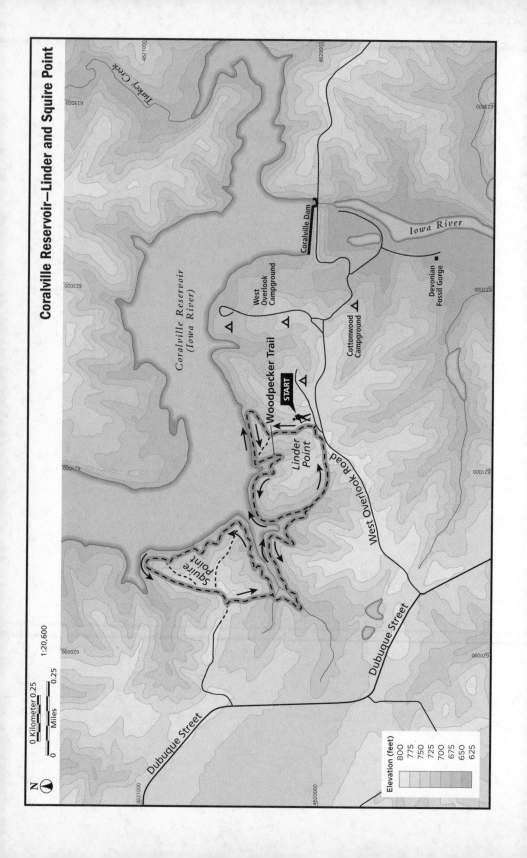

Coralville Reservoir—Linder and Squire Point

N

0 Kilometer 0.25   1:20,600

0   0.25

Miles

Turkey Creek

Coralville Reservoir
(Iowa River)

Coralville Dam

Iowa River

West
Overlook
Campground

Cottonwood
Campground

Devonian
Fossil Gorge

Woodpecker Trail

START

Linder
Point

West Overlook Road

Squire
Point

Dubuque Street

Dubuque Street

Elevation (feet)

800
775
750
725
700
675
650
625

limestone outcrops offer picturesque views of the lake as well as visual lessons in the geologic history of the area.

Both Linder and Squire Point trailheads begin where upland forest trees dominate: shagbark hickory, white and red oaks, silver maple, honey locust, and hop hornbeam. Easily distinguished amid the neighboring deciduous trees are the interspersed eastern redcedars. The eastern redcedar, a coniferous tree, normally colonizes open, sunny places, such as the pastureland this area was used as after it was logged during the early 1800s. When the Corps bought the land, domesticated animals and fences were removed, and a more typical upland forest grew in around the eastern red cedars.

In the oak-hickory forest covering the hills, you'll find wildflowers blooming throughout spring and summer. Look for anemone, bloodroot, mayapple, black snakeroot, bellwort, jack-in-the-pulpit, and lobelia. You will most likely encounter white-tailed deer nibbling on greens, as the wooded areas around the lake provide a sanctuary for deer driven from their historic range by intense agricultural cultivation in much of Johnson County.

The trail follows a contour about 50 feet above the water's edge, depending on fluctuating lake levels. On the disturbed banks next to the trail, look for moss and lichen groundcover: hair cap moss, tree moss, and fairy cups. The crossing of two bridges provides overhead views of the flood-prone sites surrounding the lake, as well as a small creek's entrance to the lake, fringed by willow thickets.

Many songbirds can be observed in the upland forest during breeding and migration times. If you're lucky you'll see prothonotary and cerulean warblers, red-eyed vireo, American redstart, blue-gray gnatcatcher, and ovenbird. (Hickory Hill Park, a city park in Iowa City, is a favorite warbler-watching sanctuary.)

While focusing on the birds, try to tell the difference between two common and extremely similar-looking woodpeckers, the downy and hairy. These are the only woodpeckers with entirely white backs, although they have the black-and-white checkers and spots common to other woodpecker species. The males have a distinguishing small patch of red on the backs of their heads. The hairy woodpecker is approximately 3 inches longer than the downy, and its call is a sharp "peek," while the downy has a slightly larger bill and calls a flat "pick."

Descending to the lake, the forest structure changes as trees that are tolerant of fluctuating water levels dominate: cottonwood, black willow, and basswood. Here you'll have the best chance to see the rare pileated woodpecker, the largest woodpecker left in America, hammering on large snags for insects. Cavity-prone tree species such as basswood, silver maple, and black cherry may also house northern flicker, red-headed woodpecker, barred owl, and eastern screech owl.

When snow is on the ground, the trails provide ungroomed cross-country skiing. (Hikers and snowshoers are asked to steer clear of established ski tracks.) Winter bird residents include black-capped chickadee, brown creeper, blue jay, northern cardinal, and tufted titmouse. Ringed-bill gulls live at the lake year-round and can

PLACES TO ROAM AROUND THE LAKES
Your trip to the Coralville Reservoir area doesn't have to end at Linder Point. Check out Sherwood Forest; Lake MacBride State Park; Lake MacBride Nature Recreation Area, home of the raptor center and cross-country ski trails; as well as Sugar Bottom Recreation Area, one of the top mountain biking trail networks in Iowa. The areas were named for ecologist Thomas MacBride, the "father of conservation" in Iowa and president of the University of Iowa from 1914 to 1916.

be seen from almost anywhere patrolling overhead. Bald eagles will occasionally fly over the lake; they winter along the Iowa River, which, unlike the Coralville Reservoir, remains unfrozen year-round. Watch for gray and fox squirrels digging for stashes of acorns when snow is heavy and all edible plants are covered.

Miles and Directions

0.0 Start from the Linder Point parking area.

0.2 At fork, turn right (northeast).

0.3 At fork at the bottom of the hill, turn left (west).

0.45 At the point, continue around the contour of the lake.

1.8 At fork, stay right and continue around the contour of the lake.

2.7 You've reached the northern boundary of the USACE property. Follow the trail left (west) and ascend the ridge to the Squire Point trailhead and parking before descending back down to the contour trail around the lake.

3.2 At the fork at the bottom of the hill, turn right (southwest) onto the contour trail.

3.9 At the fork, turn right (southeast) to return quickly to the trailhead via the long staircase, or follow the contour trail for a little more distance.

4.4 Arrive back at the trailhead.

Hike Information

Local Information
Iowa City–Coralville Convention & Visitors Bureau; (800) 283-6592, www.icccvb.org

Events/Attractions
Iowa City Jazz Festival, July, Iowa City; (319) 358-9346, www.iowacityjazzfestiva.com
University of Iowa Museum of Natural History, Macbride Hall, Iowa City; (319) 335-0482, www.uiowa.edu/~nathist

Devonian Fossil Gorge and Stainbrook State Geologic Preserve (375-million-year-old exposed fossils and bedrock with glacial grooves!); www.igwa.org/devonian.asp, www.state.ia.us/dnr/organiza/ppd/merrill.htm
Riverside Theatre, 213 North Gilbert Street, Iowa City; (319) 338-7672, www.riversidetheatre.org
Field to Family Festival, September, Iowa City; (319) 337-7885, www.fieldtofamily.org

University of Iowa Riverfest, second to last weekend in April; (319) 335-3273

Fiddler's Picnic: bluegrass, folk, and celtic music festival held late September in Iowa City. Contact Friends of Old Time Music at (319) 337-7180; http://zeus.ia.net/~mayhem/FOTM/picnic

Sugar Bottom Scramble: Annual mountain bike race held late June at Sugar Bottom Day Use Area. Contact Will Weibel at wjweibel@msn.com

Iowa City Farmers' Market, lower level, Chauncey Swan parking ramp, Iowa City; (319) 356-5110; May through October, Wednesday 5:30 to 7:30 P.M., Saturday 7:30 to 11:30 A.M.

New Pioneer Co-op, 22 South Van Buren Street, Iowa City; (319) 338-9441 or 1101 Second Street, Coralville; (319) 358-5513, www.newpi.com

Accommodations

Brown Street Inn, 430 Brown Street, Iowa City; (319) 338-0435

Haverkamps' Linn Street B&B Homestay, 619 North Linn Street, Iowa City; (319) 337-4363

Historic Phillips House, 721 North Linn Street, Iowa City; (319) 337-3223

The Golden Haug, 517 East Washington Street, Iowa City; (319) 354-4284, www.goldenhaug.com

Coralville Lake Campgrounds (U.S. Army Corps of Engineers) Coralville Lake; (877) 444-6777, www.mvr.usace.army.mil/Coralville/camp.htm

F. W. Kent Park, Tiffin; (319) 645-2315, www.johnson-county.com/conservation/camping

Restaurants

The Red Avocado, 521 East Washington Street, Iowa City; (319) 351-6088

Lou Henri, 630 Iowa Avenue, Iowa City; (319) 351-3637

The Mill Restaurant, 120 East Burlington, Iowa City; (319) 351-9529

The Sanctuary, 405 South Gilbert Street, Iowa City; (319) 351-5692

Other Resources

Prairie Lights Book Store, 15 South Dubuque Street, Iowa City; (319) 337-2681, www.prairielights.com

Iowa City Bird Club; www.icbirds.org

11 Wildcat Den State Park

The cats for which the park was named were mostly killed off in the mid–1800s, although rumors of bobcat sightings float around often enough. You can still see the Pennsylvanian sandstone outcrops, more than 300 million years after their deposition. Along Pine Creek, just a mile upstream from its confluence with the Mississippi River, you'll find exposed Devonian bedrock with a host of crinoid, brachiopod, and coral fossils. A delight to geologists and fern lovers, Wildcat Den State Park is the place to take your time on a slow walk so that you can enjoy the diversity of everything that's going on there.

Distance: 4.5-mile lollipop
Approximate hiking time: 2 to 3 hours
Total elevation gain: 787 feet
Trail surface: Forested footpath
Seasons: Year-round
Trail users: Hikers and cross-country skiers
Canine compatability: Dogs permitted on leash
Hazards: Poison ivy and ticks
Land status: State park

Nearest town: Muscatine
Fees and permits: No fees or permits required unless you are camping
Schedule: Open year-round, 4:00 A.M. to 10:30 P.M.
Map: USGS quad: Illinois City
Trail contact: Wildcat Den State Park, 1884 Wildcat Den Road, Muscatine; (563) 263-4337, www.iowadnr.com/parks/state_park_list/wildcat_den.html

Finding the trailhead: From the junction of Highways 92 and 22 in Muscatine, drive northeast on Highway 22. Drive along the Mississippi River, through the town of Fairport, and turn left (north) onto Wildcat Den Road. *DeLorme: Iowa Atlas and Gazetteer:* Page 55 C6

The Hike

Park at the northernmost picnic area, next to Wildcat Cave, a rock shelter quite possibly used by the Sauk and Fox (now Mesquakie) tribes that once lived here. Mounds have been found just outside the park, but little archaeological investigation has taken place inside the park. Following the trail southeast, the lowland forest is abloom with wildflowers during spring and summer.

To the north of Steamboat Rock, named for its shape, you'll discover a passageway known as Devil's Lane. Here you'll find carved graffiti dating from 1861, although earlier graffiti at the base of the cliffs may have been destroyed by erosion. Fat Man's Squeeze used to be located near Devil's Lane. A small opening in the rocks once wide enough to shimmy through, it has recently succumbed to erosion and collapsed.

Pennsylvanian sandstone outcrops covered in lichens ▶
in Wildcat Den State Park.

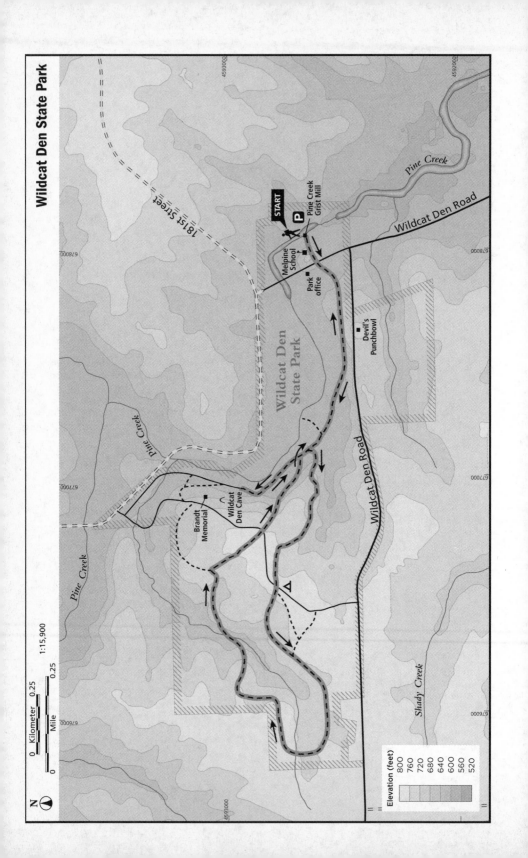

Continuing on the main trail, follow the signs to Devil's Punchbowl, a large bowl sculpted by a seasonal creek and the most visited formation in the park. Here is the best place to view the Pennsylvanian sandstone of which most of the bluffs in the park are made. Look in the sandstone for cross-bedding and ripples, suggesting that it was deposited by a shifting river channel.

The park houses a broad array of twenty-five types of ferns; on the sandstone you'll find polypody, cliff, Goldie's, and walking ferns. Look for rock-dwelling moss, liverwort, and lichen communities, especially in places where water trickles down the rocks. These nonvascular plants can go dormant during dry spells and the cold of winter; however, the first spring rains and warmer days bring them back to life. Take a break to sit in the cool shade of an overhang, examine the plant communities on the rocks, and listen to the echo of dripping water as it tumbles off the sandstone shelves into pools below.

Climb up the bluff to connect with the upland trail, or continue toward the old school and mill area, winding back down to the creek. You'll pass the park headquarters and then cross the road to see the preserved buildings.

The Blackhawk Purchase, signed in 1832 by the Sauk and Fox tribes and the federal government, ceded tribal land to the government, opening up the Upper Midwest to white settlement in mid-1833. Benjamin Nye, Muscatine County's first white settler, arrived in 1834 and within a year had opened a trading post. Within fourteen years he had built a sawmill and two gristmills along Pine Creek. The presence of the mills and an influx of agrarian settlers set the tone for the native ecosystems—the surrounding terrain was logged, and much of it was cropped and grazed.

The second mill that Nye built still stands on the banks of Pine Creek within the park and was added to the National Register of Historic Places in 1979. During the 1960s, the Melpine Country School was moved to the park for preservation. Local organizations hold interpretive tours at both of these buildings. (Check with Friends of Pine Creek Grist Mill for times.)

On your way back from the mill, take a detour down to check out the bottomland forests along Pine Creek. Walnut, green ash, elm, cottonwood, and willow grow in the moist riparian lowlands. Look for belted kingfishers and great blue herons hunting on the creek. In May look for migratory songbirds along the water's edge. Occasional nesters include cerulean and Kentucky warblers, wood thrush, scarlet tanager, and ovenbird.

The upland portion of the park provides a good opportunity to view the area, as its bluffs rise significantly above the surrounding terrain (200 feet in some places). The northwestern part of the park was grazed and logged until the 1970s, and though the black oak and ironwood trees are young, you'll find a rare orchid, oval ladies' tresses (*Spiranthes ovalis*) here. At midsummer, search beneath the colonies of white pine on top of the cliffs for rattlesnake plantain (*Goodyera pubescens*), an orchid that likes the acidic conditions formed by decaying pine needles.

Miles and Directions

0.0 Start at the parking area between Wildcat Den Cave and Pine Creek. Check out the cave and the plaque dedicated to the Brandt sisters. (FYI: These cool women donated part of their old home to the park—what a place they must've had!)

0.3 At the T-intersection turn right (west) up into the box canyon. This will take you up to the Devil's Punchbowl.

0.6 At the fork, after you've ascended the wooden staircase up to the ridge, take a left (west) onto the trail that takes you to the campground.

0.76 Walk directly west through the campground and across the road; you'll see the hiking trail sign along the edge of the forest directly in front of you. This trail curves around the uplands of a small drainage in the extreme western portion of the park and then loops around toward Pine Creek.

2.1 At the fork take a right (southeast).

2.4 Come to the clearing, cross the road, and continue on the trail out onto the ridge overlooking Pine Creek. Descend the staircase.

2.7 Arrive back at the main lowland trail and turn right (east) to get to the Pine Creek Gristmill and Melpine School.

3.1 Cross the road.

3.4 Check out the antiquities: the school, the mill, and the underlying ancient Devonian seafloor, now exposed along the creek. Backtrack on the main trail to the trailhead.

4.5 Arrive back at the trailhead.

Hike Information

Local Information
City of Muscatine; www.muscatine.com
Muscatine Chamber of Commerce; www.meetmuscatine.com

Events/Attractions
Heritage Days and Buckskinner's Rendezvous, September, Wildcat Den Park; (563) 263-4337
Muscatine Art Center, 1314 Mulberry Avenue, Muscatine; (563) 263-8282
Peal Button Museum, 117 West Second Street, Muscatine; (563) 263-1052, www.pealbutton.org
Melon City Criterium, annual bike race held Memorial Day weekend, Muscatine; (563) 263-4043, www.bikeiowa.org
Muscatine Farmers' Market, 1512 Isett Avenue parking lot, Muscatine; May through September, Tuesday 3:00 to 6:30 P.M., Saturday 7:30 to 11:30 A.M.

Accommodations
Strawberry Farm Bed & Breakfast, 3402 Tipton Road, Muscatine; (563) 262-8688
Fairport Recreation Area (Iowa Department of Natural Resources), modern campsites; (563) 263-3197
Saulsbury Bridge Recreation Area (Muscatine County Conservation Board); (563) 264-5922, www.co.muscatine.ia.us

Restaurants
El Allende, 1107 Grandview Avenue, Muscatine; (563) 262-3969
Good Earth Restaurant, 5900 Grandview Avenue, Muscatine; (563) 263-6331
Downtown Cafe, 220 Walnut Street, Muscatine; (563) 263-9813

12 Odessa-Louisa Complex

The adjoining Lake Odessa State Wildlife Management Area and Louisa Division of Port Louisa National Wildlife Refuge together encompass more than 10 square miles of public land along the Mississippi River Flyway, one of North America's most important corridors for migrating birds. Because the Odessa-Louisa Complex is dedicated to providing ample habitat for animals and plants and caters mainly to boat recreation, it offers only one designated hiking trail. However, with a little imagination you'll be able to find suitable walking areas from which to observe migrating birds, as well as diverse mammals, reptiles, amphibians, and invertebrates.

Distance: 1.5-mile interpretive trail, additional 1.0 mile along gravel road. Six-mile-long levee that can be explored to any length; about 2 miles round-trip on access road from first parking area on Toolesboro Access road.
Approximate hiking time: 1 to 6 hours
Total elevation gain: 126 feet
Trail surface: Mowed firebreak, footpath through forest. Levee is wide man-made earth mound between river and land.
Seasons: Port Louisa Division (the levee) closed September 15 through January 31; interpretive trail remains open year-round. Lake Odessa is open year-round
Trail users: Hikers, hunters, birders
Canine compatability: Dogs permitted on leash
Hazards: Poison ivy, ticks

Land status: USFWS national wildlife refuge, state wildlife area
Nearest town: Wapello
Fees and permits: No fees or permits required unless you are camping
Schedule: Port Louisa National Wildlife Refuge serves as a migratory bird refuge and is closed September 14 to February 1, open during daylight hours the rest of the year. Lake Odessa State Wildlife Management Area is open year-round, 4:00 A.M. to 10:30 P.M.
Map: USGS quad: Toolesboro
Trail contact: Port Louisa National Wildlife Refuge (USFWS headquarters), 10728 County Road X61, Wapello; (319) 523-6982, http://midwest.fws.gov/PortLouisa/ Lake Odessa (IDNR Headquarters), 9726 CR X61, Wapello; (319) 523-3102, www.iowadnr .com/fish/fishing/lakes/ode58.html

Finding the trailhead: From the junction of U.S. Highway 61 and Highway 99 in Wapello, take Higway 99 southeast. On the east side of town, turn left (north) onto I Avenue and then take a quick right (east) on County Road G62. Follow CR G62 until you come to Great River Road (County Road X61). Turn left (north) onto CR X61 and look for the USFWS Headquarters sign on the east side of the road. To reach Port Louisa Access on the north side of the levee, continue north on CR X61 past the headquarters, and turn right (east) onto 120th Street. To get to the Toolesboro Access on the south side of the levee, stay on Highway 99 all the way to Toolesboro, where you'll turn left (east) onto Prairie Road. Stop at the first parking area to walk the access road to Blackhawk, or drive all the way to the river to walk the levee. *DeLorme: Iowa Atlas and Gazetteer:* Page 54 G4

Look for chicken-of-the-woods growing on rotting logs in Port Louisa National Wildlife Refuge.

The Hike

Lake Odessa isn't really just one lake; it is an area subject to inundation, bound by bluffs on the west side and a levee around the perimeter. The northern half is the Louisa Division of the Mark Twain National Wildlife Refuge, and the southern is the Lake Odessa State Wildlife Management Area. Together, managers with the IDNR and USFWS create wetland habitat for the many birds that migrate through. But there's much more than birds to this place.

In 1930 the federal government began construction of a system of twenty-six locks and dams on the Mississippi River between St. Paul, Minnesota, and St. Louis, Missouri. The U.S. Army Corps of Engineers was given responsibility for maintaining a 9-foot-deep navigational channel for barge traffic and controlling the flooding of adjacent cultivated land. After completion of the system in the 1940s, the federal government acquired land along the Mississippi River and established several units; in 1958 these were consolidated into the Mark Twain National Wildlife Refuge, with other areas added later.

Mark Twain NWR now encompasses 45,000 acres spread along 345 miles of the Mississippi, Illinois, and Iowa Rivers. In 2000 the refuge was divided into five separate national wildlife refuges. The northernmost of these is the Louisa Division, a 2,609-acre refuge located just east of Wapello in Louisa County.

The state first obtained part of what makes up Lake Odessa WMA in 1946 and began creating wetland, bottomland forest, and backwater pond habitat for wildlife. An access road irregularly used by Department of Natural Resources staff leads from a parking area on Toolesboro Access to Blackhawk, a large pond. The road heads directly north from the westernmost parking area for 1 mile and splits just before it stops at the water's edge, jutting off to the west another 0.5 mile. During spring and fall, waterfowl will be visible from the end of the road, so bring binoculars.

The 1.5-mile interpretive trail begins at the overlook near Port Louisa refuge headquarters and descends the bluff, a reminder that the Mississippi River was once much larger. You'll pass through bottomland forests and a native prairie reconstruction on your way back up to the overlook. Just before you turn right (west) to ascend the bluff, turn north onto a 1-mile access road that ends at 120th Street. It's a wonderful place to walk at dusk on a midsummer's night, when frogs are singing, bats foraging, and nighthawks performing their aerial magic.

A walk on the levee separating the Lake Odessa complex and the Mississippi River provides a glimpse into the past, when the river's ebb and flow weren't dictated by the U.S. Army Corps of Engineers. Maintenance of the 9-foot navigational channel has entirely changed the course of the Mississippi River, altering the backwater sloughs and floodplain forests. Current management practices include flooding various areas of Lake Odessa at specific times, mimicking the river's historic fluctuations and encouraging the growth of many forms of life.

On the federal land (northern half), the levee is closed September 14 to February 1. The state land (southern half) is not mowed during summer, which can make the going pretty rough. Use the levee for late-winter cross-country skiing and early spring walks to check out the bald eagles, hundreds of which occasionally overwinter near Lock and Dam #17. A river otter sighting is uncommon but spectacular. Rare copper-bellied and diamondback water snakes, Blanding's and red-eared turtles, and small-mouthed salamanders may be seen from the levee as well.

Given the array of ecosystems contained within the Lake Odessa complex, its most important feature may be the massive tract of continuous habitat. For migratory birds, however, the complex is like a catering business: Its wetlands produce millions of invertebrates, fingerling clams, fish, and various aquatic plants that fuel the birds during migration and breeding.

Immense numbers of waterfowl visit the complex during the spring and fall migrations, at whose height almost all ducks and geese found in Iowa can be seen. On an ideal day you'll spot Canada and snow geese, wood ducks, pied-billed grebes, pintails, green and blue-winged teals, mallards, northern shovelers, common mergansers, lesser scaups, common goldeneyes, and American coots.

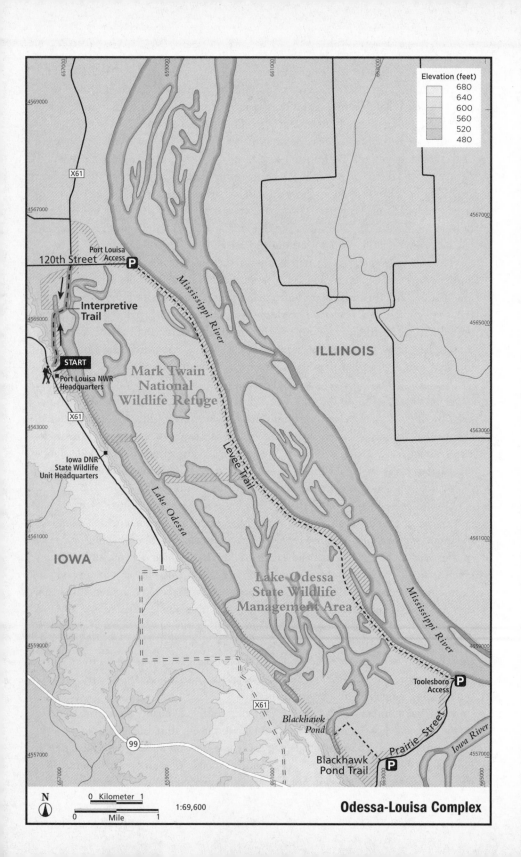

680
640
600
560
520
480

4569000

657000

4567000

X61

120th Street

Port Louisa
Access

P

Interpretive
Trail

4565000

659000

Mississippi River

661000

663000

ILLINOIS

4567000

4565000

4563000

START

Mark Twain
National
Wildlife Refuge

Port Louisa NWR
Headquarters

X61

4563000

Iowa DNR
State Wildlife
Unit Headquarters

Levee Trail

4561000

IOWA

Lake Odessa

Lake Odessa
State Wildlife
Management Area

Mississippi River

4561000

4559000

X61

4559000

Toolesboro
Access

P

99

Blackhawk
Pond

Prairie Street

Iowa River

4557000

Blackhawk
Pond Trail

P

4557000

657000

659000

661000

663000

665000

N

0   Kilometer   1

1:69,600

0   Mile   1

Odessa-Louisa Complex

From July to September the congregation of American white pelicans reaches into the thousands. These weighty birds' wings are brilliant white, with black under-wingtips. From far off, the contrast creates a magnificent sight as the birds circle and glide on updrafts. Many species of neotropical migratory songbirds can also be found in great numbers in the floodplain forests and prairie areas.

Miles and Directions

0.0 Start at the USFWS headquarters off CR G62. The interpretive trailhead is east of the observation platform. (FYI: Spend some time at the observation platform; although you are far from the river, the blufftop vista is quite a commanding view.)

0.5 If you continue on the trail (by turning left), you will ascend the bluff back to the trail-head. Turn right (north) to walk 1.0 mile north to 120th Street, passing through wetlands and ponds along the way.

1.6 Arrive at 120th Street; turn around and backtrack to the fork.

2.7 At the fork turn right (west) up the bluff to return to the trailhead.

3.2 Arrive back at the trailhead. Head over to the levee or the Blackhawk Pond hike to continue walking.

Hike Information

Local Information
City of Muscatine; www.muscatine.com
Muscatine Chamber of Commerce; www.meet muscatine.com

Events/Attractions
Heritage Days and Buckskinner's Rendezvous, September; Wildcat Den Park; (563) 263-4337
Muscatine Art Center, 1314 Mulberry Avenue, Muscatine; (563) 263-8282
Peal Button Museum, 117 West Second Street, Muscatine; (563) 263-1052, www.pealbutton.org
Melon City Criterium, annual bike race held Memorial Day weekend, Muscatine; (563) 263-4043, www.bikeiowa.org

Accommodations
Eagles Nest Bed & Breakfast, 98 Surrey Drive, Wapello; (319) 523-2111

Snively Access and Flaming Prairie Park, County Road X61; Grandview; primitive and modern campgrounds (Louisa County Conservation Board); (319) 523-8381

Restaurants
Rocky's Landing, 9673 F Avenue, Wapello; (319) 523-8115
Bootleggers Restaurant & Sports Bar, 214 Iowa Avenue, Muscatine; (563) 264-2686
Good Earth Restaurant, 5900 Grandview Avenue, Muscatine; (563) 263-6331

Other Resources
Up on the River: An Upper Mississippi Chronicle by John Madson (Nick Lyons Books)
The Iowa Breeding Bird Atlas by Laura Spess Jackson, Carol A. Thompson, and James J. Dinsmore (Bur Oak Books Series, University of Iowa Press)

LIVING LANDS & WATERS The folks who work for Living Lands & Waters, a nonprofit organization started by Chad Pregracke in 1997, wake up every morning to do some of the dirtiest, most incredible work any Mississippi river rat could ever imagine. The crew works with local volunteers on the Mississippi, Ohio, and Illinois Rivers, cleaning up garbage, planting riparian trees, and holding educational workshops. Living Lands & Waters has removed thousands of tons of refuse from these rivers since 1997, and the efforts will only continue to grow with the help of sponsors and volunteers. Contact them to donate money or elbow grease, and help take care of our rivers.

Living Lands & Waters, 17615 Highway 84 N, Great River Road, East Moline, Illinois; (309) 496-9648, www.livinglandsandwaters.org.

13 Starr's Cave Park and Preserve

The preserve is split in half by Flint Creek, which cuts through a nearly vertical 100-foot-high escarpment of fossil-rich Mississippian limestone. Starr's Cave, 300 feet long and home to several species of bats, is a great spelunking experience for folks who don't suffer from claustrophobia. Exploration of the cave isn't the only thing to do here. The forest and prairie areas of this 184-acre preserve host diverse wildflowers and birds, and the 0.25-mile Rossiter Trail is accessible to people with disabilities.

Distance: 2.8-mile loop
Approximate hiking time: 1 to 2 hours
Total elevation gain: 428 feet
Trail surface: Forested footpath mulched in places; Rossiter Trail paved
Seasons: Year-round. The nature center is open Monday through Friday 8:00 A.M. to 4:00 P.M. year-round, Saturday 9:00 A.M. to 4:00 P.M. April through September and during winter when there is enough snow to cross-country ski. Starr's Cave is open April 1 through October 1.
Trail users: Hikers and cross-country skiers
Canine compatability: Dogs permitted on leash

Hazards: Poison ivy and ticks. Flint Creek has very high fecal matter levels and should not be entered.
Land status: State preserve, managed by Des Moines County Conservation Board
Nearest town: Burlington
Fees and permits: No fees or permits required
Schedule: Year-round, 6:00 A.M. to 10:30 P.M.
Map: USGS quad: West Burlington
Trail contact: Starr's Cave Nature Center, managed by Des Moines Conservation Board, 11627 Starr's Cave Road, Burlington, Iowa 52601; (319) 753-5808, www .interl.net/~starcave, www.state.ia.us/dnr/ organiza/ppd/starr.htm

Looking up from Flint Creek into the mouth of Starr's Cave.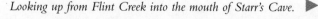

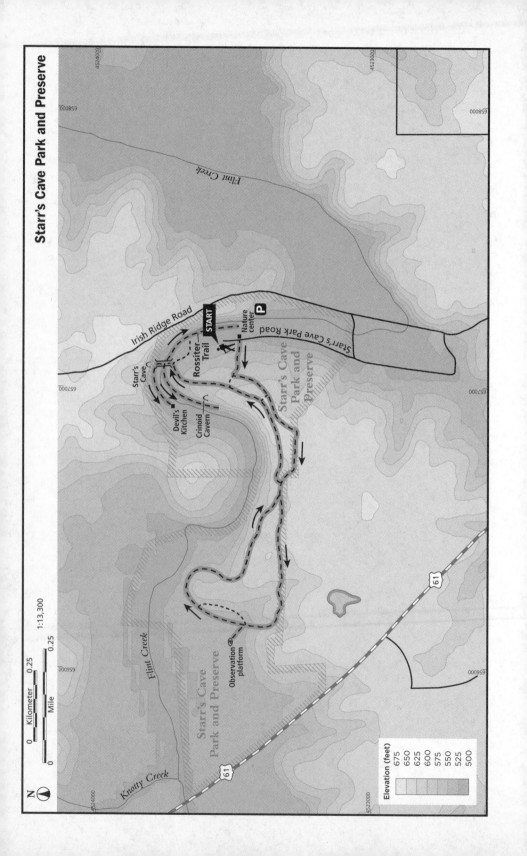

Starr's Cave Park and Preserve

1:13,300

N

Kilometer
0   0.25

Mile
0   0.25

Elevation (feet)
675
650
625
600
575
550
525
500

Flint Creek

Irish Ridge Road

START

Nature center

P

Starr's Cave Park Road

Starr's Cave

Rossiter Trail

Devil's Kitchen

Crinoid Cavern

Starr's Cave Park and Preserve

Observation platform

Flint Creek

Knotty Creek

Starr's Cave Park and Preserve

61

61

Finding the trailhead: From the junction of U.S. Highways 34 and 61 on the north side of Burlington, drive north on US 61. Turn right (east) onto Sunnyside Avenue and then left (north) onto Irish Ridge Road. Turn left (west) onto Starr's Cave Road, where there is a sign. *DeLorme: Iowa Atlas and Gazetteer:* Page 64 C 3

The Hike

There are three caves within the preserve. The largest was named for a previous landowner, the preserve's namesake. As with most caverns in Iowa, Starr's Cave is rumored to have been used as a hideout by Jesse James and his gang; it's also thought to have been a stop on the Underground Railroad. Previous explorations describe the cave as 750 feet long, and even older stories claim it once extended as far as the Mississippi River, more than a mile away.

Today an assortment of bat species enjoy the constantly fifty-five-degree temperature of Starr's Cave, which serves as a hibernacula during winter and breeding grounds during summer for big and little brown bats and quite possibly the endangered Indiana bat. Because of the sensitive nature of bat hibernation, the cave is closed from October 2 through May 31.

In the past, Starr's Cave was accessed by trail from a parking area on Irish Ridge Road. It's now reached by taking the paved Rossiter Trail along Flint Creek and crossing the new bridge that spans the creek and leads to the mouth of the cave. Bring a headlamp or flashlight and be ready to crawl in order to explore the 300 feet of narrow passage that ends in a cool, quiet room—a peaceful end to a hike on a hot day.

From the parking area in front of the nature center, walk west up the hill where oak-hickory forests form an extensive canopy. Eight species of oaks and three species of hickory live within the small preserve, a testament to its topographic variance and habitat diversity. Within the upland forests you'll find white, black, bur, and red oaks intermingling with shagbark, bitternut, and mockernut hickory, among others. The delicate spring wildflowers are in full bloom during April and May. Look for Dutchman's breeches, spring beauty, hepatica, rue anemone, bluebells, and trillium.

The trail leads down the ridge to a small prairie reconstruction area where, from the viewing platform in early morning, you may see a coyote slinking through the tall grass. Walk east up the ridge that towers 100 feet above Flint Creek, where eastern red cedars, redbuds, blue ash, and chestnut oaks hang onto the rocky bluff amid a moss and lichen bed. Don't walk too close to the edge of the steep bluffs here. The rock is somewhat unstable, and it's a long way down to the bottom of the canyon.

Follow the trail down the east side of the ridge to the cave trail, which leads to Crinoid Cavern, a small cave/room facing the creek—a good place to enjoy a snack. Check out the ceiling for fossils of brachiopods, crinoids, and cup corals, as well as a gray-green crustose lichen that can survive in environments with little light. From here you'll see black-capped chickadees flitting along green ash treetops, while belted kingfishers and great blue herons make hunting pilgrimages up and down the drainage.

Flint Creek is framed by tall sycamore and cottonwood trees, as well as thickets of peachleaf willow. Horsetails, wood and stinging nettles, and wild grapes occupy the creekside understory. Long ago, the flint deposits for which the creek was named were collected by Sauk and Fox tribes to make tools. More than a century of farming and grazing near the creek have left it with dangerously high fecal-matter levels; it's not advisable to wade in the creek.

Though it would be pretty hard to get lost, take note that all trail intersections are marked with red arrows that point away from the nature center and green arrows that point toward it. The center rents out cross-country skis during winter when there is 4 inches or more of snow and offers tours for school children during the warm seasons.

Miles and Directions

0.0 Start at the parking lot in front of nature center. The trailhead is just up the hill to the west, where several loops begin. (FYI: To follow the long loop all the way to the observation tower and back, take the left fork at each intersection.)

0.94 Descend the ridge and check out the observation platform at the prairie reconstruction. Turn left at the fork to ascend the ridge again.

2.0 Arrive at the bridge that will take you over to Starr's Cave. When you are done spelunking, return back to the south side of the creek and turn north onto the paved Rossiter Trail. Follow the sign that reads CAVE TRAIL to Crinoid Cavern.

2.6 Stop and have a break here in Crinoid Cavern, a fossil-rich cave/room. (FYI: When the trees are bare, Devil's Kitchen and Starr's Cave are both visible across the creek.) Backtrack on the Cave Trail to the Rossiter Trail, and make your way back to the trailhead. (FYI: You'll pass the foundation and remnants of an old house, probably built during the nineteenth century. The big red barn where the nature center is housed was once the Sycamore Inn and is rumored to have been a pretty happening hangout.

2.84 Return to the trailhead and check out the nature center if it's open.

ALDO LEOPOLD: IOWAN CONSERVATIONIST Aldo Leopold, an acclaimed naturalist, conservationist, and writer, was born in 1887 and grew up in Burlington, Iowa. He received a master's degree from Yale University School of Forestry, worked for the USDA Forest Service and President Franklin D. Roosevelt's Committee on Wildlife Restoration, and was a professor and chairman of the University of Wisconsin Department of Game Management. His writings on the necessity for preservation of native ecosystems have inspired conservationists all over the world. Must-reads include his best-known work, *A Sand County Almanac*, as well as the collection *The River of the Mother of God: And Other Essays by Aldo Leopold*, edited by Susan L. Flader and J. Baird Callicott.

Hike Information

Local Information

Burlington Convention and Tourism Bureau; (800) 82-RIVER

Events/Attractions

Snake Alley, called the "Crookedest Street in the World" by *Ripley's Believe It or Not;* www.snakealley.com

Snake Alley Criterium (great bike race, Memorial Day Weekend); (319) 752-0015, www.snakealley.com/criterium

Burlington Steamboat Days—American Music Festival, mid-June; (319) 754-4334, www.steamboatdays.com

Riverfront Farmers' Market, 400 Front Street, Port of Burlington; (319) 752-0015; May through September, Thursday, 5:00 to 8:00 P.M.

Accommodations

Lower Skunk River Access (west of Burlington), Des Moines County Conservation Board; (319) 753-8260

Geode State Park campground; (319) 392-4601, Geode@dnr.state.ia.us

The Shramm House Bed & Breakfast, 616 Columbia Street, Burlington; (319) 754-0373, www.visit.schramm.com

The Mississippi Manor B&B, 809 North Fourth Street, Burlington; (319) 753-2218, www.mississippimanor.com

Restaurants

Aunt Bea's Cafe/Otis Cambell's Bar and Grill, 111/113 Broadway Street, Burlington; (319) 754-1442

Ivy Bake Shoppe and Cafe, 309 South Gear Avenue #2, West Burlington; (319) 752-4981

Big Muddy's, 710 North Front Street, Burlington; (319) 753-1699

Other Resources

A Sand County Almanac, with Essays on Conservation from Round River by Aldo Leopold (Oxford University Press, Inc)

14 Geode State Park

Take a creek walk in Geode State Park, named for Iowa's state rock, and you may find several of the beautiful stones—but it's illegal to take them home with you. Early spring and summer are the best times to visit, when wildflowers blanket the forest floor and migratory ducks find themselves at home. A 7.0-mile trail around the lake drops in and out of small ravines and is popular with hikers and bikers.

Distance: 7.0-mile loop
Approximate hiking time: 2 to 3 hours
Total elevation gain: 975 feet
Trail surface: Forested footpaths
Seasons: Year-round; great cross country-skiing in winter
Trail users: Hikers, mountain bikers
Canine compatability: Dogs permitted on leash
Hazards: Poison ivy, ticks

Land status: State park
Nearest town: Burlington
Fees and permits: No fees or permits required unless you are camping
Schedule: Open year-round, 4:00 A.M. to 10:30 P.M.
Map: USGS quad: Lowell
Trail contact: Geode State Park; (319) 392-4601, www.iowadnr.com/parks/state_park_list/geode.html

Finding the trailhead: From the junction of U.S Highways 34 and 61 on the north side of Burlington, drive west on US 34. At the fork, when US 34 turns to the northwest, continue straight ahead on Highway 79, which will take you directly west to the park. *DeLorme: Iowa Atlas and Gazetteer:* Page 64 C1

The Hike

Geode comes from "geoides," the Latin word for "earthlike," and some exceptionally beautiful specimens can be found within a 35-mile radius of Keokuk, Iowa. Located in tributary valleys of the Des Moines River, geodes are spherical rocks with usually hollow cavities lined with mineral crystals. World-famous Keokuk geodes originated in the clays of the Mississippian seafloor, around 340 million years ago. Their enigmatic formation validates how unique they are. Iowa adopted the geode as its state rock in 1967. It is illegal to remove any geodes from the state park.

From the parking area northeast of the beach, you'll see a small peninsula jutting out into the lake that serves as an annual nesting ground for Canada geese. During very early spring you may flush common goldeneye, greater scaup, bufflehead, common loon, or northern shoveler. Blue-winged teals, wood ducks, and mallards spend the summer in the lake.

Follow the trail south along the developed side of the lake, following a contour in and out of the inlets. You'll pass the beach, the boat ramp, and several picnic shelters

Canada geese nest on the small peninsula on the northeast side of the lake at Geode State Park.

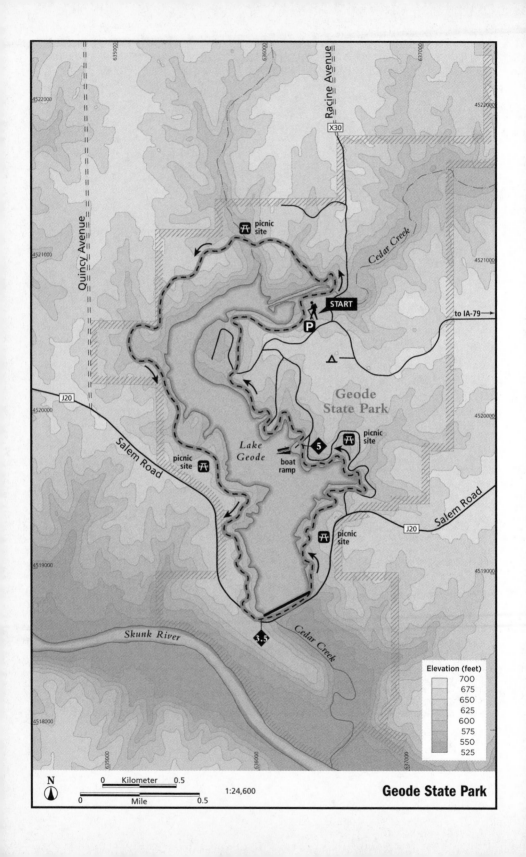

Racine Avenue

Quincy Avenue

X30

picnic site

Cedar Creek

4522000
4521000

START

to IA-79→

P

Geode State Park

J20

Salem Road

Lake Geode

5

picnic site

boat ramp

picnic site

4520000

J20

Salem Road

picnic site

Skunk River

Cedar Creek

3.5

4519000

Elevation (feet)
700
675
650
625
600
575
550
525

4518000

N

0   Kilometer   0.5
0   Mile   0.5

1:24,600

Geode State Park

before crossing the dam. A small interpretive trail leads from the beach up to the campground (brochures available at park office), where you'll find a display of Keokuk geodes.

Continue west, across the dam that was built in 1950 just before the park's opening. The introduction of nonnative carp and their subsequent predation on native fish, along with the siltation of Lake Geode, compelled the Department of Natural Resources to drain the lake in 1981. The silt was removed and the lake was refilled and restocked with fish; however, the siltation problem is still present. Even more destructive to lake habitat is the excessive fecal matter detected in the waters each year.

Following the west side of the lake back up to the parking area, you'll find a much more diverse forest habitat. Instead of following a contour, the trail dips in and out of ravines and can get very muddy during rainy periods. Water from runoff and many small springs drains into Lake Geode, with several species of ferns hanging over the small riparian areas. Dense mats of mosses flank the sides of the trail. During April and May look for wild blue phlox, wild geranium, Jacob's ladder, and downy yellow violet.

If you'd like a great hike-and-bike trip, try the Southeast Iowa Bike Route, which connects Lacey-Keosauqua and Geode State Parks. The 46-mile ride winds through the rolling hills of southern Iowa on county roads. Cross the Des Moines River, pass through the historic towns of Bentonsport and Bonaparte, and navigate the forests and cultivated fields of southern Iowa.

Miles and Directions

0.0   Start at the picnic area to the northeast of the beach. The trail leaves from the north side of the parking area and heads east.

3.5   Cross over the dam and follow the trail along the lakeside.

5.0   Cross over the boat ramp.

6.1   Walk past the beach and continue north. **Options:** Turn to the east to follow the Fallen Oak Interpretive Trail up to the campground.

7.0   Arrive back at the trailhead.

SMART STUDENTS OF THE SKUNK
No other watershed in Iowa houses more institutions of higher education. The oldest college in the state, Iowa Wesleyan in Mt. Pleasant, was established in 1842. Other nearby schools include Grinnell College (Grinnell), Iowa State University (Ames), Vennard College (University Park), Maharishi University of Management (Fairfield), and William Penn University (Oskaloosa).

Hike Information

Local Information
Burlington Convention and Tourism Bureau; (800) 82-RIVER

Events/Attractions
Snake Alley, called the "Crookedest street in the world" by *Ripley's Believe It or Not;* www.snakealley.com

Riverfront Farmers' Market, 400 Front Street, Port of Burlington; (319) 752-0015; May through September, Thursday 5:00-8:00 P.M.

Snake Alley Criterium (great bike race, Memorial Day weekend); (319) 752-0015, www.snakealley.com/criterium

Burlington Steamboat Days—American Music Festival, mid-June; (319) 754-4334, www.steamboatdays.com

Accommodations
Lower Skunk River Access (west of Burlington), Des Moines County Conservation Board; (319) 753-8260

Geode State Park campground; (319) 392-4601, Geode@dnr.state.ia.us

The Shramm House Bed & Breakfast, 616 Columbia Street, Burlington; (319) 754-0373, www.visit.schramm.com

The Mississippi Manor B&B, 809 North Fourth Street, Burlington; (319) 753-2218, www.mississippimanor.com

Restaurants
Aunt Bea's Cafe/Otis Cambell's Bar and Grill, 111/113 Broadway Street, Burlington; (319) 754-1442

Ivy Bake Shoppe and Cafe, 309 South Gear Avenue #2, West Burlington; (319) 752-4981

Other Resources
Iowa's Minerals: Their Occurrence, Origins, Industries, and Lore by Paul Garvin (University of Iowa Press)

15 Brinton Timber

Perched on the hills overlooking the Skunk River, 320-acre Brinton Timber is part of a 1,000-acre swath of forests along the riparian corridor. Mature oak-hickory forests cover the hills, and in springtime the understory is an explosion of blooming wildflowers. To help hikers avoid getting lost, trails are named and labeled with colored symbols painted on trees. The trails are a favorite among cross-country skiers when the snow is deep.

Distance: 5.3-mile loop
Approximate hiking time: 3 to 4 hours
Total elevation gain: 699 feet
Trail surface: Forested footpaths
Seasons: Year-round, although muddy in spring; heavy horse traffic
Trail users: Hikers, equestrians, and cross-country skiers
Canine compatability: Dogs permitted on leash
Hazards: Poison ivy, ticks
Land status: Washington County Conservation Board Park

Nearest towns: Brighton, Washington
Fees and permits: No fees or permits required
Schedule: Open year-round during daylight hours
Map: USGS quad: Brighton
Trail contact: Washington County Conservation Board, Marr Park, 2943 Highway 92, Ainsworth; (319) 657-2400, http://co.washington.ia.us/departments/conservation/index.htm

Finding the trailhead: From the junction of Highways 1 and 92 on the west side of Washington, take Highway 1 south. One mile west of the town of Brighton, turn right (north) onto Fir Avenue (County Road W21; the road to the south leads to Pleasant Plain). This will lead you the 3 miles to the parking area. You will drive "through" several farm areas, so be respectful and drive slowly. *DeLorme: Iowa Atlas and Gazetteer:* Page 53 F7

The Hike

Six different loops, each named and associated with a symbol (painted onto trees along the trail), traverse the forested bluffs overlooking the Skunk River. The total combined length of the loops is 6.0 miles, but you can choose your hike depending on the amount of energy you have. At each trail intersection there is an area map posted; an arrow points to where you are, so you won't get lost amid the maze.

From the parking area, take the Grandfather Trail (red feather) down to the creek and cross it, following Indian Ridge Trail, marked with orange arrowheads, to the right (northwest). Almost immediately you'll turn right (north) onto the Wood Duck Trail (dark blue wood duck). You'll follow the creek down into the forested bottomlands of an old Skunk River terrace. During early spring, ground-nesting wild turkeys will wait until just before you step on them to flush, startling the whole

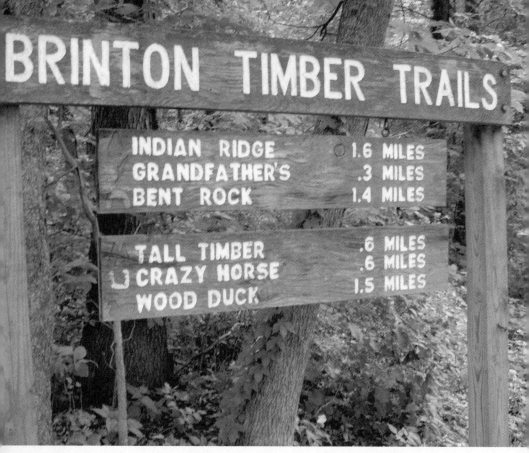

A sign in the parking area shows the trail markings and lengths for Brinton Timber hikes.

forest with a great commotion. Be respectful of the nests by leaving quickly so that the females can return to their eggs.

The name of this trail reflects the fact that riparian forests are favored by wood ducks, which require cavities in trees to lay their eggs. By the early 1900s wood ducks were close to extinction because of habitat loss and extensive hunting for their plumage and eggs. The discovery in 1937 that wood ducks readily adapt to laying eggs in nesting boxes, and a surge of nest box programs since then, have enabled populations to grow steadily.

At the intersection of Wood Duck and Bent Rock Trails (light blue half moon), turn right (north). This trail loops south and connects with the Tall Timber Trail (violet double tree). Though the hills have been logged multiple times since first being settled by the Brinton family in the early 1800s, this swath of forest along the Skunk River still serves as habitat for many birds. Listen for pileated woodpeckers drumming on large snags and the echoing, metallic song of the wood thrush. Large numbers of warblers use Brinton Timber during migration. During spring look for cerulean and Kentucky warblers, Louisiana waterthrush, and northern parula.

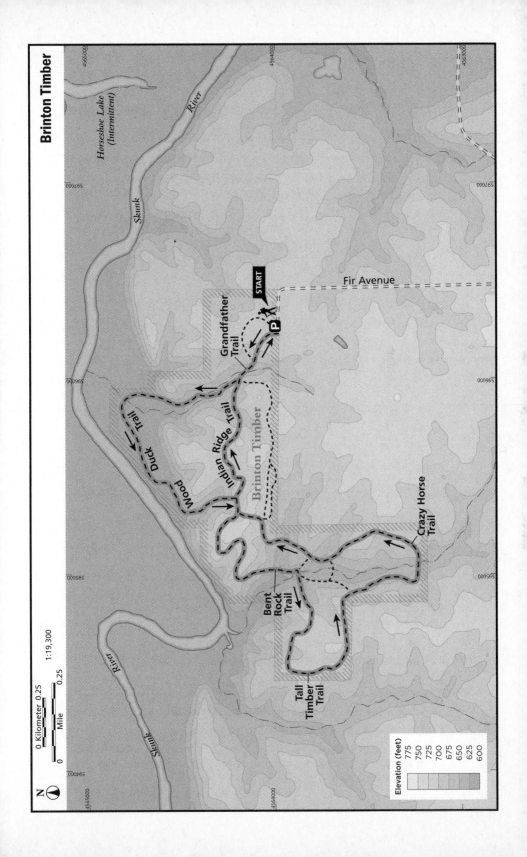

Brinton Timber

DOES THE SKUNK STINK? The origin of the Skunk River's name is unknown, but several theories exist.

When explorer-naturalist Giacoma Beltrami rode the steamship *Virginia* up the Mississippi River in 1823, it passed the mouth of the Skunk River south of Burlington; he called the river a "stinking beast." The river's name might also have come from the large population of skunks, or skunk cabbage, that live along its banks or as a modification of "checauque," an Algonquin word meaning "a rank and offensive odor like onions."

Follow the Tall Timber Trail around to the Crazy Horse Trail (yellow horseshoe). When you reach the intersection with the Bent Rock Trail, turn left (west) and walk down to the drainage to find the "bent rock," an outcrop exposed by erosive powers of the small creek.

Backtrack to the Bent Rock Trail and head northeast toward the parking lot. Spring wildflowers abound on the slopes. In April you'll find small clusters of hepatica blooming before anything else. The flowers emerge before the leaves and range in color from white to soft pink and purple to a deep lilac. Also look for Dutchman's breeches, bloodroot, nodding trillium, and spring beauty just as the trees are beginning to leaf.

You'll encounter two successive forks that diverge back onto the south part of the Indian Ridge Trail to walk though the shrub area on your way back to the trailhead. Walk just a little farther to take the north part of the Indian Ridge Trail, past three vernal pools that are home to several species of breeding frogs during spring. Listen for the spring peepers' short, loud "peep," repeated every one or two seconds. You may also hear western chorus frogs' fingernail-on-a-comb call, or the banjo-tuning notes of green frogs. Cross the creek, hop back on the Grandfather Trail, and cruise up to the trailhead.

Miles and Directions

0.0 Start from parking area and follow Grandfather Trail (red feather) down to the creek.

0.3 At the fork, turn left (north) onto the Indian Ridge Trail (orange arrowhead), and make a quick right onto the Wood Duck Trail (dark blue wood duck).

1.5 Arrive back at Indian Ridge Trail; turn right (west). You'll quickly approach another fork.

1.6 At the fork turn right (northwest) onto the Bent Rock Trail (light blue half moon).

2.2 At fork, turn right (west) onto the Tall Timber Trail (violet double tree). Cross the creek and climb up to the ridge.

3.0 At fork, turn right (south) onto the Crazy Horse Trail (yellow horseshoe).

3.9 At fork, continue straight (north) onto the Bent Rock Trail.

4.3 You'll come to two successive forks; stay left (north) at both of them. **Option:** If you turn right at the first fork, you'll wander through a shrubby area, rife with birds, on your way back to Grandfather Trail and the trailhead.

4.4 At the third fork, turn right (east) to check out the vernal pools.

5.1 Cross creek and follow Grandfather Trail back up to the trailhead.

5.3 Arrive back at the trailhead.

Hike Information

Local Information

Washington Area Chamber of Commerce; (319) 653-3272, www.washingtoniowachamber.com, **Fairfield;** www.fairfieldiowa.com

Events/Attractions

Conger House Museum, 903 East Washington, Washington; (319) 653-3125

Maharishi University of Management, Fairfield; (800) 369-6480, www.mum.edu

Live on the Square Summer Concert Series, June through September, Fairfield; www .fairfieldiowa.com

Fairfield Bike Fest, October, Fairfield; (641) 472-2600

Washington Farmers' Market, Central Park Square, Washington; (319) 653-4888; May through October, Thursday, 5:00 to 7:30 P.M.

Fairfield Farmers' Market, Howard Park, Fairfield; May through October, Wednesday 3:30 to 8:00 P.M., Saturday 7:30 A.M. to 1:00 P.M.

Accommodations

Lake Darling State Park, campsites and cabins; (319) 694-2323, www.iowadnr.com/ parks/state_park_list/lake_darling.html

Burr Oak Lodge and Spa, 1804 315th Street, Brighton; (319) 694-3066

Roses and Lace Bed & Breakfast, 821 North Second Avenue, Washington; (319) 653-2462

Restaurants

Winga's Restaurant, 106 West Main, Washington; (319) 653-2093

Washington Cafe, 121 North Iowa Avenue, Washington; (319) 653-4339

Coffee Corner, 104 West Main Street, Washington; (319) 653-3663

The Raj, 1734 Jasmine Avenue, Fairfield; (641) 472-9580

Everybody's, natural food store and buffet, 501 North Second Street, Fairfield; (641) 472-5199

Honorable Mentions

F. Cairo Woods

Approximately 5 miles of trails wind through forests, food plots, and prairie remnants. Several sightings of Henslow's sparrow, white-eyed and Bell's vireos, and yellow-breasted chat have earned this park Important Bird Area Status. Park at the East Access to hike the trails in the eastern half of the park; there are three connected loops. From the junction of U.S. Highway 61 and County Road G62 on the west side of Wapello, take CR G62 west. At the T-intersection with County Road X37, turn right (north) and drive 2 miles north. Turn left (west) onto 105th Street and then left (south) onto Q Avenue. Turn right (west) onto 100th Street, which will lead you to the parking area. Trails are also accessible from the Main Access, located 1.5 miles north of CR G62 on S Avenue. For information: Louisa County Conservation Board; (319) 523–8381, www.lccb.org/cairoparkmap.htm.

G. Gibson Wildlife Area

From the junction of Highways 218 and 34 in Mt. Pleasant, head west on Highway 34. Turn south onto County Road W55 (Franklin Avenue). Just after you cross the Skunk River, turn west onto County Road H46 (260th Street). Fifteen hundred feet before you cross Big Cedar Creek, turn north onto a small gravel road, which will lead to the parking area and east entrance to the park. Camping is free here, on the mowed area next to the parking area. Two loop trails up on the ridge form a 1.0-mile-long figure eight. When you get to the northwest arc of the figure eight, another 0.75-mile trail diverges to the west. This leads you down through reconstructed prairie, around the five-acre pond, and to the west entrance parking area. Here you'll be able to see the cottonwoods and willows fringing the banks of Big Cedar Creek. For information: Henry County Conservation Board, 2591 Nature Center Drive, Mt. Pleasant; (319) 986–5067, www.henrycountyconservation.com. The Old Threshers Reunion is held annually during early September just south of Mt. Pleasant; www.oldthreshers.org

H. Sockum Ridge

Located on a ridge of hills overlooking Crooked Creek, this park, covered in dense oak-hickory forests, is the perfect place to spend a day. Four loops and one out-and-back trail totaling nearly 7 miles of trails make this a favorite for hikers, mountain bikers, and equestrians. Spring-blooming wildflowers will knock your boots off. Fern Cliff, a smaller park located 2.0 miles upstream on Crooked Creek, doesn't have quite the length of trails but is worth the side trip. From the junction of Highway 92 and County Road W55 in Washington, take CR W55 south. Turn left (east) onto 305th Street and drive 0.5 mile to the parking area. For information: Washington County Conservation Board; (319) 657–2400, http://co.washington.ia.us/departments/conservation/parks.htm

I. F. W. Kent Park

With the help of conservation board staff and local volunteers, the once prairie-covered hills of northeastern Johnson County are slowly returning to their previous state. Numerous small ponds and wetlands are great spots to watch waterfowl, and you may flush a woodcock or two on the edges. Mowed loop trails and a crushed-rock path around the lake total 9.5 miles of hiking trails within the 1,082-acre park. This is a cross-country skiing hot spot in winter. Located 3.0 miles west of Tiffin on U.S. Highway 6. For information: Johnson County Conservation Board; (319) 645–2315, www.johnson-county.com/conservation/index.shtml.

J. Amana Trail to Indian Fish Trap State Preserve

Three loops totaling just over 4 miles lead from the parking area down to a bluff overlooking the Iowa River and to a very old fishing hole. The only known fish trap in the state is a V-shaped pile of glacial boulders (moved from the adjacent bluff) positioned on a bend in the river. It was probably used to funnel fish into an area where spearing or netting them was easily done. The Amana Society uses this area for small-time logging operations, but contrary to what you might think, the forests are incredible. Early autumn's colors are not to be missed and, if the river is low, the perfect time to see the fish trap. When water is high in the Coralville Reservoir, it backs up and covers the fish trap, but even if it isn't visible, it's worth the hike. The preserve is closed during shotgun deer season. At the T-intersection of U.S. Highways 151 and 6, look for the NATURE TRAIL sign and drive onto the small gravel road. When it forks, take a left (west) and drive 0.25 mile to the parking area. For information: Amana Society Forestry Office; (319) 662–7554.

K. Big Hollow Creek Recreation Area

Des Moines County's largest park is located on a tributary of Cedar Fork Creek, just before it flows into Flint Creek. (Starr's Cave Park is located about 10 miles downsream). Nearly 5 miles of trails loop around Big Hollow Creek. The John H. Witte Observatory, run by the Southeastern Iowa Astronomy Club, is open to the public the first and third Fridays of the month. For information: Des Moines County Conservation Board; (319) 753–8260, www.dmcconservation.com/Woods.html#BigHollow.

L. Linn County Conservation Board Parks

Four parks within a twenty-minute drive of Cedar Rapids offer a total of nearly 18 miles of trails. Camp at one of the parks, and spend a few days exploring the land between the Wapsipinicon and Cedar Rivers. The 6.2-mile Pine & Prairie Trail winds around the wetlands, pine plantations, floodplain forests, and remnant prairies at 1,624-acre Matsell Bridge Natural Area, located along the Wapsipinicon River. At Morgan Creek Park, a 0.75-mile trail explores the arboretum, where more than one hundred species of shrubs and trees are planted. The Arboretum Trail connects with several loops that travel through prairie and forest uplands above Morgan Creek and add 3.0 miles onto the total. At Pinicon Ridge Park, the Flying Squirrel, White Oak, Whip-poor-will, and Woodpecker Hill Trails add up to a sweet 9.0 miles on either side of the Wapsipinicon River. The 4.0-mile trail at Squaw Creek Park winds through forests surrounding Squaw Creek. For information: Linn County Conservation Board; (319) 892–6450, www.linncountyparks.com.

Hill Country

As you cruise across the Southern Iowa Drift Plain on Interstate 80, you'll observe what many consider to be quintessential Iowa landscape—pastoral scenes painted onto a canvas of billowy hills. Artist Grant Wood captured the essence of these southern Iowa hills in his paintings *Fall Plowing, Near Sundown, Spring Corn,* and *Stone City.*

The ancient plain was composed of glacial till deposited by Pre-Illinoian ice sheets more than a half million years ago. Today the Southern Iowa Drift Plain, the largest landform region in the state, bears the mark of its age. Drainage networks have carved out the once-level glacial plateau, forming the rills, streams, creeks, and major rivers that now define the landscape. The only remainders of the plain are today's hill summits, which reveal the parts of the plain that have not been carried away by water. Standing atop these ancient hills brings perspective on change in landscape and form.

During the Pennsylvanian period, 290 to 365 million years ago, a vast shallow sea covered the bulk of the continent, with Iowa sitting near the equator. Tropical swamps fringed the coastline, which migrated with the rising and falling ocean levels. The swamps flooded periodically, and the organic matter decomposed and was covered by sand and mud. South-central Iowa's coal deposits, interbedded with Pennsylvanian sandstones and shales, are reminders of these swamps.

From 1874 to 1900, Iowa produced more coal than any other state west of the Mississippi. For a brief time Iowa was the last place that westward-bound coal-burning trains could stock up before their trip over the Great Plains. Thriving during the 1870s, Buxton, in Monroe County, was the largest unincorporated town ever in Iowa. Buxton once housed nearly 8,000 coal miners and their families, the majority of whom were African Americans recruited from the South to man the mines. The need for higher grade coal and discoveries of deposits elsewhere put an end to boom times, and Buxton was a ghost town by 1925. Many other southern hills towns survived the coal bust—but as much quieter reflections of their coal boom heyday.

Although the hills of southern Iowa seem to be uniformly curved, they are anything but homogenous. For the most part, loess deposits sit atop various layers of ancient soils, or palesols. These clayey strata have been leached of nutrients and covered by windblown loess. The clay nature of the hills allowed for most of Iowa's man-made lakes to be created in southern Iowa. Farm ponds are found throughout, and the bulk of state parks and wildlife management areas are situated around the larger lakes: Ahquabi, Bobwhite, Icaria, Little River, Nine Eagles, Rathbun, Three Fires, Twelve Mile, and Wapello, to name a few. As elsewhere in the state, the endless prairies of the region have been converted to agriculture and have undergone a succession into forests and shrubs due to overgrazing and the suppression of fire.

16 Lake Ahquabi State Park

Ahquabi, a Sauk and Fox word for "resting place," is an apt name for the park, given its popularity among migratory songbirds. Warblers arrive in multitudes in early spring to take a breather on their journey north, and at least eight species stay for the summer to raise their young. A 4.0-mile loop traverses the forested hills around the lake, and several spur loops add nearly 3 additional miles to explore.

Distance: 6.75 miles round-trip
Approximate hiking time: 2 to 4 hours
Total elevation gain: 735 feet
Trail surface: Well-worn footpaths, mowed paths
Seasons: Year-round
Trail users: Hikers, cross-country skiers
Canine compatability: Dogs permitted on leash
Hazards: Poison ivy, ticks

Land status: State park
Nearest town: Indianola
Fees and permits: No fees or permits required unless you are camping
Schedule: Open year-round, 4:00 A.M. to 10:30 P.M.
Map: USGS quad: Indianola
Trail contact: Lake Ahquabi State Park; (515) 961-7101, www.iowadnr.com/parks/state_park_list/lake_ahquabi.html

Finding the trailhead: From the junction of Highway 92 and U.S. Highway 65/69 in Indianola, take US 65/69 south. Where the two highways split, turn right (west) onto Highway 349 (County Road G58). This leads into the park, where you will follow the signs to the beach. *DeLorme: Iowa Atlas and Gazetteer:* Page 50 F2

The Hike

Visit Lake Ahquabi during early spring and you'll witness the forest emerging from winter in a brilliant display of violet and indigo. In April, before any trees have leafed out, the eastern redbud (*Cercis canadensis*) produces brilliant pinkish-purple flowers. At the same time, Virginia bluebells (*Mertensia virginiana*) blanket the forest floor, adding another hue of color to the drab early-spring landscape.

A flash of yellow flitting in the trees will remind you to keep your eyes out for the many wood warblers that shoot through in spring and fall on their way to and from breeding grounds. An outstanding twenty-nine species have been sighted at Lake Ahquabi during migration, and eight of them are known to stay and nest. Look for the ovenbird high-stepping and head-bobbing its way around on the ground. The prothonotary warbler, with its brilliant yellow head, can be seen flitting around woody debris in the siltation pond north of the campground. Yellow warbler nests can be viewed by wading through dense willow thickets in the small coves.

To explore Ahquabi, start by walking the 4.0-mile loop around the lake. Park at the beach and follow the trail to the south along the shore. At the second fork in the trail, turn left to view the monument erected by the Iowa Federation of

Northern water snakes inhabit Lake Ahquabi.

Women's Clubs in honor of Cora Whitley. As IFWC president in the early 1900s, she spread her conservation ethic among thousands of club members, as well as fostered relationships with the male-dominated conservation organizations in Iowa. Whitley served on the board of directors of the Izaak Walton League and testified before Congress in support of a wildlife refuge in the Upper Mississippi River Valley. Perhaps most famous for the "Outdoor Good Manners" campaign she started in 1925, Whitley worked through clubs and organizations to spread the message that "to abuse the hospitality of parks and forests is . . . a breach of good manners."

Continue toward the southern tip of the lake, where the trail swings sharply to the right (west) and ascends a large hill. To the south of the park is Hooper Wildlife Area, where bushwhacking may yield a look at long-eared owls that show up in winter to roost in pine plantings. Other owls to be seen at Lake Ahquabi during winter are barred, eastern screech, great-horned, and saw-whet.

Along the west side of the lake, you'll find numerous gnawed tree stumps; the trees have been used by beavers to build their lodge dwellings. The best time to see beavers is at dusk, when they're most active, usually swimming around the lake.

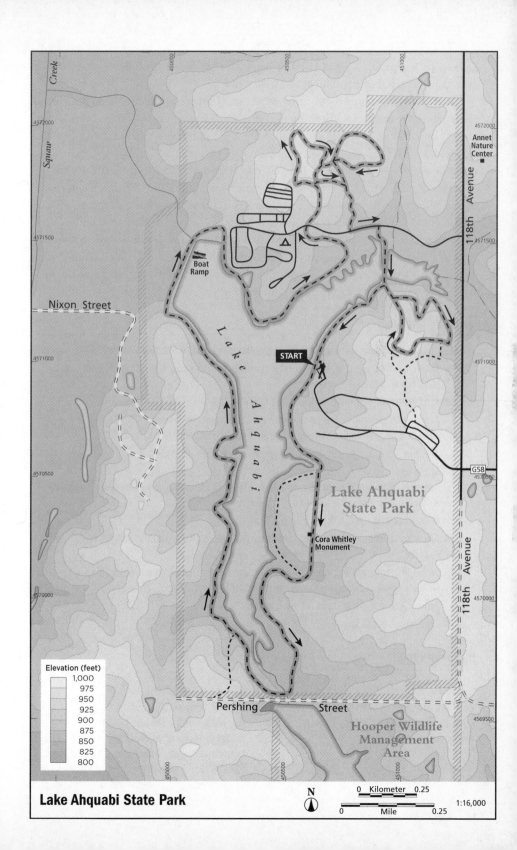

Lake Ahquabi State Park

Beavers have a paddle-shaped tail; another park resident—the muskrat—has a similarly shaped body but a rounded, rudderlike tail.

As you continue north over the dam toward the campground, keep your eyes peeled for the bobcat that's been sighted frequently in recent years. When you arrive at the campground, continue east around the shore to return to the trailhead, or walk north to access the 1.4-mile loop through scrubby uplands. You'll pass several siltation ponds used to dump the material dredged from the lake in the early 1990s.

Directly east, across the road from Lake Ahquabi, is the Annet Nature Center, run by the Warren County Conservation Board. Water that flows through the pond and wetlands next to the nature center eventually drains into Lake Ahquabi and is home to forty species of dragonflies and damselflies. Look for common green darner, American rubyspot, saffron-winged meadowhawk, and vesper bluet around the water. The nature center has several natural history exhibits, as well as aquariums with native turtles, fish, salamanders, and snakes.

Miles and Directions

0.0 Start at the beach parking area. You'll see the trail down to the south at the water's edge.

0.35 At the fork take a left to check out the Cora Whitley Monument; this trail will bring you back down to the lake loop.

0.69 At intersection with main trail, turn left (south) to continue around the lake.

1.3 At the southern end of the park, Hooper Wildlife Management Area is just south of where you are standing. Follow the trail as it turns north, and climb the steep hill.

3.2 Arrive at the campground; follow the lakeshore until you come to a fork.

3.7 At the fork turn left (north) onto this trail to cross the road in order to explore the scrubby uplands and siltation ponds to the north of the campground. **Bailout:** Continue along the lakeshore to return to the parking area.

4.0 At the fork turn left (north) to take the loops.

5.25 Arrive back at the road. You'll road hike for 0.1 mile until you see the bridge to cross over the lake.

5.5 At the fork after you've crossed the bridge, turn left (northeast) onto a short loop. **Bailout:** Continue along the lakeshore to return to the trailhead.

6.3 Arrive back at the lakeshore on the lake loop.

6.75 Arrive back at the trailhead.

Hike Information

Local Information
Chamber of Commerce, 515 North Jefferson, Suite D, Indianola; (515) 961-6269, www.indianolachamber.com

Events/Attractions
National Balloon Museum, 1601 North Jefferson, US 65/69; (515) 961-3714
Indianola Farmers' Market, Highway 92 at fairgrounds west gate, Indianola; (515) 961-7031; June through October, Wednesday 2:00 to 6:00 P.M., Saturday 8:00 A.M. to noon

Accommodations

Summerset Inn and Winery, 15101 Fairfax, Indianola; (515) 961–3545, www.summersetwine.com

Gallery and Galley Bed & Breakfast, 1321 Jefferson Way, Indianola; (515) 961–4305, www.galleryiowa.com

Restaurant

Harvest Restaurant, 10 East Salem, Indianola; (515) 962–0466

17 Stephens State Forest–Woodburn Unit

Stephens State Forest is the largest in Iowa, with seven separate units totaling 14,112 acres. The Woodburn Unit is designated as the backpacking unit and contains 2,011 acres of rolling hills dissected by Sand and Bluebird Creeks. A gravel road divides the unit into two parts, allowing hikers to follow the two 2.5-mile loop trails in a figure-eight fashion to maximize trail length. There are five "backcountry" campsites in the unit, but because none is more than 2 miles from the parking area, you may want to walk the loop several times before calling it a day and pitching your tent.

Distance: 6.2 miles round-trip

Approximate hiking time: 2-to 3-hour day hike or an overnight with stops at primitive campsites

Total elevation gain: 808 feet

Trail surface: Dirt path; bridges over creeks

Seasons: Year-round; good cross-country skiing in winter

Trail users: Hikers only

Canine compatability: Dogs permitted

Hazards: Poison ivy, ticks

Land status: State forest

Nearest towns: Osceola, Chariton

Fees and permits: No fees or permits required

Schedule: Open year-round

Map: USGS quad: Le Roy

Trail contact: Stephens State Forest, 1111 North Eighth Street, Chariton, IA 50049; (641) 774–4559, www.iowadnr.com/forestry/stephens.html

Finding the trailhead: From the junction of Highways 34 and 65 east of Chariton, head south on Highway 65. Take a right (west) onto 480th Street, a gravel road. Take a left (south) onto 110th Street and a quick right (west) onto 440th Street (you'll pass Last Chance Church). Take a right (north) onto 330th Avenue, and soon see a brown STATE FOREST sign. Look for the small parking area on the west side of the road 0.75 mile north of 440th Street. *DeLorme: Iowa Atlas and Gazetteer:* Page 60 A2

The Hike

During warm seasons, brown thrashers, red–winged blackbirds, and eastern towhees will greet you noisily in the parking area and can be found on the forest-grassland

A fresh bur oak acorn.

edges throughout the unit during late spring and summer. Setting out east from the parking area, follow the Bur Oak Trail through the upland oak/hickory–dominated forests, where typical spring wildflowers abound. Scattered amid the uplands, several large burr oaks form huge canopies that provide ample shade for a midafternoon picnic or nap.

In the fields that are plowed and planted as wildlife food plots, look for chipping, field, and white-throated sparrows, which forage on barren or broken ground but find solace in the thick rose, sumac, and chokecherry shrubs at the edge of the forest. Here you'll also see many wild turkeys, once eradicated from the state because of habitat destruction and excessive hunting. After the DNR released the birds in Stephens State Forest, their population grew rapidly; turkey hunting has been allowed in the park since 1971.

Just east of the Bur Oak trailhead are two small ponds, hidden by conifer plantings. Both ephemeral ponds are fringed with cattails and rife with aquatic plants. Early in spring, when the ponds are full, you may catch a turtle sunning itself, hear a chorus of frogs singing, or flush a woodcock hiding in cattails at the water's edge.

The Woodburn Unit (the designated hiking-trail unit) is a mosaic of native upland and bottomland forests, nonnative hardwood and softwood plantings, and leased-out agricultural land. The unit's dynamic ecological communities make it home to diverse plant and animal species.

You'll still find Stephens an exceptional place. The Ridge Trail climbs through oak/hickory–dominated forest, where typical spring wildflowers abound. Look for hepatica, bloodroot, nodding trillium, false rue anemone, and trout lily, followed by bellwort, Virginia bluebells, wild geranium, and blue woodland phlox. Moister slopes will boast columbines, Virginia waterleaf, and jack-in-the-pulpit. The Sand Creek riparian area is dominated by huge cottonwoods and water birches, with dense blankets of flowers forming in the understory in early spring. Among the trees, you'll hear and see a variety of woodpeckers, as well as blue jays, northern cardinals, scarlet tanagers, and blue-gray gnatcatchers.

In the past year there have been several mountain lion sightings in the Stephens State Forest vicinity. Though you're unlikely to glimpse a cougar, if you camp out you will hear coyotes at dusk. In the early morning you may catch a red fox slipping through the underbrush.

The five campsites—Bur Oak, Bottom Oak, South Slope, White Oak, and Black Oak—are all equipped with a picnic table, fire pit, and ample space for several tents. I would recommend the Bur Oak site, because it is the farthest from the trailhead.

Miles and Directions

0.0 Start at the trailhead in middle of unit. Cross gravel road to east side of unit, and follow Bur Oak Trail to the left (north).

0.82 Arrive at White Oak campsite.

1.15 Cross Sand Creek.

1.4 At the fork take left (north) fork to continue on Bur Oak Trail.

1.5 Arrive at Black Oak campsite.

1.8 Emerge from forest into wildlife food plot. Cross to the south side of field, and continue onto Ironwood Trail by turning to the right (west) and following the edge. If you follow the edge left (east), Bur Oak trailhead is only 0.2 mile away. (FYI: Look here for the marshy forest openings.)

2.0 Follow Ironwood Trail west through break in hedgerow; continue due west until you hit the forest edge and see the Ironwood Trail.

2.4–2.7 Cross Sand Creek three times.

3.1 Emerge from forest where trail parallels the wildlife food plot, or "cornfield." The trail is severely clogged by multiflora rose; to avoid being ripped to shreds, walk along the edge of the field rather than on the trail.

3.4 Cross 330th Avenue and continue downridge on the Prairie Trail.

3.8 Arrive at South Slope campsite.

3.9 At the fork turn left (south) onto the Ridge Trail.

4.5 At the fork turn right (north) and head downslope.

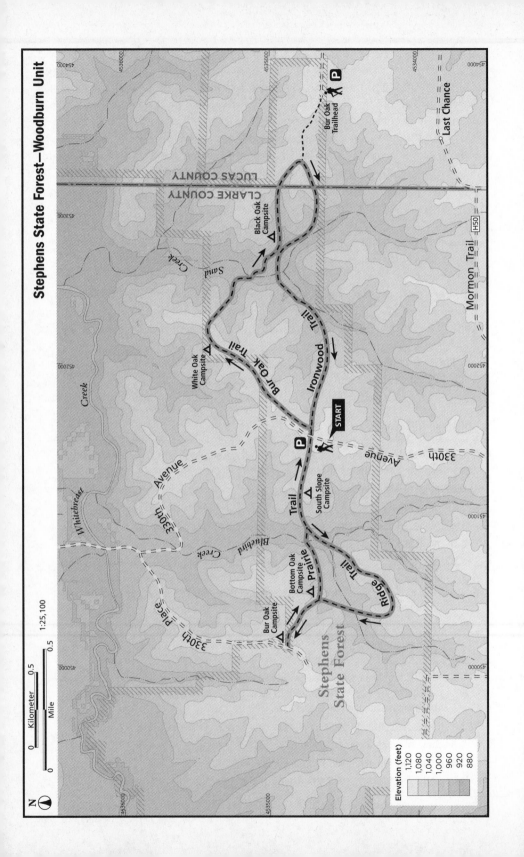

Stephens State Forest—Woodburn Unit

N

Kilometer
0   0.5
Mile
0   0.5

1:25,100

Elevation (feet)
1,120
1,080
1,040
1,000
960
920
880

5.0 At the fork turn left (northwest) to reach the Bur Oak campsite. (FYI: Sign posts point you north (left) toward Bur Oak campsite, 0.2 mile away, or east (right) toward Bottom Oak Campsite, 0.2 mile away.)

5.2 Arrive at Bur Oak campsite. Backtrack down the hill to return to the trailhead.

5.5 At the fork turn left (east); arrive at Bottom Oak campsite.

5.7 At the fork turn left (east); continue up the hill past the South Slope campsite.

6.2 Arrive back at trailhead.

Hike Information

Local Information

Chariton Chamber and Development Corp; (515) 774-4059

Events/Attractions

John L. Lewis Memorial Museum of Mining and Labor, 102 Division Street, 2 blocks north of junction of Highways 34 and 65, in Lucas; (641) 766-6831

Cinder Path Rail-to-Trail, (14.0-mile multiuse, the first in Iowa); (641) 872-2004

Pin Oak Marsh Recreation Area, on Highway 14 south of Chariton; (641) 774-2438

Prairie Trails Museum, Corydon; (641) 872-2211, www.prairietrailsmuseum.org

Wayne County Farmers' Market, Corydon Square, Corydon; (641) 872-1755; June through October; Thursday 5:00 to 7:00 P.M.

Accommodations

Camping on-site (free) or at the Whitebreast or Lucas Units to the northeast; (641) 744-4459

Red Haw State Park, Chariton; (641) 774-5632, www.iowadnr.com/parks/state_park_list/red_haw.html

StorieTime Bed & Breakfast, 735 Braden Avenue, Chariton; (877) 378-6743, www.storietime.com

Restaurants

Whiteway Cafe, 123 North Main Street, Osceola; (641) 342-4621

Sangini's Pizza, 228 North Eighth Street, Chariton; (641) 774-4074

18 Nine Eagles State Park

Just 2 miles north of the Missouri border, sixty-two-acre Nine Eagles Lake nestles among a large band of forested hills. Spring-blooming wildflowers abound below the oak-hickory canopy. A short jaunt on the 3.1-mile loop trail around the lake, equipped with a fishing rod and binoculars, will land you a nice pan-fried dinner and a glimpse of migrating warblers or waterfowl in spring and fall. If you want, 4.1 miles of equestrian trails add some length to the walk.

Distance: Hiking trail, 3.1-mile loop; equestrian trail, 4.1 miles round-trip
Approximate hiking time: 2 to 5 hours
Total elevation gain: Hiking trail, 439 feet; equestrian trail, 829 feet
Trail surface: Mowed forest footpath
Seasons: Year-round
Trail users: Hikers, equestrians, cross-country skiers
Canine compatability: Dogs permitted on leash

Hazards: Poison ivy, ticks
Land status: State park
Nearest towns: Davis City, Leon
Fees and permits: No fees or permits required unless you're camping
Schedule: Open year-round, 4:00 A.M. to 10:30 P.M.
Map: USGS quad: Akron
Trail contact: Nine Eagles State Park; (641) 442-2855, www.iowadnr.com/parks/state_park_list/nine_eagles.html

Finding the trailhead: From the junction of U.S. Highways 69 and 2 in Leon, drive south on US 69. Just south of Davis City, turn left (east) onto County Road J66. Three miles north of the Missouri state line, you'll see the sign and turnoff for the state park. *DeLorme: Iowa Atlas and Gazetteer:* Page 60 F1

The Hike

In the summer of 1949, local residents purchased the land for $10 per acre and then donated it to the state, which provided matching funds to develop the park. The dam to create Nine Eagles Lake was built in 1952. During summer, before you start your hike look for swarms of barn and northern rough-winged swallows foraging over the lake. Of the five species of swallows that visit Decatur County, the barn swallow is the easiest to recognize with its navy-blue back, buffy-peach underside, rufous throat, and long, forked tail. Overall, the northern rough-winged swallow is much more drab, with a brown body and a short, unforked tail.

In 1862 European water clover (*Marsilea quadrifolia*) was brought to Connecticut and afterward joined other Old World invasive species in colonizing much of the Northeast. How this aquatic fern ended up in Nine Eagles Lake, we'll never know, but it's the only lake in Iowa that contains the plant. A native cousin, the hairy water clover (*M. vestita*) is found in Iowa only in Gitchie Manitou State Preserve in the northwest. Water clover leaves look like four-leaved shamrocks and also resemble the

European water clover, a floating fern, flourishes near the dam in Lake of Nine Eagles.

leaves of wood sorrel (*Oxalis* sp.). In shallow water next to the spillway, you'll find a large colony of water clover growing below arrowhead and cattail.

Park at the beach and walk the 3.1-mile loop around the lake for starters. If you're taking a stroll around the lake, you might as well bring a fishing rod with you. The many inlets and rocky areas along the dam are home to largemouth bass, bluegills, channel catfish, crappie, and northern pike. Only rowboats and electric motor–powered boats are allowed on the lake, keeping noise and water pollution to a minimum.

Because the lake is filled by surface runoff water and the forested state park occupies 90 percent of the watershed, the water is exceptionally clean. Low phosphorus and nitrate levels help keep algae blooms from killing aquatic vegetation and animals. However, the hills, composed mainly of clay, have been eroding rapidly in the gullies of the four main creeks that flow into the lake. This has introduced high levels of turbidity; because of its suspension of solids, Nine Eagles Lake is on the EPA's impaired waters list.

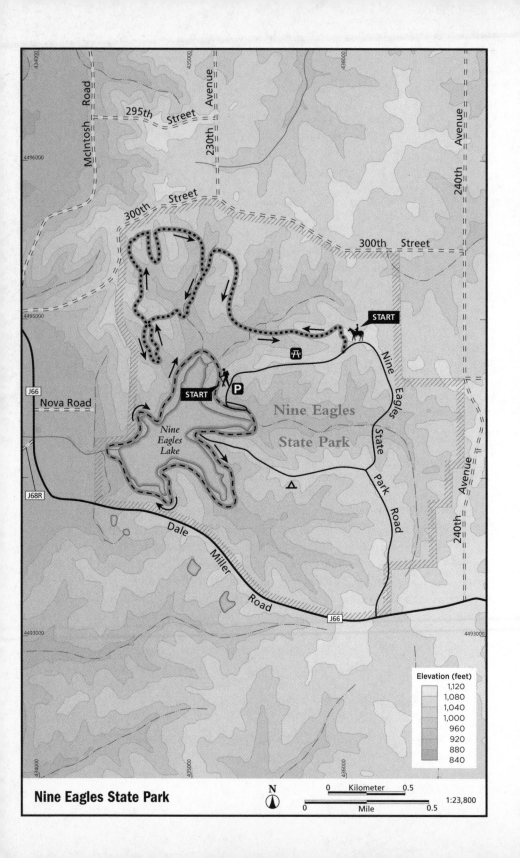

295th Street

McIntosh Road

230th Avenue

240th Avenue

300th Street

300th Street

START

Nine Eagles State Park Road

J66

Nova Road

START

P

Nine Eagles Lake

Nine Eagles

State Park

J68R

Dale

Miller

Road

240th Avenue

J66

Elevation (feet)
1,120
1,080
1,040
1,000
960
920
880
840

Nine Eagles State Park

N

0   Kilometer   0.5

0   Mile   0.5

1:23,800

You can check out the equestrian trails on the north side of the park, although they aren't as walker-friendly as the loop around the lake. From the southeast end of the beach, a small trail will take you up to the northeast to the equestrian day-use parking area. The trails that lead to the northwest corner of the park see heavy traffic during summer and with rain can become extremely muddy. You'll pass three siltation ponds, created to help keep the lake free of sedimentation. Various prairie restoration projects have seeded native grasses and removed shrubs that overwhelm the native plants. During winter, the trails are perfect for cross-country skiing if there is enough snow.

Miles and Directions

The hikes are a simple loop and a lollipop as described in the text.

Hike Information

Local Information

Leon; www.netins.net/ricweb/community/ leon/leon.htm
Decatur County Development; www.grm.net/ ~dcdc/

Events/Attractions

SIANOMO (Southern Iowa and Northern Missouri), September, 12-, 30-, or 52-mile bike ride, Lamoni; (641) 784-8344, www.bikeiowa.com

Accommodations

Little River Wildlife Management Area and Slip Bluff Park, (Decatur County Conservation Board); (641) 446-7307
Double Stitch B & B, 23734 US 69, Leon; (641) 446-8088
Arbor Inn, 107 Northwest Fourth Street, Leon; (641) 446-4595

Restaurants

Davis City Cafe, 217 Bridge Street, Davis City; (641) 442-3900
Linden Street Coffee House, 104 South Linden Street, Lamoni

19 Clanton Creek Recreation Area

Although Madison County is best known for its covered bridges and for being the birthplace of John Wayne, sadly no feature flick has been made about Clanton Creek Recreation Area. Hike the 2.0-mile loop or the 8.0-mile out-and-back trail that goes up and down—and up and down—over the real hills of south-central Iowa. Three hike-in campsites make this an ideal place to spend the weekend.

Distance: 9.4 miles round-trip

Approximate hiking time: 4 to 5 hours

Total elevation gain: 1,551 feet

Trail surface: Forested footpaths, mowed swaths

Seasons: Year-round

Trail users: Hikers, cross-country skiers

Canine compatability: Dogs permitted

Hazards: Poison ivy, ticks

Land status: Madison County Conservation Board Park

Nearest town: Winterset

Fees and permits: No fees or permits required

Schedule: Open year-round during daylight hours

Map: USGS quad: East Peru

Trail contact: Madison County Conservation Board; (515) 462-3536, www.madisoncountyparks.org

Finding the trailhead: From Highway 92 and U.S. Highway 169 just west of Winterset, take US 169 south for 9 miles. Turn left (east) onto 310th Street, which will quickly jog to the north and then continue east. At the T-intersection with Millstream Avenue, turn left (north) onto Millstream Avenue. Turn right (east) onto 305th Street; pass a Clanton Creek Recreation Area sign and parking area (access to a 0.25-mile trail around a prairie reconstruction). Turn right (south) onto Clanton Creek Road and drive 0.5 mile up the hill to the hiking trail parking lot. Another parking lot is located at the west end of the recreation area, mainly for folks interested in the pond. This lot is off Millstream Avenue (County Road G8P), just south of the intersection with 310th Street. *DeLorme: Iowa Atlas and Gazetteer:* Page 49 G9

The Hike

From the east access parking lot, before entering the forest you'll take a quick jaunt in the uplands, where prairie reconstruction has yielded big and little bluestem, Indian grass, sideouts grama, purple coneflower, and several species of goldenrod. You'll be able to tell the seeded prairie from the unrestored uplands on the west side, which are scrubby and invaded by bromegrass and eastern red cedar. The bonus of the scrub is the colonies of black raspberry bushes, bursting with fruit in mid to late summer.

It seems that each time I've been to Clanton Creek, the fungal diversity has been amazing. This hike write-up is dedicated to some of the most important and over-looked parts of our woodland ecosystems, mushrooms. The extent of most Iowans'

Hedgehog mushrooms are a tasty surprise in Clanton Creek Recreation Area.

mycological knowledge is that "morels taste really good." Morels are important, for they feed a good number of us each spring when the oak leaves "are as big as a squirrel's ear." However, another several hundred species of fungi inhabit the state. Almost none of them taste as good as the sought-after morel; in fact, many of them will make you violently ill—even kill you—if you eat them. Edible or not, fungi are a vital part of most ecosystems; they are beautiful and mysterious organisms as well. Mushrooms grow in a variety of environments; with regards to Clanton Creek, we'll focus on woodland fungi.

Within the forest, certain mushrooms live off decaying organic matter; some are parasitic and draw sugars from living plants, while others form a mycorrhizal relationship with various plants, receiving sugars in exchange for nutrients (particularly phosphorus) via root systems. From spring through fall, the mushrooms that we see growing off trees or out of the soil and leaf litter are just the tip of the fungal iceberg. The most important part of mushrooms, their fungal hyphae, are small tubelike structures that spend most of the time underground or in rotting wood, collecting

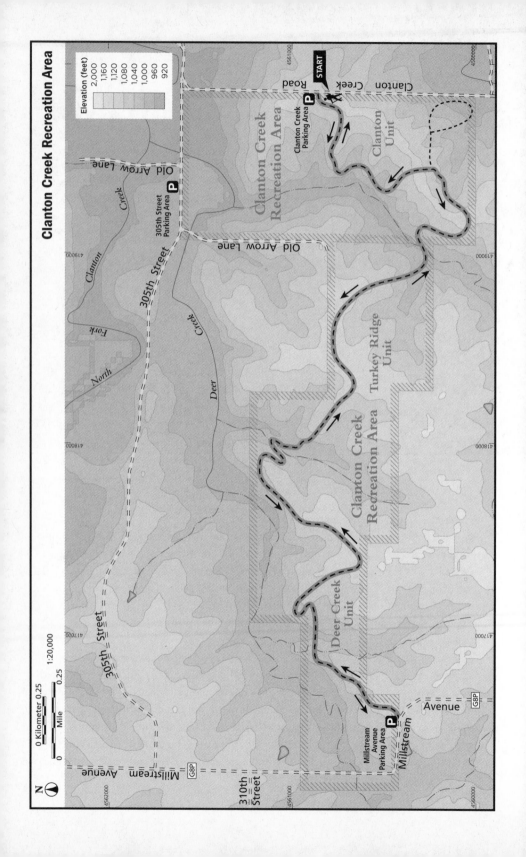

Clanton Creek Recreation Area

Elevation (feet)
2,000
1,160
1,120
1,080
1,040
1,000
960
920

N

0 Kilometer 0.25
1:20,000
0 Mile 0.25

START

Clanton Creek Road

Clanton Creek Parking Area

Clanton Unit

Clanton Creek Recreation Area

Old Arrow Lane

Old Arrow Lane

305th Street Parking Area

305th Street

Clanton Creek

North Fork

Deer Creek

Turkey Ridge Unit

Clanton Creek Recreation Area

Deer Creek Unit

305th Street

Millstream Avenue

Millstream Avenue Parking Area

Millstream Avenue

310th Street

G8P

G8P

nutrients. If you turn over a pile of leaves or knock open a downed log, occasionally you'll see a network of fine strands, the hyphae. Interwoven mats of hyphae look like cotton and are called mycelium.

Mushrooms can take many forms: your basic cap-on-stalk mushroom, jelly fungi, slime molds, club fungi, cup fungi, and shelf fungi, among many others. Start learning about fungi by going on walks with someone who knows them; take a mycology class, or thoroughly steep yourself in fungal literature and identification keys. Study the various mushrooms you find, examining what they grew out of; what their gills look like, if they have them at all; the texture of the cap; the length of the stalk. These macroscopic characteristics are not always all the information you'll need to identify any mushrooms you'll find, but they'll at least get you on the right path. If you want to collect wild mushrooms to eat, know what you're doing, use good identification keys, and don't be stupid: **Never eat fungus unless you are 100 percent sure they are nonpoisonous.**

If you visit a few days after a good rain during spring or fall, you're likely to find numerous mushrooms: The golden chanterelle (*Cantharellus cibarius*) is one of the most sought after wild edibles, and it's delicious. These bright-orange fungi grow individually or in clusters out of the soil. Their creamy yellow undersides have gills that look more like ridges. Oyster mushrooms (*Pleurotus* spp.) are white and fan shaped; they grow in overlapping clusters that are laterally attached to dead trees. Stumble upon a bitter bolete (*Tylopilus felleus*) growing out of the ground and you won't believe your eyes. The caps are café-con-leche in color and can grow up to 6 inches in diameter! Purple-gilled Laccaria (*Laccaria ochropurpurea*) are almost unmistakable with their bright violet gills. At the height of their growth, giant puffballs (*Calvatia gigantea*) can be more than 1.5 feet in diameter. The bright orange topside of chicken-of-the-woods, or sulphur shelf (*Laetiporus sulphureus*), will catch your eye as you pass a stump or downed log it may be growing on.

Miles and Directions

0.0 Start at the trailhead on Clanton Creek Road.

0.2 At the fork turn left to do the 2.0-mile loop; turn right for the 8.0-mile out-and-back trail. From here on, the directions will be for the 8.0-mile out-and-back.

4.7 Arrive at the parking lot off CR G8P; turn around and head back the way you came.

9.4 Arrive back at the trailhead.

PICK WITH CARE Mushrooms can affect people in different ways. Individual sensitivity makes it impossible to say that any particular mushroom is safe to eat, and some types of fungi are downright deadly. However, this doesn't prevent amateur mycologists from learning all they can in order to enjoy the many wild edibles found in Iowa.

Hike Information

Local Information

Madison County Chamber of Commerce; (515) 462-1185 or (800) 298-6119, www.madisoncounty.com

Events/Attractions

Covered Bridges (obtain map from Madison Chamber of Commerce; see above)

Covered Bridge Festival, October, Winterset; www.madisoncounty.com/bridge_fest.html

Birthplace of John Wayne, 216 South Second Street, Winterset; (515) 462-1044

Madison County Farmers' Market Town Square, Winterset; (515) 462-3894; May through October, Thursday 3:00 to 7:00 P.M., Saturday 7:30 to 11:30 A.M.

Accommodations

Summerset House Inn, 204 West Washington, Winterset; (515) 462-9014

Clanton Creek Recreation Area; free camping

Pammel State Park (managed by Madison County Conservation Board); (515) 462-3536

A Step Away, 104 West Court Street, Winterset; (515) 462-5956

Restaurants

Northside Cafe, 61 West Jefferson, Winterset; (515) 462-1523

Nature's Cupboard & Down to Earth, 105 North John Wayne Drive, Winterset; (515) 462-3579

Other Resources

Mushrooms and Other Fungi of the Midcontinental United States by D. M. Heffman, L. H. Tiffany, and G. Knaphys (Iowa State University Press)

Mushrooms Demystified: A Comprehensive Guide to the Fleshy Fungi by David Aurora (Ten Speed Press)

20 Lake of Three Fires State Park

Lake of Three Fires, the largest fragment of preserved land in Taylor County, provides vital habitat for wildlife, including sixty-five species of nesting birds. It becomes quite apparent after several steps that the loop trail around the lake was built for equestrian and snowmobile usage. The 10-foot-wide swath can get quite muddy after heavy rains, but if the trail is moderately dry, it's worth it. Check out the siltation ponds on the northwest side of the lake. They help keep the lake clean and provide habitat for wetland plants and animals.

Distance: 10.5 miles out and back with loop
Approximate hiking time: 3 to 4 hours
Total elevation gain: 911 feet
Trail surface: Well-worn footpaths, mowed paths
Seasons: Year-round, but very muddy in spring
Trail users: Hikers, equestrians, and cross-country skiers
Canine compatability: Dogs permitted on leash
Hazards: Poison ivy, ticks

Land status: State park
Nearest towns: Bedford, Mt. Ayr
Fees and permits: No fees or permits required unless you are camping
Schedule: Open year-round, 4:00 A.M. to 10:30 P.M.
Map: USGS quad: Bedford
Trail contact: Lake of Three Fires State Park; (712) 523-2700, www.iowadnr.com/parks/state_park_list/lake_three_fires.html

Finding the trailhead: From the junction of Highway 2 and U.S. Highway 169 to the west of Mt. Ayr, take Highway 2 west. Just outside (to the east of) the town of Bedford, turn north onto Highway 49. Look for the sign on the west side of the road. *DeLorme: Iowa Atlas and Gazetteer: Page 58 E3*

The Hike

Originally from the northern Great Lakes Region, the Potawatomi, Ojibwe, and Ottawa peoples once constituted the Confederacy, or Council of Three Fires. When President Andrew Jackson signed the Indian Removal Act of 1830, these tribes, along with many others, were forced from their homelands. Groups split and went in different directions—to Canada, southern Illinois, Minnesota, Missouri, and Wisconsin. Others were pushed to a settlement in southwestern Iowa near present-day Council Bluffs. It's thought that the now-flooded valley of Lake of Three Fires was a site for council meetings and that smoke signals from three fires (representing the three tribes) summoned people to the meetings. In 1846 a treaty ceding the Potawatomi's lands in Iowa to the government forced them to move to Kansas and Oklahoma.

Lake of Three Fires was constructed in 1935 at the height of the lake-creation boom in Iowa's state parks. Because of high carp populations and heavy siltation, the

An American lotus blossom accents the beauty of Lake of Three Fires State Park.

lake was drained in 1980. Jetties were built along the shore to reduce erosion, and the lake was refilled and restocked with bass, bluegill, crappie, bullhead, channel catfish, and tiger muskie. During summer 2004 the lake was again dredged to remove 500,000 cubic yards of silt and to add rock reefs for fish habitat. The lake is still on the EPA's list of impaired waterways, with extremely high phosphorous levels supporting algae blooms that kill aquatic plants and animals.

Park at the equestrian staging area on the north side of the park if there's room; otherwise, spaces are usually open at the adjacent campground. As you begin walking, you'll notice that the trails were built with equestrians in mind—they're 10 feet wide. Walking north, you're on the first straightaway along the park's boundary; the trail can become extremely muddy after heavy rain or horse traffic. As the trail turns westward, climb a small hill that overlooks most of the 1-mile-long lake. Prairie probably once covered this hill, but because of previous cultivation, planted pines, eastern red cedars, and bromegrass now abound. During August look for the small yellow flowers of partridge pea, which prefers disturbed areas, blanketing the area.

If you want a short hike, bypass spur loops and head directly south down to the three inlets on the northwest side of the lake. Walk the loops and you'll pass several cattail- and sedge-fringed ponds, all created in an attempt to reduce the amount of silt entering the lake. As you round one of the small coves, look for dabbling ducks or a great blue heron hiding out among the American lotus plants, whose stunning flowers bloom after midsummer.

Moving south you'll enter dense forests that surround the south side of the lake. In the southwest corner of the park, the trail follows around one larger inlet before crossing the dam. Follow the intermittent footpath along the lake's edge past the boat ramp and cabins on your way back up to the trailhead. The nine-hole disc golf course near the central picnic area will make the last 0.5 mile more interesting. To double your hike's mileage, backtrack around the west side of the lake, taking the trails you missed on the way down.

Miles and Directions

0.0   Start at the trailhead on the north side of the lake, next to the equestrian staging area.

1.0   After you've rounded the north side of the lake, you'll come to a series of loops that cruise down to the water's edge and around the siltation ponds. **Options:** If you want to keep your hike short, take the "outer loop," which totals 7.3 miles. For a longer and more visually interesting hike, follow the winding loops by turning left at each of the forks. (The following milepoints describe the longer route.)

1.5   Take a left at the fork.

2.5   Take a left at the fork.

3.3   Take a left at the fork.

4.8   Take a left at the fork.

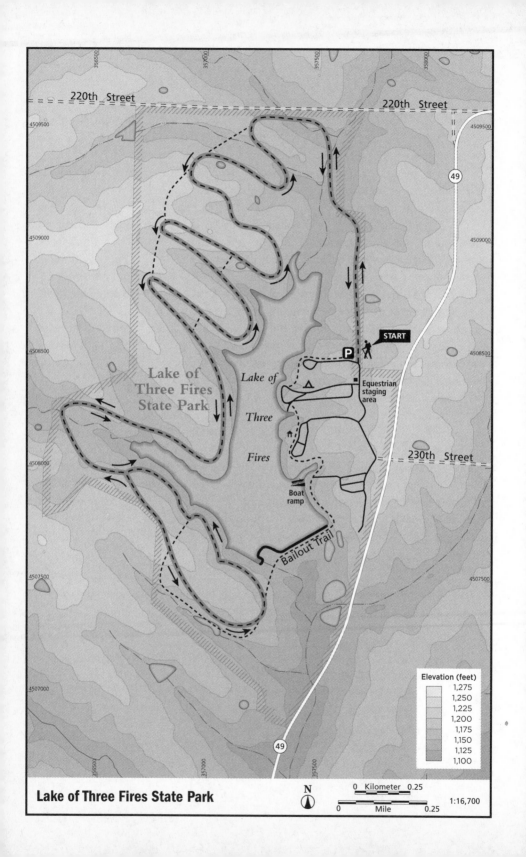

220th Street
220th Street

49

START

P

Lake of Three Fires State Park

Lake of Three Fires

Equestrian staging area

230th Street

Boat ramp

Bailout Trail

49

Elevation (feet)

| 1,275 |
| 1,250 |
| 1,225 |
| 1,200 |
| 1,175 |
| 1,150 |
| 1,125 |
| 1,100 |

Lake of Three Fires State Park

N

0   Kilometer   0.25

0   Mile   0.25

1:16,700

5.7 When you reach the dam, follow the loop around back to the main trail on the west side of the lake. Return the way you came, or shorten the trail by taking the outer loop. **Bailout:** Continue across the dam and walk 1.0 mile north on the developed east side of the lake back to the trailhead instead of backtracking on the west side.

10.5 Arrive back at the trailhead.

Hike Information

Local Information

Mount Ayr Chamber of Commerce; (641) 464-3234, http://mtayr.heartland.net/rdevco/mtayr.htm

Ringgold County Tourism; (515) 464-3704

Events/Attractions

Kellerton Bird Conservation Area and Ringgold Wildlife Management Area (prairie chickens booming in early spring); (641) 464-2220, www.iowadnr.com/wildlife

Le Festival de L'Heritage Francais, June, Corning; (515) 322-5229

Ayr Days (Scottish Festival), September, Mt. Ayr; (515) 464-2756

Accommodations

Charlie-Jane's, 400 West Madison Street, Mt. Ayr; (641) 464-2564

Sands Timber Recreation Area (Taylor County Conservation Board); (712) 523-2762

Fife's Grove Park (Ringgold County Conservation Board); (641) 464-2787

Restaurants

Lefty's Club Tavern (prairie-chicken watchers welcome!), 111 East Madson, Mt. Ayr (no phone)

Bedford Cafe, 320 Main Street, Bedford; (712) 523-2973

Skylark Cafe, Old Highway 2 East, Bedford; (712) 523-2847

Honorable Mentions

M. Two Hikes on Two Raccoon Rivers—Voas Nature Area and Keuhn Conservation Area

When the Des Moines Lobe surged to its southernmost terminus 12,000 to 14,000 years ago, it formed the Raccoon River drainage. The forks of the Raccoon River are situated in a very diverse area, with the woodlands of southern Iowa and wet-prairie influences of north-central Iowa. Four miles of trails at Voas Nature Area, east of the North Raccoon River, take you around an old farmstead that was donated to the county by a local family. The tile lines were broken and the wet-lands expanded, and a prairie restoration project has transformed the place. Another 2.0 miles of trails are located at Keuhn Conservation Area, on the south side of the South Raccoon River.

To Keuhn CA: From Interstate 80 take the U.S. Highway 6 exit and drive north 1.6 miles. Turn right (east) onto 345th Street, which becomes Bear Creek Road. At the T-intersection with Houston Trail, go north and stay north when the road gets quite windy before stopping at the nature center. *To Voas NA:* At the junction of U.S. Highway 169 and County Road F31 in Minburn, take CR F31 west. Just before you cross the North Raccoon River, turn north onto Lexington Road and go 1.2 miles. Before the road jogs to the west, you'll see the entrance on the east side of the road. For information: Dallas County Conservation Board; (515) 465–3577, www.dallascountyconservation.org.

N. Woodland Mounds State Preserve and Wildlife Area

A group of seven burial mounds built 900 to 1,600 years ago perch atop a bluff over-looking the South River, on the north end of Woodland Mounds State Preserve. The footpath that leads through forested uplands to the mounds is just under 1.5 miles long. The adjacent Woodland Mounds Wildlife Area has a 1.0-mile out-and-back trail and a 1.0-mile loop that will bring you back to the parking area. Two words: spring wildflowers! From the junction of U.S. Highway 65/69 and Highway 92, take Highway 92 east for 3.5 miles. Turn right (south) onto County Road S23 (165th Avenue). Turn left (east) onto Kennedy Street, and then make another left (east) onto Kirkwood Street. This will become Keokuk Street at the southward jog. Just after the jog, look for the WOODLAND MOUNDS STATE PRESERVE sign on the north side of the road, where a 0.25-mile access road takes you to the parking area. For information: Warren County Conservation Board; (515) 961–6169, www.warrenccb.org.

O. Sharon Bluffs Park

This area used to be a state park but is now managed by the Appanoose County Conservation Board, which runs a small nature center out of the park. Just over 3 miles of trails traverse the bluffs overlooking the Chariton River, dipping down into the floodplain as well. From the junction of U.S. Highway 2 and Highway 5 in Centerville, take US 2 east 3 miles. Look for the old brown state park sign that points you right (south) onto 248th Avenue. Stay on 248th Avenue for 1 mile and then turn left (east) onto 520th Street, which will take you past the nature center and to the parking area. The trailhead is directly east of the parking area. For information: Appanoose County Conservation Board; (641) 856–8528.

P. Honey Creek State Park–Prairie Peninsula Addition

The future site of Honey Creek Resort on Rathbun Lake, the state's first destination park, comprises 800 acres recently sold by the U.S. Army Corps of Engineers to the Iowa Department of Natural Resources. Two and a half miles of lime-chip trails wind around the lobed prairie peninsula that juts into the north side of Lake Rathbun. Multiple state-threatened species live on the ephemeral wet-prairies that occur on the hillsides leading down to the lake. Henslow's sparrow (*Ammodramus henslowii*) and the slender glass lizard (*Ophisaurus attenuatus*) make their home here. From the junction of Highways 142 and 5 just west of Moravia, head west on Highway 142 for 5.5 miles. Just before you enter the town of Iconium, turn south onto 185th Avenue (the name of this road may change with the development of the resort park). At 1.5 miles, park and walk east through a break in the fenceline that will lead you to the trail. For information: Honey Creek State Park; (641) 724–3739, www.state.ia.us/dnr/organiza/ppd/honeycrk.htm

Q. Ken Sidey Nature Area, Nodaway Lake, and Lake Greenfield

Located between the town of Greenfield and the Middle Nodaway River, the Ken Sidey Nature Area, Nodaway Lake, and Lake Greenfield Parks are connected by more than 10 miles of walking trails. Camp at Nodaway Lake in order to explore the parks. The Land Between Two Lakes Trails connect the two lakes, which both have loop trails around their perimeters. Three miles of trails at the less developed Ken Sidey Nature Area wander through beautiful forests. While you're in the area, check out Jesse James Historical Park near Adair, where in 1873 he and his gang successfully stole $3,000 in the first-recorded robbery of a moving train. For information: Adair County Conservation Board; (641) 743–6450, www.nod-valley.k12.ia .us/community/lakes/index.html.

Des Moines River

For years the name Des Moines was said to be a French derivation of the word "Moingona," thought to be the name of a tribe who once lived along the banks of the Des Moines River. However, recent linguistic investigations have left some certain that the name was instead a somewhat foul term for a tribe used by a Peoria chief to explain the other inhabitants of the region to Father Jacques Marquette in 1673. These differing explanations represent just one of the many mysteries that flow within the banks of the Des Moines.

The West Fork of the Des Moines starts from Lake Shetek in southwest Minnesota. The East Fork splits its headwaters with the Blue Earth River that flows north into Minnesota. Union Slough National Wildlife Refuge, which straddles the headwaters of the East Fork and the Blue Earth, is where millions of organisms hatch and grow each summer—predominantly freshwater invertebrates and the birds that eat them.

The east and west forks merge just south of Humboldt, Iowa, and flow into the Mississippi below Keokuk in the extreme southeast corner of the state, 320 river miles downstream. In his book *Iowa: The Rivers of Her Valleys,* writer William Petersen calls the Des Moines River, which flows a total of 535 miles, "a river of superlatives." With good reason: It is the only river to fully traverse Iowa from north to south; it possesses the widest valley and largest watershed of any of the state's rivers; and it houses the bulk of our human population along its banks.

The Des Moines River has been used by humans as a route for travel since the first mastodon hunters saw its banks. Conical burial mounds perched atop bluffs overlooking the river, summer camps, remnants of small-scale agriculture, and animal-processing sites found along the terraces tell us that the early inhabitants were drawn to the river. So were the steamships, which traveled up the great Des Moines before any other river in Iowa. From 1834 to the 1870s, the Des Moines was the main artery for transportation and commerce—a role that faded as the railroads began crisscrossing the state. Today many state and county conservation board parks are located along its banks, and the Des Moines River Trail is a favorite of kayakers and canoeists.

Just below the confluence of the east and west forks, traveling the Des Moines River or hiking along its banks means getting a visual lesson in the erosional forces of glacial meltwater. Several stretches of the Des Moines feature exposed outcrops of Pennsylvanian sandstone. Dolliver, Ledges, and Lacey Keosauqua State Parks contain several of these outcrops, and more can be found at Cedar Bluffs State Preserve in Mahaska County and Garrison Rock Park in Wapello County.

Saylorville Reservoir and Lake Red Rock, north and south of the state capital Des Moines, are two of the largest lakes in Iowa. Constructed and managed by the U.S. Army Corps of Engineers, they provide drinking water for countless mammals, habitat for aquatic plants and fish, nesting grounds for waterfowl and riparian songbirds, and recreational opportunities for many.

Down in the Big Bend country of Van Buren County, the Des Moines River pauses and swings around in a slow, graceful arc before its final rapid sweep to the Father of Waters. Lacey-Keosauqua State Park sits on the forested hills of the bend's southern bank. The Villages of Van Buren County, some of the oldest and most quaint towns in southern Iowa, lie along the lower Des Moines between Lacey-Keosauqua State Park and Shimek State Forest, the largest block of forests in southeast Iowa. The Des Moines River forms the extreme southeast Iowa boundary for 34 miles until its mouth at Keokuk.

As with many of the rivers in Iowa, the Des Moines's beauty has been marred by pollution. Even one hundred years ago, Thomas MacBride lamented at the state of the river: "I am not a very old man," he said in 1902 at age fifty-four, "but I have dipped oar in the Des Moines River away down near its mouth and seen the netted sunbeams on its gravel-colored bottom all the way across. Who looking now upon the muddy channel would think such a thing possible?" In 1985 Congress authorized the Des Moines Recreational River and Greenbelt to fund projects aimed at providing streambank stabilization and recreational opportunities and improving the health of the river. Each year, volunteers with Central Iowa Paddlers and the Iowa DNR clean up portions of the river. Much more attention is needed, and this mighty river requests your help.

21 Shimek State Forest—Farmington and Donnellson Units

The largest block of contiguous forest in the state, Shimek was named for one of Iowa's most important conservationists. The first unit was purchased in the mid-1930s after a century of logging and farming had left it infertile. In the late 1930s the Civilian Conservation Corps planted thousands of evergreen trees to demonstrate a reforestation regime for state parks and private landowners. An old railroad bed serves as the main thoroughfare in the adjoining Farmingon and Donnellson Units, the designated hiking-only units. Mowed firebreaks and several dirt roads spur off onto small loops through tree plantings and to Shagbark, Black Oak, and White Oak Lakes.

Distance: 9.1 miles round-trip
Approximate hiking time: 3 to 4 hours
Total elevation gain: 896 feet
Trail surface: Portion of the trail is on old railroad bed. Mowed firebreaks and gravel roads form the rest of the trail
Seasons: Year-round; however, in high water the creek crossings may involve some wet feet
Trail users: Hikers, cross-country skiers
Canine compatability: Dogs permitted on leash
Hazards: Poison ivy, ticks, rattlesnakes

Land status: State forest
Nearest towns: Farmington, Bentonsport
Fees and permits: No fees or permits required unless you are camping
Schedule: Open year-round, 4:00 A.M. to 10:30 P.M.
Map: USGS quad: Farmington
Trail contact: Shimek State Forest, 33653 County Road J56, Farmington; (319) 878-3811, www.iowadnr.com/forestry/shimek.html

Finding the trailhead: From the junction of Highways 2 and 1 south of Keosauqua, take Highway 2 east. Cross the Des Moines River and enter the town of Farmington, where Highway 2 turns southeast. Look for the County Road J56 and turn left (east). This will take you out of town, become a gravel road, and pass the Shimek State Forest Headquarters. Just after the headquarters, turn right (south) toward the Black Oak Lake parking area. *DeLorme: Iowa Atlas and Gazetteer:* Page 63 F8

The Hike

The southern boundary of Iowa is formed by a straight line following the approximate arc of parallel 40° 35' north latitude. When the line intersects with the Des Moines River, the river becomes the state boundary. The bulk of Shimek State Forest is located just east of the intersection, 34 river miles north of the Mississippi River.

Three trailheads provide access to the Farmington and Donnellson Units, open to hikers and mountain bikers only. You'll have to do a little bit of road-hiking and backtracking to traverse the unit, but it's worth it. The old railroad bed that runs

east-west through the unit serves as its backbone, and the bulk of the spur trails are mowed firebreaks. Visible from the railroad bed trail are wet lowlands housing walnut, swamp white oak, silver maple, green ash, hackberry, and elm trees. You'll cross Lick Creek, which is shaded by willow thickets and tall cottonwoods. Three lakes are located within the unit, and just southeast of Shagbark Lake there's a primitive campsite available to backpackers.

Among Iowa's ninety-nine counties, heavily forested Lee County has the highest amount of rainfall and the lowest elevation. Such tree-friendly conditions are exactly what the state was seeking when it first purchased the land. The Civilian Conservation Corps (CCC) began planting demonstration plots with softwoods, many of them nonnatives such as eastern white, red, jack, and Virginia pines, as well as several spruces and larches. Sit down and have your lunch in one of the plantings, where shafts of light break the thick canopy and the smell of sunlight on pine will tickle your nose.

To the south the Lick Creek and Croton Units house one of the most popular trail-riding systems in the state, a maze of paths surrounding Lick Creek just before its confluence with the Des Moines River. The trails are extensive; however, many are seriously eroded muddy swaths rather than footpaths. On weekends during summer, the horse traffic can be substantial. Exploration by foot in early spring and late fall or on cross-country skis in winter is your best bet at avoiding the crowds and scat. The Croton Unit has long been known as a birding hot spot; ten of the twelve warblers you may see are annual nesters here, and both scarlet and summer tanagers can be found.

Wild turkeys were abundant in the state during presettlement times (the Turkey River in northeast Iowa was named for high gobbler populations). Rampant hunting led to near extirpation of the birds, and by the early 1900s there were only random sightings. After several attempts to reintroduce game-farm birds failed, eleven wild turkeys were obtained from Missouri and released in Shimek in 1965. The population exploded, and less than ten years later, a limited hunting season was opened. Today wild turkey populations are enormous and the birds can be found almost everywhere in the state.

Miles and Directions

0.0   Start at Black Oak Lake parking area; walk south on the trail until you arrive at the railroad bed. Turn west (right) at Signpost 6.

0.82   At fork (Signpost 2) turn south (left).

1.34   At fork (Signpost 1) turn left (east). (Note: Turning right here would take you to the Highway 2 trailhead/parking.)

1.75   At fork (Signpost 20) turn left (northeast) and cross the dam at White Oak Lake.

2.24   At fork (Signpost 19) turn left (east). **Option:** Follow any of the trails that wind through a pine planting. They all loop around to Signpost 18, where you want to end up.

2.46   At fork (Signpost 18) turn left (north) onto a dirt access road; walk 0.25 mile.

◄ *Sunlight filters through a pine planting at Shimek State Forest.*

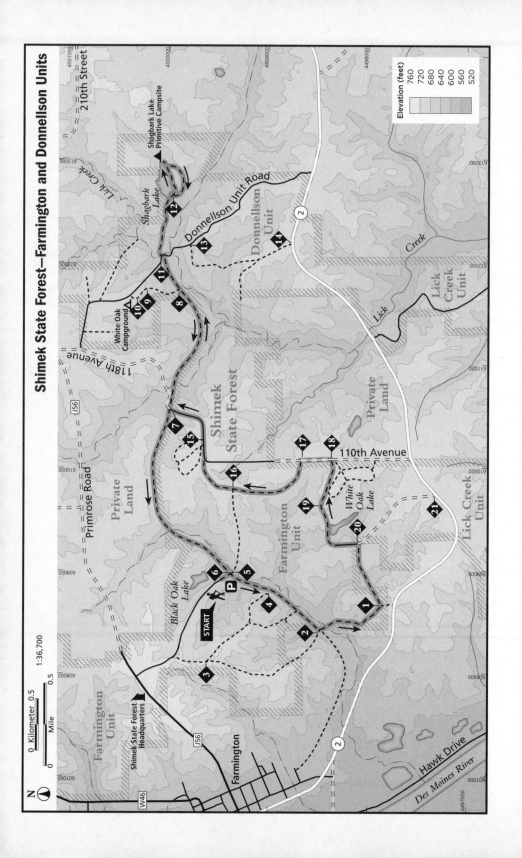

Shimek State Forest—Farmington and Donnellson Units

1:36,700

2.63 At fork (Signpost 17) turn left (west) and walk through pine planting.

3.15 At fork (Signpost 16) turn right (north). **Option:** Loop around another pine planting, or just continue on main trail.

3.5 At fork (Signpost 15) turn right and emerge onto dirt access road once again; walk north.

3.9 At fork (Signpost 7) turn right (east) back onto railroad bed.

5.0 At Donnellson Unit Road (Signpost 11) turn left (north) and then make a quick right (east) onto the access road for Shagbark Lake. This will end at a parking lot.

5.4 From the parking lot walk due east over the dam and turn left (north) onto the small footpath that fringes the southeast side of the lake. At the fork walk left (west) for the last 50 feet before the campsite.

5.7 Arrive at Shagbark Lake primitive campsite. To return to the parking lot, backtrack and take the left (east) fork around in a small loop before climbing back up on the dam and walking into the parking lot.

6.0 Arrive back at the Shagbark Lake parking area. Follow the access road back down to the Donnellson Unit Road.

6.5 Hop back onto the railroad bed and take this all the way back to the trailhead.

9.1 Arrive back at the trailhead.

BEWARE OF TICKS AND POISON IVY
Tiny deer, or blacklegged ticks (*Ixodes scapularis*), which transmit Lyme disease, draw nourishment from attaching themselves to warm-blooded animals and sucking their blood. During spring and summer, when larvae are hatching, it is best to wear light-colored clothing and long sleeves and pants, tuck in your socks, and frequently check yourself for ticks. If you do find a tick on your body, use tweezers to grasp the entire tick and pull it straight off your skin. (Make sure you remove the entire tick; leaving any part embedded in your skin exposes you to additional infections.) Wash the bite area with soap and water. Lyme disease symptoms can include headaches, fever, chills, swollen glands, flulike fatigue, muscle and joint pain, and rashes in the form of bulls-eyes around the initial bite. If you experience any of these symptoms, immediately consult a doctor.

Poison ivy (*Toxicodendron radicans* and *T. rydbergii*) can grow as a woody shrub on the forest floor or in disturbed areas or as a vine with distinctive aerial roots that wind up trees in Iowa forests. All parts of poison ivy, including the roots, contain an oil that can cause an extremely irritating skin reaction on most people. The blistery rash is usually very itchy. Oils can be transmitted to humans via pets' fur or the smoke from a burning poison plant. The best way to avoid contact with poison ivy is to know how to identify it. If you are exposed to it, thoroughly wash the area with water (and soap if available) as soon as possible. Although humans should follow the "leaves of three, let them be" mantra, the white, waxy berries serve as food for migrating songbirds and for hungry American robins during winter.

Hike Information

Local Information

Villages of Van Buren County;
www.800-tourvbc.com/
Famington; http://farmingtoniowa.com
Bonaparte; http://bonaparte-iowa.com

Events/Attractions

Bentonsport Arts Festival, mid-October,
Bentonsport; (319) 592-3579, www
.bentonsport.com/events.htm
Farmington Strawberry Festival, June,
Farmington; (319) 878-3313, www
.farmingtoniowa.com
Historic Bonaparte Pottery Tour, September,
Bonaparte; (319) 592-3620
Morel Mushroom Festival, early May, Bona-
parte; (319) 592-3400
Bike Van Buren, late August (approximately
110 miles from Keosauqua to outlying vil-
lages); (800) 868-7822, http://showcase
.netins.net/web/villages/bike.htm

Keokuk Farmers' Market, Rivercity Mall parking lot, Keokuk; (319) 524-1021; May
through October, Saturday 7:00 to 11:00 A.M.

Accommodations

Shimek State Forest, equestrian and primitive
camping; (319) 878-3811
RiverView Canoes & Campground, cabins and
campground, Farmington; (319) 878-3715
Indian Lake Park, cabins and campground,
Farmington; (319) 878-3706
The Cottage Bed & Make Your Own Breakfast,
507 First Street, Bonaparte; (319) 592-3620
Mason House Bed & Breakfast, Hawk Drive,
Bentonsport; (319) 592-3133

Restaurants

Bridge Cafe, 101 Olive Street, Farmington;
(319) 878-3315
Bonaparte Retreat Restaurant, Bonaparte;
(319) 592-3339
4th Street Cafe, 22 South Fourth Street,
Keokuk; (319) 524-9354

22 Lacey-Keosauqua State Park

The unparalleled beauty of the forested bluffs rising from the huge horseshoe bend in the Des Moines River reveal each season's spectacular show. Winter's snow cover forms a contemplative silence followed by spring's diverse wildflower display and budding trees. The shade of the tall forest canopy is a perfect respite from the heat of summer, while autumn yields one of the most vividly colorful scenes in Iowa.

Distance: 9.5 miles round-trip
Approximate hiking time: 3 to 4 hours
Total elevation gain: 1,380 feet
Trail surface: Forested footpaths
Seasons: Year-round
Trail users: River Trail and Lake Lacey Loop for hiking and cross-country skiing only. Trails on northwest corner and going through the Keosauqua Unit of the Shimek State Forest are used by snowmobiles as well
Canine compatability: Dogs permitted on leash
Hazards: Poison ivy and ticks

Land status: State park; bordered by Shimek State Forest–Keosauqua Unit and Lake Sugema Wildlife Management Area, managed by Iowa Department of Natural Resources and Van Buren County Conservation Board
Nearest town: Keosauqua
Fees and permits: No fees or permits required unless you are camping
Schedule: Year-round, 4:00 A.M. to 10:30 P.M.
Map: USGS quad: Keosauqua
Trail contact: Lacey-Keosauqua State Park, P.O. Box 398, Keosauqua, IA 52565; (319) 293-3502, www.state.ia.us./dnr/organiza /ppd/laceykeo.htm

Finding the trailhead: From Keosauqua drive south on Highway 1; cross the bridge and immediately turn west (left) onto Park Road. At the second fork in the road, follow the right fork, continuing on Park Road. Just before you exit, park at the westernmost shelter. *DeLorme: Iowa Atlas and Gazetteer:* Page 63 E6

The Hike

Walking along the Des Moines River at 1,653-acre Lacey-Keosauqua State Park elicits Van Buren County's motto: "The rush of life races the blood, but the quiet life restoreth the soul." For reasons unknown to geologists, the Des Moines River decided to slow down a little here at Keosauqua, deviating from its normally linear course to form the largest oxbow in southeast Iowa. Lacey-Keosauqua lies on the south side of the oxbow, almost 49 river miles from the Mississippi River at Keokuk. Across the river from the park, sandy alluvial deposits underlie the terraced farmland inside the river's bend. The park sits atop deeply cut older bedrock.

When the former Big Bend Park was dedicated in 1921, it was renamed Keosauqua. A good deal of controversy surrounds the origin and meaning of Keosauqua, first used as a second name for the Des Moines River on Charles de

Wild geraniums bloom in May in Lacey-Keosauqua State Park.

Wards's 1835 map. It is believed that Keosauqua is a Fox word, though there are varied speculations of its meaning. Several theories, taken from early settlers' accounts, include "the stream bearing a floating mass of snow, slush, or ice," "clear broad river," and "great bend." In 1926 the name Lacey was added to the park in honor of Major John F. Lacey from Oskaloosa. Lacey fought in the Civil War, was a member of the Iowa House of Representatives and the U.S. Congress, and campaigned for and wrote conservation legislation.

The River Trail extends from the farthest west shelter in the park 3.0 miles along the Des Moines to the bridge to Keosauqua. Late Woodland peoples buried their dead in the conical mounds they built atop the bluffs along the river. Nineteen are visible now. Pottery shards and tools such as spear points and animal-bone scrapers have been discovered by recent archaeological explorations in the beds of Wesley, Ely, and Thatcher Creeks.

Several connector trails access the 1.0-mile upland forest loop in the northwest section of the park, a 2.5-mile loop trail around Lake Lacey, and a 3.0-mile trail connecting Lake Lacey to Lake Sugema Wildlife Management Area and camping area.

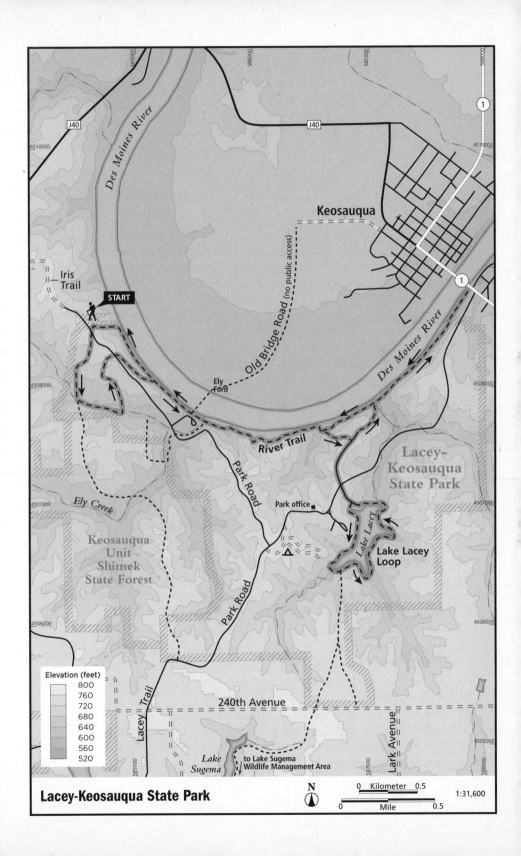

Lacey-Keosauqua State Park

These all ascend the forested bluffs and meander over the rich upland oak-hickory forest that dominates the park.

Ely Ford, named for the Mormon expedition that crossed the Des Moines River here, is a popular picnicking and birding spot along the River Trail. Sit in the shade of the tall sycamore and elm trees and look for such exciting birds as northern parula; yellow-throated, worm-eating, cerulean, Kentucky, and hooded warblers; summer and scarlet tanagers; ovenbird; and Louisiana waterthrush. Follow a small trail south of Ely Ford up a forested ravine where Ely Creek has dissected the terrain to expose the Keosauqua sandstone formation hidden beneath alluvium in the rest of the park.

If you want a really decent-length hike, park at Lake Sugema and walk all the loops in the park, including the snowmobile trail that winds through the Keosauqua Unit of Shimek State Forest. Leave early, and spend the whole day enjoying the Big Bend; you can even stop in Keosauqua for a midday treat.

Miles and Directions

Option: To explore most of the trails, use the following directions. If you're just looking for a nice walk, follow the River Trail to Keosauqua Bridge and back.

0.0 Start at the westernmost shelter. Cross Park Road and take the trail that heads south, down the ridge. At the creek turn left (east) onto the trail that loops back north again. **Option:** Going straight will take you through the Keosauqua Unit of Shimek State Forest. This is a great place to cross-country ski when there aren't a bunch of snowmobiles cruising through.

1.2 Arrive back at Park Road and cross it, connecting with the River Trail. (FYI: Here lie the bulk of the visible burial mounds.)

1.8 Arrive at Ely Ford Monument; cross the bridge and continue east. (FYI: Bald eagles have been known to nest in the cottonwood trees on the other side of the river just east of Ely Ford.)

2.7 Turn right (southeast) onto a trail that takes you up the ridge.

2.9 Arrive at a shelter. Walk due south next to the road to get to the Lake Lacey Loop.

3.2 Cross Park Road. Walk down the hill to the boat ramp and hop onto the Lake Lacey Loop. **Option:** At the southern tip of Lake Lacey, the Lake Sugema Trail diverges from the Lake Lacey Loop. The trail is 3.0 miles, if you're looking for a super-duper day.

5.2 Arrive back at the boat ramp and backtrack up to the River Trail.

5.7 Arrive back at the River Trail; turn right (east) to walk over to Keosauqua Bridge, or turn left (west) to head back to the trailhead.

6.7 Arrive at Keosauqua Bridge; head over for a treat in town, or turn around and backtrack along the River Trail.

8.6 Arrive back at Ely Ford. **Option:** Check out Ely Creek sandstone exposures by following the trail to the left (south). It will loop around to the south and bring you back to Park Road, where you can connect back with the River Trail to return to the trailhead.

9.5 Arrive back at the trailhead.

Hike Information

Local Information

Villages of Van Buren County, P.O. Box 9, Keosauqua, IA 52565; (800) 868-7822, www.800tourvbc.com

Keosauqua Community, web site: www.keosauqua.com

Events/Attractions

Forest Crafts Festival, October, Lacey-Keosauqua State Park

Bike Van Buren, late August (approximately 110 miles from Keosauqua to outlying villages); (800) 868-7822, http://showcase.netins.net/web.villages/bike.htm

Des Moines River Canoe Trail; www.desmoinesriver.org, www.state.ia.us/parks/canoe/dsmrvr2.pdf

Keosauqua Farmers' Market, City Shelter; May through October, Friday 2:00 to 6:00 P.M.

Accommodations

Lacey-Keosauqua State Park (cabins and campground); (319) 293-3502

Hotel Manning, 100 Van Buren Street, Keosauqua; (800) 728-2718, http://showcase.netins.net/web/manning/index.htm

Mansion Inn Hotel, 500 Henry Street, Keosauqua; (800) 646-0166, http://mansion-inn.com

Restaurants

Village Cup and Cakes, 202 Main Street, Keosauqua; (319) 293-8200

Riverbend Pizza and Steakhouse, 603 First Street, Keosauqua; (319) 293-9900

Red Barn Bistro, 21268 Fir Avenue, Keosauqua; (319) 293-6154

George's Pizza and Steakhouse, 607 First Street, Keosauqua; (319) 293-3999, www.georgespizzaandsteakhouse.com

Tillie's Tap, 711 First Street, Keosauqua; (319) 293-9985

Other Resources

Paddling Iowa by Nate Hoogeveen (Trails Books)

23 Cedar Bluffs Natural Area and State Preserve

The 2.0-mile Lacey Memorial Nature Trail takes you across prairie and oak–savanna restoration areas, down into a box canyon, along a 100-foot-high bluff overlooking Cedar Creek, past a several-thousand-year-old burial mound, and through forests that house spring-blooming wildflowers galore. If you visit Cedar Bluffs in early May and like wild edible mushrooms, I can predict what you'll be eating for dinner (as long as you look in the right spots).

Distance: 2.0 miles
Approximate hiking time: 1 to 2 hours
Total elevation gain: 152 feet
Trail surface: Mowed trails, forested footpaths
Seasons: Year-round.
Trail users: Hikers, hunters
Canine compatability: Dogs permitted on leash
Hazards: Poison ivy, ticks, steep bluff faces
Land status: State preserve, owned and managed by Mahaska County Conservation Board

Nearest town: Oskaloosa
Fees and permits: No fees or permits required
Schedule: Year-round during daylight hours
Map: USGS quad: Leighton
Trail contact: Mahaska County Conservation Board; (641) 673-9327
Iowa Department of Natural Resources Web site: www.state.ia.us/dnr/organiza/ppd/cedarblf.htm

---

Finding the trailhead: From the junction of Highway 92 and U.S. Highway 65 in Oskaloosa, take US 65 south; turn right (west) onto Eleventh Avenue. When the road curves, turn left onto Beacon Road (County Road T39) and take this through town. Turn right onto Kilbourn Street, which becomes Indian Way. Just after you cross the Des Moines River bridge, turn right (west) onto 290th Street. Turn right (north) onto County Road G62, which becomes 280th Street. Follow 280th Street until you see the sign and parking area on the north side of the road. *DeLorme: Iowa Atlas and Gazetteer:* Page 51 F9

The Hike

A bobolink sitting atop a compass plant is a special treat, and at Cedar Bluffs in late July, you're likely to enjoy such a sight before you've even started hiking on the Lacey Memorial Trail (named for former Oskaloosan, John F. Lacey). After checking out the prairie reconstruction, follow the old road that heads directly north from the parking area. The shrubby fence line along the road is a good place to look for eastern kingbirds, brown thrashers, and American goldfinches. Also look for Eastern bluebirds using the nesting boxes set up along the trail.

At 0.4 mile, continue due north on the main road or detour to the east, following the forest edge around in a short loop. You'll arrive back at the main trail just before it enters the forest, on the way to the bluff's edge.

Of the five species of morels that grow in Iowa, you'll surely find one on a spring visit to Cedar Bluffs.

Follow the steps leading down into the box canyon and cross a small bridge. Between the bridge and the interpretive sign describing ancient swamps, a small footpath leads toward Cedar Creek and then veers east to traverse the base of the bluffs. This trail is somewhat rough going and can be very slippery when wet, but it's greatly worth the detour. The fractured cliffs tower above you, while below at the base of the bluff are piles of broken boulders from the escarpment.

Similar to exposures at Wildcat Den, Ledges, and Dolliver State Parks, these Pennsylvanian sandstone bluffs are remnants of ancient river channels that once flowed through Iowa. Looking closely, you'll see cross-bedding and swirled ripples in the sandstone, evidence of the rivers' movement 305 million years ago. Mosses and liverworts cover the limestone and shale that underlie the sandstone, while hepatica, columbine, walking fern, goldie's wood fern, and silvery spleenwort grow out of the cracks and crevices. The footpath extends 0.25 mile to the east, where you can turn around and head back to the bridge to walk the second half of the Lacey Trail.

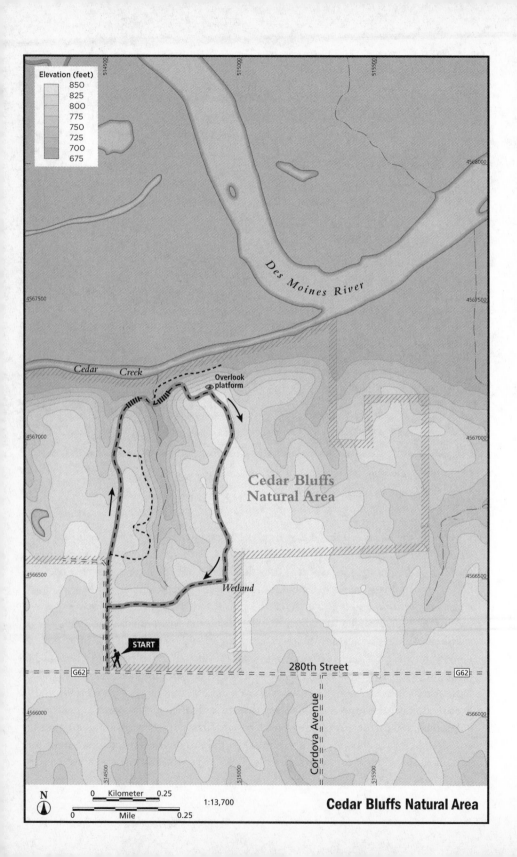

Elevation (feet)
850
825
800
775
750
725
700
675

Des Moines River

Cedar Creek

Overlook platform

Cedar Bluffs
Natural Area

Wetland

START

G62 — 280th Street — G62

Cordova Avenue

N

Kilometer   0.25
0

Mile   0.25
0

1:13,700

Cedar Bluffs Natural Area

At the top of the ninety-nine stairs going up the east side of the ravine, stop to catch your breath and look for birds from your stance within the canopy. Prescribed burns along the blufftop have uncovered a community of prairie plants within the forest, and you'll see leadplant and yellow stargrass growing along the trail. Just before you come to the overlook platform, a conical Woodland-period burial mound comes into view. In 1999 archaeological investigations uncovered stone-tool processing and habitation sites, evidencing nearly 8,000 years of human use of the area.

The confluence of Cedar Creek and the Des Moines River hasn't always been where it is today. Earlier located 0.25 mile upstream on Cedar Creek at the west end of the preserve, it moved to its current position sometime between 1878 and 1884. During the early 1800s the Des Moines River was a major commercial shipping route, and steamboats passing Cedar Bluffs would sound their horns, for which the outcrop was nicknamed "Echo Rock."

Bald eagles have been known to nest along the Des Moines River within sight of the overlook. After spending sufficient time gazing at the bends in the river, continue southward on the trail. You'll exit the forest and walk through a wildlife food plot before turning west to follow the forest edge. Stop at the small pond, fringed in cattails and teeming with turtles and red-winged blackbirds, before you arrive back at the trailhead.

Miles and Directions

0.0 Start from the parking lot, and walk on the access road due north. At the fork continue straight (north).

0.8 Arrive creekside, after having descended the many stairs. Now you get to climb some—ninety-nine of them on the way to the overlook. **Option:** Just after you've crossed to the east side of the bridge, you'll see a small footpath off to the left (north). If you want to explore the base of the sandstone cliffs, this is the trail. Once you've walked toward the river, you'll have a choice to take the precipitous path midway up the bluff or the safe path along the river terrace. You'll still be able to see the magnificent sandstone if you take the low road.

0.8 + ninety-nine stairs; take a deep breath and check out the canopy view.

1.0 Arrive at the overlook. You'll be able to see the bend in the Des Moines River and the cropped floodplain below. Check out the bluffs across the river; they may yield a big bird nest surprise if you look hard enough. Continue on the loop through the forest, which you'll emerge from after 0.25 mile.

1.5 Arrive at the pond fringed with cattails and sedges.

1.8 Arrive back at the main access road; turn left (south) to return to the trailhead. Take another loop if you aren't worn out.

2.0 Arrive back at the trailhead.

Hike Information

Local Information

Oskaloosa Area Chamber and Development Group; (641) 672-2591, www.oskaloosa chamber.com

Events/Attractions

Tulip Time Festival, May, Pella
Nelson Pioneer Farm and Museum; (641) 672-2989, www.nelsonpioneer.org
Bluegrass Festival, third week in August, Southern Iowa Fairgrounds, Oskaloosa (largest four-day bluegrass festival in Iowa); (641) 673-7004
Oskaloosa Farmers' Market, Town Square, Oskaloosa; (641) 673-7357, May through October, Tuesday 4:00 to 6:00 P.M., Saturday 8:00 to 11:00 A.M.

Accommodations

The Clover Leaf, 314 Washington Street, Pella; (641) 628-9045

Restaurants

Dutch East Indies Coffee Company, 804 East First Street, Pella; (641) 628-9723
Smokey Row Coffee House, 639 Franklin Street, Pella; (641) 621-0008
Hunters, 113 High Avenue, Oskaloosa; (641) 673-9991
Big Ed's BBQ, 104 First Avenue East, Oskaloosa; (641) 672-2680

Other Resources

Paddling Iowa by Nate Hoogeveen (Trails Books)
The Guide to Iowa's State Preserves by Ruth Herzberg and John Pearson (Bur Oaks Books Series, University of Iowa Press)

24 Ledges State Park

Picturesque sandstone bluffs line the canyon of Pea's Creek just before it enters the Des Moines River. Take the 5.4-mile loop around the upland prairie reconstruction, down to the canyon, over to the interpretive trail around Lost Lake, and back again. Or just spend the day exploring the ledges. If you like climbing stairs or just want a nice steep hike, this is the place.

Distance: 5.4-mile loop
Approximate hiking time: 2 to 4 hours
Total elevation gain: 866 feet
Trail surface: Forested footpaths, a little road-hiking
Seasons: Year-round, although steps into canyon become dangerously slippery when wet or icy
Trail users: Hikers only
Canine compatability: Dogs permitted on leash

Hazards: Poison ivy, ticks, steep bluffs
Land status: State park
Nearest town: Boone
Fees and permits: No fees or permits required unless you're camping
Schedule: Open year-round 4:00 A.M. to 10:30 P.M.
Maps: USGS quads: Madrid NW, Boone W
Trail contact: Ledges State Park; (515) 432-1852, www.iowadnr.com/parks/state_park_list/ledges.html

Look for orb weaver spiders in the upland restored prairie of
Ledges State Park.

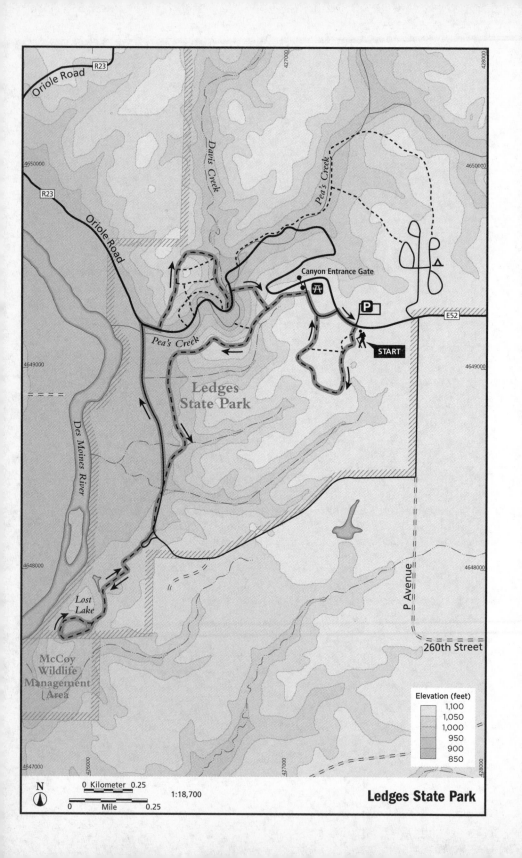

Oriole Road

R23

Davis Creek

Pea's Creek

R23

Oriole Road

Canyon Entrance Gate

P

Pea's Creek

START

Ledges
State Park

Des Moines River

Lost
Lake

McCoy
Wildlife
Management
Area

P Avenue

E52

260th Street

Elevation (feet)
1,100
1,050
1,000
950
900
850

N

0 Kilometer 0.25

0   Mile   0.25

1:18,700

Ledges State Park

Finding the trailhead: From the junction of Highway 17 and U.S. Highway 30 southeast of Boone, take Highway 17 south. Turn right (west) onto County Road E52, which will take you the 3 miles into the park. *DeLorme: Iowa Atlas and Gazetteer:* Page 39 E10

The Hike

The Pennsylvanian sandstone for which Ledges State Park is so well known was deposited some 300 million years ago, when Iowa was located just south of the equator. Large rivers flowed northeast-southwest through the state, draining into the shallow sea that covered much of the western United States. The sea's coastline was constantly in flux, migrating back and forth between Oklahoma and Illinois, periodically flooding the coastal swamps and tropical forests of Iowa (the source of our coal deposits). The rivers deposited clay, mud, and sand, which today can be found in the park's Pennsylvanian rock record of sandstone, shale, coal, and limestone.

In geologic time, the sandstone was sculpted into the ledges overlooking Pea's Creek Canyon much more recently, only 12,000 to 13,000 years ago. As the Des Moines Lobe of the Wisconsinan ice sheet was melting, massive amounts of water drained off it. The routes the meltwater took carved out the steep-sided Pea's and Davis Creek valleys.

To maximize trail length, park at the lot north of the prairie area, which lies on the uplands above the canyon. A summer stroll around the Ledges prairie reconstruction will give you a look at yellow and purple coneflowers, rattlesnake master, big bluestem, Indian grass, Missouri goldenrod, and several species of gentian. Continue west past the shelters and onto the trail that parallels the road heading into the canyon. Descend the 200-plus steps made of native stone, which can be very slippery when wet. Search the ground for a multitude of ferns as well as reindeer lichen, a boreal species that looks like small piles of gray-green steel wool and can be found growing amid beds of mosses and liverworts.

The trail will fork twice; keep left both times, heading past Council Ring and Table Rock. Archaeological explorations at Ledges found a record of continuing habitation for the past 4,000 years. Before Euro-American settlement, Sauk and Fox (now Mesquakie) and Sioux peoples lived in the area, and the park's canyon is thought to have been a site for their council meetings.

Follow the trail south (you'll have to road-hike the last 0.4 mile from the shelter) to the Lost Lake trailhead, where there's a relaxing interpretive loop trail around the lake. In late summer you'll find abundant fungi growing on rotting wood; coral tooth (*Herecium corraloides*), chicken-of-the-woods (*Laetiporus sulphureus*), and honey mushrooms (*Armillariella mellea*) are three edibles that are quite common during wet summers.

After walking around the lake, continue north up the road that parallels the river. At the bridge that crosses Pea's Creek, follow the opening in the floodplain willow thickets down to the Des Moines River for a great view of the valley. You'll

IF YOU'RE STILL NOT TIRED

McCoy Wildlife Management Area lies just to the south of Ledges State Park and can be accessed from the Lost Lake trailhead. Just past the trailhead you'll come to a three-way intersection. Take the trail closest to the Des Moines River, and you'll traverse a narrow path along the cliff's edge. The trail is very slippery and dangerous and shouldn't be attempted unless you are sure of yourself, but it offers an astounding view of the river valley.

find evidence of Ledges' flood history on the telephone pole/flood-level marker in the parking lot just before you enter Lower Ledges via the road.

Returning into the lower canyon, take the second trail to the left that heads up the stairs to the bluff. You'll wind around the top in a small maze, ending up in the Crow's Nest. When the trees have shed their leaves, it's a perfect spot to see the canyon, but during spring and summer the view is a splendid wall of green.

The trail leads back down to the canyon and passes the confluence of Davis and Pea's Creeks. The staircase that lies just across the road and north a skosh from where you emerged will take you back up to the trailhead. Otherwise, you can follow the Pea's Creek drainage north and in a loop back to the campground (see Miles and Directions).

Miles and Directions

0.0 Start at parking area just north of the prairie area. Walk across the road onto the mowed trails through the prairie restoration.

0.67 Arrive at the picnic area, just outside the CANYON ENTRANCE on the road. Follow the trail that parallels the road before descending into the canyon.

0.95 At fork turn left (south) toward Council Ring.

1.4 After descending to the floodplain, continue due south until the trail ends, then hop onto the road until you reach the parking area for Lost Lake.

2.1 Arrive at Lost Lake trailhead. The trail forks three times. Choose whichever way you'd like to loop around the lake; it's not difficult to find your way back to the trailhead.

3.3 Arrive back at the Lost Lake trailhead and road-hike to the north, parallel to the river.

4.0 Arrive at the bridge over Pea's Creek; turn right on the road to enter the canyon. **Option:** Instead of going directly back into the canyon, follow Pea's Creek west, through the willow thickets, to its confluence with the Des Moines River, then return and go up into the canyon.

4.1 Turn left (north) onto the (staircase) trail that heads up the ridge toward the Crow's Nest.

4.6 Arrive back down in the canyon. Cross the road and look straight east for your trail, the staircase leading back up out of the canyon. **Option:** Follow the road to the north to take the long way back to the trailhead, via upper Pea's Creek and the campgrounds. You'll see the trail diverging off to the north the last time Pea's Creek crosses under the road and just before the road climbs out of the canyon.

5.1 Arrive back at the picnic area just west of the prairie area. You can walk back through the prairie or just cross the road and follow the small footpath to the parking area.

5.4 Arrive back at the trailhead.

Hike Information

Local Information

Ames Convention and Visitors Bureau, Ames; (515) 232-4032 or (800) 288-7470, www.acvb.ames.ia.us/
Boone Chamber of Commerce; (800) 266-6312, www.booneiowa.com

Events/Attractions

Iowa Arboretum, 1875 Peach Avenue (between Ledges State Park and Madrid, south of County Road E57); (515) 795-3216; directions: http://iowa.sierraclub.org/arboretumdirections.htm
Midnight Madness Road Races, July, Ames (5k and 10k); (515) 233-6057, www.fitnesssports.com/july_races/Madness/MidnightMadness_info.html
Boone & Scenic Valley Railroad, Eleventh & Division Streets, Boone; (800) 626-0319
Ames Farmers' Market, North Grand Mall parking lot, Ames; (515) 827-5360; May through October, Wednesday 3:00 to 6:00 P.M., Saturday 8:00 A.M. to noon
Boone Farmers' Market Association, Wal-Mart parking lot, Boone; (515) 432-4480; seasonal, Thursday 2:00 to 6:00 P.M.

Accommodations

Bluebird B&B, 1372 Peony Lane, Boone; (515) 432-5057
Green Belt Bed & Breakfast, RR2, Ames; (515) 232-1960

Restaurants

Thai Kitchen, 2410 Chamberlain Street, Ames; (515) 292-4788
The Cafe, 2616 Northridge Parkway, Ames; (515) 292-0100
Dutch Oven Bakery, 219 Duff, Ames; (515) 232-9244

Other Resources

Big Table Books, 330 Main Street, Ames; (515) 232-8976
Big Bluestem Audubon; www.wyalusing.org/BBAS.htm
Iowa's Geological Past: 3 Billion Years of Change by Wayne I. Anderson (Bur Oak Books Series University of Iowa Press)
Paddling Iowa by Nate Hoogeveen (Trails Books)

25 Brushy Creek State Recreation Area

Brushy Creek contains 35 miles of multiuse trails and offers a multitude of recreational opportunities, including hunting, fishing, boating, and equestrian and hiking trails. A controversial 1967 proposal to flood Brushy Creek's stunning forested canyon led to a twenty-year struggle over future development. In the end, the Iowa Department of Natural Resources created a state preserve to protect an extremely sensitive tract (260 acres), impounded a smaller lake than earlier proposed (690 acres), and acquired additional land to build more equestrian trails (1,750 acres). Though not every group involved was satisfied with the outcome, many people now enjoy the multiuse aspect of Brushy Creek.

Distance: 35 miles of multiuse trails
Approximate hiking time: As long as you want
Trail surface: Forested footpaths, mowed swaths, paved trails
Seasons: Year-round; multiuse trails very muddy in spring, heavily used by hunters during deer, pheasant, and turkey seasons
Trail users: Hikers, equestrians, hunters, cross-country skiers, snowmobilers
Canine compatability: Dogs permitted on leash

Hazards: Poison ivy, ticks
Land status: State recreation area, state preserve
Nearest towns: Fort Dodge
Fees and permits: No fees or permits required unless you're camping
Schedule: Open year-round, 4:00 A.M. to 10:30 P.M.
Maps: USGS Quads: Duncombe, Stratford
Trail contact: Brushy Creek State Recreation Area; (515) 543–8298, www.iowadnr.com/parks/state_park_list/brushy_creek.html

Finding the trailhead: From the junction of U.S. Highways 20 and 169 south of Fort Dodge, take US 20 east. Turn right (south) onto County Road P73, and at the T-intersection turn left (east) onto County Road D46. Turn left (north) onto Brushy Creek Road to access the park office, beach, and various trailheads. *DeLorme: Iowa Atlas and Gazetteer:* Page 28 H4

The Hike

In 1967 the Iowa legislature appropriated monies to begin development of a 1,000-acre lake in Brushy Creek Canyon. Land acquisition began, but it was discovered that two neighboring communities' sewage systems, as well as an industrial plant, were discharging waste into the proposed area. Property owners refused to sell land to the state for what they saw as unfairly low prices, while various interest groups each wanted a say in the future of the project. The development was put on hold.

In 1975, with lawsuits resolved and land acquisition completed, a master plan for development was next on the line. However, in 1969 a landmark piece of federal

Late-blooming forest wildflowers like woodland aster and tall bellflower extend the season at Brushy Creek.

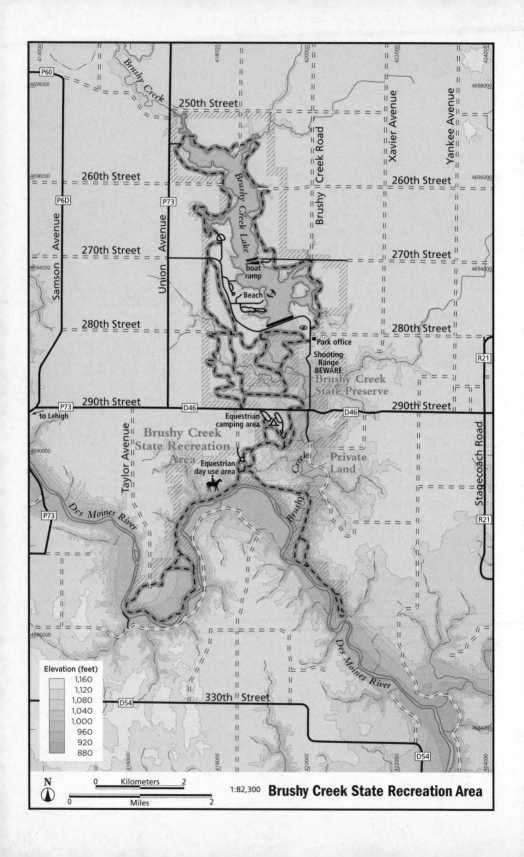

Brushy Creek State Recreation Area

Elevation (feet)
1,160
1,120
1,080
1,040
1,000
960
920
880

Kilometers
0   2
Miles
0   2

1:82,300

N

legislation had been enacted. The National Environmental Policy Act required preparation of an environmental impact statement before any development could take place at Brushy Creek. When surveys uncovered several native forest and prairie communities, endangered species, and prehistoric American Indian burial mounds and sites, plans for the lake project were set aside until 1988.

In the end, the sensitive habitat and archaeological sites within Brushy Creek were protected by establishing Brushy Creek State Preserve, and a 690-acre lake was created to the north of the protected canyon. Today almost 35 miles of trails wind around the lake, through the preserve, and along the Des Moines River. This nearly 6,500-acre tract demonstrates the state's commitment to establishing multiuse conservation areas, which provide both critical habitat for plant and animal communities and a variety of recreational opportunities.

The best place to start exploring Brushy Creek is within Brushy Creek State Preserve, located in the center of the area. Lower Brushy Creek Canyon, carved out by huge flows of Des Moines Lobe meltwater, contains bedrock exposing the ancient Pre–Des Moines Lobe landscape. Plant fossils found within the outcrops indicate that about 37,000 years ago the area was covered in spruce forests, much like present-day Canada.

While the hilltops are home to bur-oak savanna, oak-hickory forests, and prairie openings, the moist, cool ravines house maple-basswood forests. Black maple (*Acer nigrum*) trees predating Euro-American settlement of the area can be seen on steep, north-facing slopes. In one of the forested ravines, the state-threatened woodland vole burrows in loose soils and dense leaf litter. Deep forest birds such as American redstart, red-shouldered hawk, ovenbird, and yellow-throated vireo can also be found here.

Archaeological excavations have unearthed several campsites from the Middle Archaic period (6,500 to 4,000 years ago) to the more recent Late-Woodland period (750 to 1,400 years ago). Among the many sites discovered are a bison kill site, various campsites, and several conical mounds.

The land within Brushy Creek State Recreation Area (surrounding the preserve) still shows the effects of almost 150 years of cultivation, grazing, and draining of wetlands. Soil testing here has shown that before Euro-American settlement, roughly two-thirds of the uplands were covered in tallgrass prairie, and almost all the rest was savanna. It's hard to imagine that only a tiny fraction of the area was once forest, whereas today, young woodlands flourish. While a complete return to native communities may not be feasible, projects promoting prairie reconstruction and wetland creation are helping the land recover.

Many of the trails throughout the state recreation area are heavily used by hunters and equestrians and thus not as hiker-friendly. However, if you want some length to your hike and don't mind running into a few folks or getting muddy, this is the place. Numbered posts along the trail correspond to numbers on the main Department of Natural Resources map, which can be obtained from the Web site listed earlier or at Brushy Creek State Recreation Area.

Miles and Directions

Choose your trail or trails, and wander to your heart's content.

Hike Information

Local Information

Fort Dodge Chamber of Commerce; www
.dodgenet.com/~chamber/

Events/Attractions

The Fort Museum, South Kenyon and Museum
Road, Fort Dodge; (515) 573-4231, www
.fortmuseum.com

Frontier Days, June, Fort Dodge; (515)
573-4231

Fort Dodge Farmers' Market, northwest
corner of Crossroads Mall, Fort Dodge; (515)
955-8433; May through October, Wednesday
2:00 to 6:00 P.M., Saturday 8:30 A.M. to
1:00 P.M.

Accommodations

Stephen H. Taft House B & B, 809 First
Avenue North, Humboldt; (515) 332-3167

Hook's Point Country Inn, 3495 Hook's Point
Drive, Stratford; (515) 838-2781

**Brushy Creek State Recreation Area Camp-
ground** (equestrian and nonequestrian); (515)
543-8298

Dolliver Memorial State Park, Webster; (515)
359-2539

Restaurants

Tropical Smoothie Cafe, 2813 ½ Fifth Avenue
South, Fort Dodge; (515) 573-1199

Hickory House/Family Restaurant Bar-B-Q,
3022 Fifth Avenue South, Fort Dodge; (515)
955-2722

Organizations

Brushy Creek Trail Advisory Board; www
.iowadnr.com/bcreek

Other Resources

Book Shelf, 919 Central Avenue, Fort Dodge

The Guide to Iowa's State Preserves by Ruth
Herzberg and John Pearson (Bur Oaks Books
Series, University of Iowa Press)

*Places of Quiet Beauty: Parks, Preserves, and
Environmentalism* by Rebecca Conard (University of Iowa Press)

Paddling Iowa by Nate Hoogeveen (Trails
Books)

Honorable Mentions

R. Carlson Recreation Area

Several miles of trails explore the Des Moines River Valley, 22 river miles downstream from Dolliver State Park. Upland prairie and woodlands are separated from the riparian forests by huge bluffs and can be traversed by a network of footpaths and deer trails. The area is heavily used by hunters during fall; be sure to let them know of your presence. A canoe/kayak access point for the Des Moines River Trail is located on the eastern edge. From the junction of Highway 175 and U.S. Highway 169 between Dayton and Harcourt, drive east on Highway 175, through Dayton. Just before the bridge over the Des Moines River, turn right (south) onto River Road. Drive 1.5 miles south and look for the sign and parking area. For information: Webster County Conservation Board; (515) 576–4258, www.webstercountyia.org.

S. Pioneer Ridge Nature Area

Located on an old farmstead, this park is now undergoing prairie and oak savanna restoration. The park sits on the southwest side of Little Soap Creek, about 15 river miles before its confluence with the Des Moines River. The hummingbird garden at the nature center is planted with native plants and can draw quite a crowd. Fifteen miles of trails wind through the property, and the long loops will keep you content for at least a day. Spend another day checking out Garrison Rock, another Wapello County Conservation Board property, where bluffs of Pennsylvanian sandstone (the same formation exposed at Cedar Bluffs Natural Area to the north in Mahaska County) tower over the Des Moines River. From the junction of Highways 34 and 63, drive south on Highway 63 and look for the signs on the left (east) side of the road. For information: Wapello County Conservation Board; (641) 682–3091.

T. Lake Wapello State Park

The 7.5-mile loop trail around the lake isn't entirely on footpaths (you'll have to walk the park road for approximately 0.75 mile), but this shouldn't hold you back from the hike. The trail winds around inlets where in late summer American lotus, a beautiful aquatic plant, grows densely. You'll flush wood ducks, blue-winged teal, and great blue heron and find healthy populations of Canada geese. Trumpeter swans have been released at Lake Wapello since 2001, and you will find them near the park office or in the westernmost pond-wetland area. Check out the floodplain forests along the edges of the lake, and climb up onto the oak-hickory uplands. Cross-country skiing is a must when there's enough snow, although you'll have to share the trails with snowmobiles. From the junction of Highway 2 and U.S. Highway 63 in Bloomfield, head north on US 63 for 4 miles. Turn left (west) onto Highway 273 and keep right at the fork in the road; continue on Highway 273, which leads you straight into the park. The best place to access the trails is from the north end of the campground. For information: Lake Wapello State Park; (641) 722–3371, www.iowadnr.com/parks/state_park_list/lake_wapello.html.

U. Union Slough National Wildlife Refuge

Union Slough National Wildlife Refuge was established in 1937 as Union Slough Migratory Waterfowl Refuge to preserve and restore tallgrass prairie and wetland areas located at the "union" of two watersheds—the Blue Earth River (which flows into Minnesota) and the East Fork of the Des Moines River. The 9- by 0.5-mile-long refuge serves as a stopover point for migratory ducks, geese, shorebirds, and pelicans, as well as a grassland home for various sparrows, bobolink, dickcissel, and northern harrier. A 1.0-mile trail on the south end of the refuge is the only developed one (open April 15 through September 15), but there's good wildlife viewing from the several county roads that bisect the area. From the junction of U.S. Highways 18 and 169 in Algona, take US 169 north. Just before you enter the town of Bancroft, turn right (east) onto County Road A42 (360th Street) for 6 miles to the refuge office, located at 1710 360th Street. For information: United States Fish and Wildlife Service; (515) 928–2523, http://midwest.fws.gov/unionslough.

V. Dolliver Memorial State Park

The Pennsylvanian sandstone outcrops that people flock to view at Ledges State Park are also exposed at Dolliver State Park, towering 100 feet above Prairie Creek. Seven miles of trails wind over forested bluffs above the Des Moines River. Several Woodland period burial mounds sit atop these bluffs. Explore Bone Yard Hollow, in the northern reaches of the park, where early settlers found tremendous amounts of bison bones in the canyon. It is thought that previous inhabitants of the area drove herds of bison off the cliffs or into the narrow canyon in order to kill them for food, clothing, and tools. From the junction of County Road P73 and Highway 50 in Lehigh, take Highway 50 west for 2 miles; turn right (north) onto County Road D33, which will take you into the park. Park at the lot just north of the park office or in the northern section of the park near Bone Yard Hollow for best access to the trails. For information: Dolliver State Park; (515) 359–2539, www.state.ia.us/dnr/organiza/ppd/dolliver.htm.

Kettle and Knob, Paha and Prairie

Three of Iowa's distinct landform regions are covered within this overarching category, which diverges from the other regions in this book. The common link among these protected areas is their presence as islands within a sea of modern agriculture. The locations are a blend of geologically and biologically unique areas and a testament to the richness of Iowa's northern and central regions, places that most people find entirely uninteresting. The protection of these sites has allowed for the reconstruction and restoration of ecosystems previously in peril.

Beginning with the youngest landscape in the state, you'll find the descriptively named "knob and kettle" terrain in the north-central tongue of Iowa. The Des Moines Lobe of the Wisconsinan glacier finally removed its icy grip from Iowa a short 10,500 years ago, leaving in its wake vast amounts of glacial till, the original ingredient of the region's later superfertile soils.

Also left behind were interesting formations called kames, also known as knobs. Pilot Knob in Hancock County is one of the best representations of these glacial-debris domes, deposited when silt- and gravel-laden meltwater drained through holes and crevices in the receding glacier. Kettles—usually marsh-filled bowl-like dimples—were created when isolated blocks of ice broke off the glacier and melted into place. Drainage networks never developed, and the kettles are annually filled with snowmelt, rain, interesting plants, and tons of ducks.

Each spring and summer the vast pothole marshes are breeding grounds for hundreds of thousands of waterfowl. At Fossil and Prairie Nature Center in Floyd County you can learn how during the 1800s the bulk of Iowa's wetlands were drained with clay tiles, and then walk outside and hike around a restored wetland— a transformation that's appreciated by the blue-winged teals that spend summers there.

The geologic grandparent to north-central Iowa resides just next door, to the east, and is known as the Iowan Surface. Located in Tama County, Casey's Paha in Tama County ("paha" is the Dakota Sioux word for "hill" or "ridge") was deposited by the Pre-Illinoian glaciers 500,000 years ago. For some reason, while the rest of the landscape was being wiped away by the intense erosive forces of nearby glaciers, the paha stood fast. More than one hundred paha can be found in Benton, Linn, and Tama Counties and for the most part make up the few isolated tracts of upland forest to be found in those areas.

Twenty miles east of Des Moines, the 5,200-acre Neal Smith National Wildlife Refuge comprises the largest tallgrass prairie reconstruction in the United States. In Jasper County, both Jacob Krumm Prairie and Rock Creek State Park were farmed and grazed for more than a century before becoming public land. Restoration efforts can be seen at both these sites and a feeling of hope for the future derived from them. To the northeast lies Hayden Prairie's 240 heavenly acres, the largest black-soil prairie remnant in the state.

It takes a little investigation to truly see how these locations are related. One of the subtleties of Iowa life is learning how to step back and see how everything fits together. Enjoy!

26 Jacob Krumm Prairie

When Jacob Krumm bequeathed his farm to the Jasper County Conservation Board, he did so with the express intention that it become a wildlife refuge. The board followed through, and reconstruction efforts have jump-started the improving health of prairie, wetland, savanna, and forest. Today, muskrats build dens on the site of a former hog lot, and fish use junked cars at the bottom of ponds as breeding habitat. Prairie is reseeded both by human hand and from the railroad right-of-way seedbank.

Distance: 5.25-mile figure eight

Approximate hiking time: 2 to 3 hours

Total elevation gain: 611 feet

Trail surface: Dirt footpath, mowed swath through grassland/prairie

Seasons: Year-round; good cross-country skiing in winter

Trail users: Hikers, bikers, cross-country skiers

Canine compatability: Dogs permitted on leash

Hazards: Poison ivy, ticks

Land status: Jasper County Conservation Board park

Nearest towns: Newton, Grinnell

Fees and permits: No fees or permits required

Schedule: Year-round, during daylight hours

Map: USGS quad: Oakland Acres

Trail contact: Jasper County Conservation Board; (641) 792-9780, www.co.jasper .ia.us/conservation.htm

Finding the trailhead: From Interstate 80, take exit 179 (Lynnville), and drive north on County Road T38. At the T-intersection, turn right (east) onto Jacob Avenue and follow the curve. You'll see the sign and parking area on the north side of the road, just after you've rounded the curve. *DeLorme: Iowa Atlas and Gazetteer:* Page 41 H9

The Hike

Following the death of Jacob Krumm in 1976, his will provided for the transfer of his 300-acre farm to the Jasper County Conservation Board "to be retained as a wildlife refuge." A bachelor-farmer who was more a steward of the land than its owner, Krumm shunned destructive agricultural practices. However, he did allow townspeople to junk nearly 300 cars on his land. During the park's development, gas tanks were removed from the cars and the frames bulldozed together. The mass of metal now functions as a fish habitat at the bottom of the three ponds on Sugar Creek.

Because more than 99.9 percent of Iowa's native prairie is gone, the hunt for prairie remnants usually takes you to places you least expect. Railroad rights-of-way—the unplowed swaths on the sides of train tracks—have long served as refuges for prairie plants. On the north side of Jacob Krumm Prairie, land adjacent to the train tracks has visibly benefited from the right-of-way seedbank and is the best prairie remnant in the park.

Sparks flying from the coal engines of passing trains probably started small fires that helped rejuvenate the prairie. In 1977 several other areas within the park were seeded to native prairie grasses. Try to discern the difference between the seeded tracts and prairie south of the train tracks by assessing the forb diversity. You'll find big and little bluestem, Indian grass, Canada wild rye, and switchgrass throughout, but wildflowers such as pale purple coneflower, wild rose, cream gentian, butterfly milkweed, compass plant, and several species of goldenrod usually can be found only south of the railroad.

The mystery of the missing oak savanna has long been a matter of distress to Iowa naturalists. Historically, savanna, or prairie with interspersed bur oak trees, made up an estimated 10 percent of the state's ecosystems. The open, spreading canopies and gnarly, grubby trunks of fire-resistant bur oaks are signs they were once surrounded by savanna. However, systematic logging, cultivation, and suppression of prairie fires have virtually extirpated this ecosystem, allowing woody growth to invade and choke out the native understory of grass, sedge, and wildflower. With next to nothing of our oak savanna remaining, Iowans are forced to rely on knowledge of plant interactions and imagination to re-create the savanna of the past. At Jacob Krumm Prairie, prescribed burns and the removal of shrubs around bur oak trees in the north end of the park are jump-starting the return of the savanna.

In 2003 a wetland that was to be destroyed by a nearby road-building project was bulldozed and the soils brought to Jacob Krumm. The excavated earth was placed near the bridge in the east side of the park. Plant seeds hitchhiked for the ride, and within months sedges, rushes, cattails, and wildflowers germinated. Voila! Instant wetland!

It may be hard to believe, but the area now covered by the twenty-five-acre lake at Ahren's Access was once described by a director of the Jasper County Conservation Board as "one of the most disgusting hog lots you've ever smelled." In 1996 local businessman Claude Ahrens bought the eighty-acre hog lot and generously donated the land to the board. Several rat-infested buildings were disassembled, the manure-choked lagoon was dredged, and its contents were spread out to compost into soil. The dam was built—and a former environmental disaster zone is now a place where Canada geese raise their young.

In past years, cross-country ski races have been held at Jacob Krumm Prairie. Wide trails that wind over rolling uplands provide excellent cross-country skiing when more than a few inches of snow cover the ground.

Miles and Directions

0.0 Start by walking west across the dam; the trail fringes the west side of the lake.

◀ *The northeast corner of Jacob Krumm Prairie holds forests and an instant wetland.*

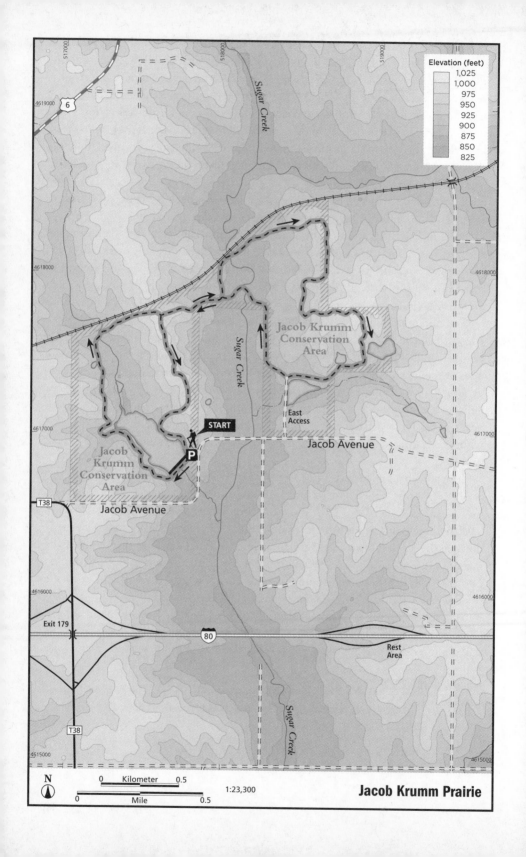

Elevation (feet)
1,025
1,000
975
950
925
900
875
850
825

Sugar Creek

6

Jacob Krumm
Conservation
Area

Sugar Creek

START

P

East
Access

Jacob Avenue

Jacob
Krumm
Conservation
Area

Jacob Avenue

T38

Exit 179

80

Rest
Area

Sugar Creek

T38

Sugar Creek

N

0   Kilometer   0.5

0   Mile   0.5

1:23,300

Jacob Krumm Prairie

1.2 After looping around the north side of the lake, you'll be walking next to the train tracks. (FYI: During the growing season, you're going to want to spend a little time here checking out prairie plants.)

1.4 At the fork go straight (east) to continue into the eastern portion of the park. **Bailout:** If you're close to being done walking, take a right (south) and head back the 0.6 mile to the trailhead.

1.7 At the fork turn left (northeast) to explore the savanna area in the northeast corner of the park.

3.7 At the fork you'll be able to see the east parking area directly to the south. Take a right (north) to get back to the other trailhead.

4.0 After the trail has gone due north and just as it begins to curve to the west, check out the newly created wetland described above, amazing stuff.

4.3 At the fork turn left (southwest).

4.5 At the fork at the top of the hill, turn left to cruise down to the lake.

5.25 Arrive back at the trailhead.

Hike Information

Local Information
Grinnell Chamber of Commerce; www .grinnellchamber.org

Events/Attractions
Happy Days Festival, September, Grinnell; (641) 236-8065, www .grinnellchamber.org
Grinnell Farmers' Market, Central Park, Grinnell; (515) 236-6555; May through October, Thursday and Saturday 3:00 to 6:00 P.M.

Accommodations
Carriage House Bed & Breakfast, 1133 Broad Street, Grinnell; (641) 236-7520
Marsh House, 833 East Street, Grinnell; (641) 236-0132, www.marshhousebnb.com
Rock Creek State Park Campground; (641) 236-3722, www.iowadnr.com/parks/ state_park_list/rock_creek.html
Mariposa Conservation Park Campground (Jasper County Conservation Board); (641) 792-9780, www.co.jasper.ia.us/ conservation.htm

Restaurants
Pagliai's Pizza, 816 Fifth Avenue, Grinnell; (641) 236-5331
Grinnell Coffee Company, 915 Main Street, Grinnell; (641) 236-0710

Other Resources
Juli's Health & More Food Store, 931 West Street, Grinnell; (641) 236-7376
Tallgrass Prairie Audubon; www.iowabirds .org/birdingiowa/clubs.asp
Grinnell College, Center for Prairie Studies; (641) 269-4720, web.grinnell.edu/cps/ Index.html
Grinnell College Bookstore, Grinnell College; (641) 269-3424
An Illustrated Guide to Iowa Prairie Plants by Paul Christiansen and Mark Muller (Bur Oak Books Series, University of Iowa Press)
Where the Sky Began: Land of the Tallgrass Prairie by John Madson (Houghton Mifflin Company)
Restoring the Tallgrass Prairie: An Illustrated Manual for Iowa and the Upper Midwest by Shirley Shirley (Bur Oak Books Series, University of Iowa Press)

27 Rock Creek State Park

The 10.5-mile loop trail around Rock Creek Lake gives you quite the look into native ecosystems and those changed by development. Several managed prairie remnants spend the summer blooming a sheer blaze of color, while previously overgrazed areas now left undisturbed are clogged with multiflora rose and honey locust. Most of the south side of the lake is built up with roads and houses, but walk a few steps into the forested southeast corner of the park and all you'll hear is birdsong.

Distance: 10.5-mile loop
Approximate hiking time: 3 to 5 hours
Total elevation gain: 1,091 feet
Trail surface: Forested footpaths, mowed swaths
Seasons: Year-round; great cross-country skiing in winter
Trail users: Hikers, equestrians, cross-country skiers
Canine compatability: Dogs permitted on leash

Hazards: Poison ivy, ticks
Land status: State park
Nearest towns: Newton, Grinnell
Fees and permits: No fees or permits required unless you are camping
Schedule: Year-round, 4:00 A.M. to 10:30 P.M.
Map: USGS quad: Newburg
Trail contact: Rock Creek State Park, 5627 Rock Creek East, Kellogg; (641) 236-3722, www.state.ia.us/dnr/organiza/ppd/rockcrk.htm

Finding the trailhead: From Interstate 80, take exit 182 (toward Grinnell) and drive north on Highway 146. In the middle of Grinnell, turn left (west) onto U.S. Highway 6 and drive 2 miles. Turn right (north) onto County Road T38 and then left (west) onto County Road F27. This will lead you to the north end of the park. Turn left toward the campground to park at the east access, or cross the bridge and turn left toward the boat ramp to park at the west access. *DeLorme: Iowa Atlas and Gazetteer:* Page 41 H8

The Hike

When it was dedicated in 1952, Rock Creek Lake was touted as the "largest lake in the United States constructed solely for recreational purposes." From 1933 to 1952, when artificial lake construction was a hot new thing in Iowa, twenty-four such lakes were built in state parks. Over the years the focus changed from the creation of small bodies of water for beach activities and fishing during the 1930s, to construction of large lakes accessible to motorboats after 1950. Each weekend, Rock Creek Lake is covered with boats from which anglers are trying to catch largemouth bass, channel catfish, walleye, and crappie.

On the 10.5-mile multiuse loop trail around the lake, most people you'll encounter will be on horseback. Several reasons keep folks from walking around the lake, including the length of the walk and the 3.0-mile portion of the loop with no

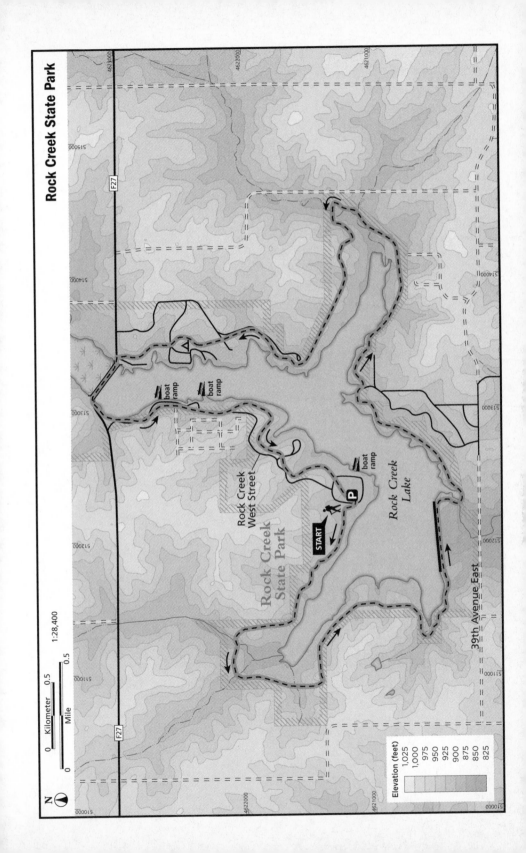

Rock Creek State Park

designated trail. Most of the south-central portion of the lake is bordered by residential neighborhoods, and you'll be walking through what feels like a mowed backyard between the boat ramps. It may seem a nuisance to "hike" the developed part of the park, but if you're looking for a long walk on a beautiful day, it's worth it.

Stroll through the campground and over the bridge, stopping to check out the Rock Creek Wildlife Area to the north of the bridge. You'll see ducks, geese, various shorebirds, gulls, and terns. This marshy area was once home to hundreds of muskrats; however, the heavy silt levels have clogged the water and left it uninhabitable by the rodents.

Since it will determine the direction you take around the lake, your most important decision is whether to do the road-hiking at the beginning or end of your hike. This will cause you to park at the northwest boat ramp or the parking area south of the campground. Instead of taking the loop around the whole lake, you can also park on either side of the lake, hike as far as you'd like, and then turn back.

Undulating hills surround the lake, the majority of them covered in scrubby woodlands. Much of the young forests are composed of box elder, honey locust, and gray dogwood growing under random larger walnut and bur oak trees. During spring, trout lilies virtually blanket the forest floor on the west side of the dam.

Several healthy prairie remnants remain among the overgrown shrubs and young trees, reminders that historically the hilltops were probably dominated by prairie. Many small openings have been created by park staff, who've removed shrubs and burned the area, allowing prairie plants to flourish once again.

On the northwest side of the lake, you'll find several of these openings, and during mid- to late summer, the wildflower display is worth the walk. Blazing star, compass plant, pale purple coneflower, field milkwort, and rattlesnake master bloom June to August. August and September they are followed by round-headed bush clover, downy gentian, giant lobelia, and nodding ladies' tresses.

After you cross the dam, the lake is bordered by residential neighborhoods, and the trail leads around a mowed, developed tract for several miles before it reenters the woodlands around the easternmost inlet. If you're up for a really long walk, tough it out and cruise through the lawns and road-hike; otherwise, double back and loop the way you came.

Miles and Directions

0.0   Start at the boat ramp parking loop on the northwest side of the lake. Walk onto the trail that leads to the west, along the lake.

3.1   Cross over the dam. For the next 2.0 miles the south side of the park is quite developed. Look for waterfowl in the lake to your left instead of at the people mowing their lawns to the right.

◀ *Flowering wild plum is one of the springtime highlights of Rock Creek State Park.*

4.7 Arrive at the boat ramp on the south side of the lake.

7.0 Arrive in the developed area on the northeast side of the lake. Follow the lakeshore.

7.7 Arrive at the campground.

8.3 Cross the bridge. Start your next-to-the-road hiking. (FYI: Look to the northeast to the Rock Creek Marsh Wildlife Area; there are usually some good birds up there.)

8.5 At the intersection of CR F27 and Rock Creek West Street, turn left (south) onto Rock Creek West Street. From here back to the trailhead, walk along the road, or find a more fun way to travel: along the lakeshore, bushwhacking through the scrubby forests, or on blacktop while your mind wanders over the prairie-covered hills that once were.

10.5 Arrive back at the trailhead.

Hike Information

Local Information

Newton Convention and Visitors Bureau, Newton; (800) 798-0299, www.visitnewton.com

Events/Attractions

Iowa Sculpture Festival at Maytag Park, June, Newton; (641) 792-0882

Chichaqua Valley Recreational Trail; 20.0-mile rail-to-trail through Baxter, Ira, Mingo, and Bondurant; (641) 792-9780

Grinnell Happy Days Bike Ride, September, Grinnell; (641) 236-7401, www.bikeiowa.com

Jasper County Farmers' Market, West Second Street North, Newton; (515) 674-3910; June through October, Tuesday 2:00 to 6:00 P.M.

Accommodations

Aerie Glen Bed & Breakfast, 2364 First Avenue West, Newton; (641) 792-9032, www.midiowa.com/aerieglen

Rock Creek State Park Campground; (641) 236-3722, www.iowadnr.com/parks/state_park_list/rock_creek.html

Mariposa Conservation Park Campground (Jasper County Conservation Board); (641) 792-9780, www.co.jasper.ia.us/conservation.htm

Restaurant

La Cabana Mexican Restaurant, 2002 First Avenue East, Newton; (641) 791-1932

Other Resources

Mattingly & Sons, 113 West Second Street North, Newton; (641) 792-3250

28 Neal Smith National Wildlife Refuge

Less than 0.1 percent of the original native tallgrass prairie that once covered Iowa remains in existence today. That's why the reconstruction of 5,000 acres of tallgrass prairie at Neal Smith National Wildlife Refuge is truly inspirational. Three miles of trails lead you through the reconstructed prairie's tallgrasses and wildflowers, into a piece of oak savanna, and within view of the bison and elk range. The Friends of the Prairie Learning Center, which serves as a base for the restoration and ongoing research, features in-depth exhibits.

Distance: Tallgrass Trail: 2.5-mile loop (including 0.5-mile overlook loop), Savanna Trail: 0.5-mile loop
Approximate hiking time: 1 to 3 hours
Total elevation gain: Tallgrass Trail: 197 feet
Trail surface: Paved
Seasons: Year-round; June through September best for wildflowers and birds
Trail users: Hikers, hunters
Canine compatability: Dogs not permitted (unless you are using them to hunt)
Hazards: Ticks

Land status: U.S. Fish and Wildlife Service national wildlife refuge
Nearest towns: Prairie City, Des Moines
Fees and permits: No fees or permits required
Schedule: Open year-round during daylight hours
Map: USGS quad: Runnells
Trail contact: Friends of the Prairie Learning Center, 9981 Pacific Street, Prairie City; (515) 994-3400, www.tallgrass.org; USFWS: http://midwest.fws.gov.nealsmith/

Finding the trailhead: From Interstate 80 take exit 155 (Colfax/Prairie City) onto Highway 117 south. Go through Prairie City and follow the signs over the Highway 163 bridge and onto Pacific Street, the refuge entry road. *DeLlorme: Iowa Atlas and Gazetteer:* Page 50 B5

The Hike

Created by an act of Congress in 1990, this refuge is the largest tallgrass prairie reconstruction project in the United States. After plans for a nuclear power generating station fell through in the late 1970s, the U.S. Fish and Wildlife Service purchased 3,622 acres in the Walnut Creek watershed from Redlands Coporation, a subsidiary of Iowa Power. Neal Smith, a longtime congressman from Iowa, supported the tallgrass reconstruction project and helped obtain federal funding. Formerly known as Walnut Creek National Wildlife Refuge, it was renamed to honor Smith's dedication and service.

The reconstruction itself is quite an undertaking: Annually, millions of seeds are collected from surrounding prairie remnants and various parts of the refuge; the land within the refuge is burned or tilled and planted; and the natural process of grassland succession is left to destiny.

Bison once again roam at Neal Smith National Wildlife Refuge.

Bison were introduced in 1996 and elk in 1997, and they can be seen happily munching on prairie grasses and forbs. Although it will take time before all the floral and faunal components of the prairie return, and they may not, the infancy of the refuge prairie is a spectacular thing just the same. In *Sand County Almanac,* writer-ecologist Aldo Leopold wrote: "What a thousand acres of *Silphiums* [compass plants] looked like when they tickled the bellies of the buffalo is a question never again to be answered, and perhaps not even asked." We don't yet know, but Leopold's question may yet be worth asking. The creation and ongoing management of the refuge wouldn't have been possible without the work of many committed volunteers who accepted Leopold's challenge.

There are four short hiking trails within the refuge (Basswood, Savanna, Overlook, and Tallgrass), as well as a 10-kilometer road/firebreak hike that can be walked when it's mowed. (The 0.5-mile Basswood Trail is far from the learning center and is not covered here.) The auto tour takes you through the bison and elk range and gives you a landscape view of the Walnut Creek watershed.

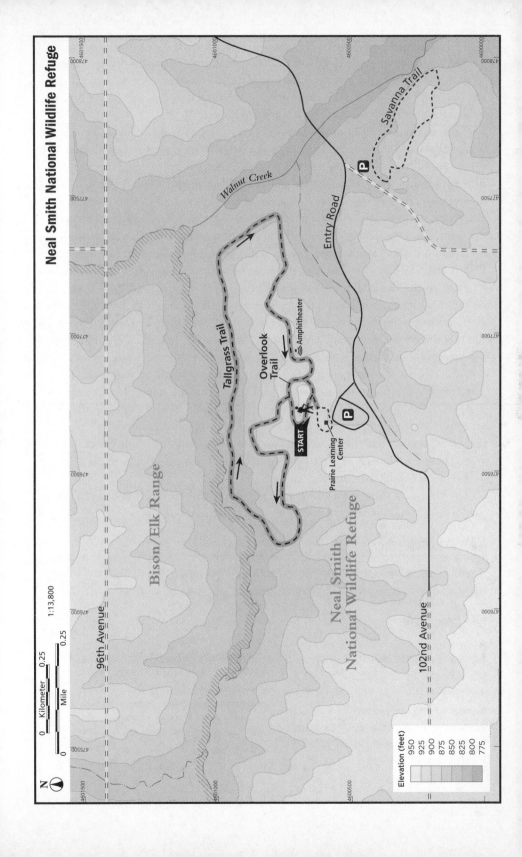

Neal Smith National Wildlife Refuge

Stop at the Prairie Learning Center, which features exhibits on prehistoric cultures that inhabited the area, presettlement natural history, various ecosystems currently present in the refuge, and the prairie reconstruction process. Check out the under-the-prairie maze—but look out for the badger!

Walk out the east side of the learning center and onto the 0.5-mile Overlook Trail, following signs onto the Tallgrass Trail, a paved 2.0-mile walkway with benches every one-third mile. Here is where you'll really start to feel prairie: big and little bluestem, Indian grass, and sideoats grama undulate in the wind. Scores of wildflowers, including cup plants, butterfly milkweed, yellow and purple coneflowers, tick trefoil, Culver's root, and bee balm, among countless others, add vivid colors to the scene. Black swallowtails, clouded sulphurs, great spangled fritillary, and monarch butterflies are seen flitting from flower to flower, gathering nectar. Listen for the flight calls and songs of several typical prairie birds that flush as you walk: the American goldfinch's descending *ti-di-di-di;* dickcissel's buzzy *fpppt;* and bobolink's soft *bink.* During spring, you'll undoubtedly hear the classic *wichety-wichety-wichety* of the common yellowthroat. Surveys of the refuge in 2003 by Drake University Professor Keith Summerville and his students found more than 500 species of moths, including one species new to science.

At 0.75 mile the trail makes a 180-degree turn and begins to follow the fence that separates the bison and elk range from the rest of the refuge. If you're lucky, some of the animals may be down by the creek for a drink or foraging in the lush vegetation surrounding it. It's estimated that thirty million bison once roamed the prairies of Iowa, while their extermination from the landscape took less than 150 years. The reintroduction of these beacons of the prairie has restored a sense of hope to this devastated landscape.

On your way to or from the learning center, take a stroll around the Savanna Trail. The 0.5-mile gravel path winds through ancient oaks.

Miles and Directions

The 0.5-mile Overlook Trail is a loop inside the 2.0-mile Tallgrass Trail loop. Both trails are easy to navigate and have interpretive signs to guide you.

Hike Information

Local Information
City of Prairie City; (515) 994-2649, www .prairiecityiowa.us/

Events/Attractions
Des Moines Botanical Center, 909 Robert D. Ray Drive, Des Moines; (515) 323-6290, www.botanicalcenter.com

Living History Farms, Urbandale; (515) 278-5286, www.lhf.org (LHF Off-Road Race in November for the strong)

Downtown Des Moines Farmers' Market, Fourth Avenue and Court Avenues, Des Moines; (515) 286-4928, May through October, Saturday 7:00 A.M. to noon.

New City Market Natural Grocery, 4721 University Avenue, Des Moines; (515) 255-7380

Accommodations
The Country Connection B&B, 9737 West Ninety-third Street South, Prairie City; (515) 994-2023

Restaurants
Raccoon River Brewing Company, 200 Tenth Street, Des Moines; (515) 283-1941
Home Team Pizza, 3801 Southwest Ninth Street, Des Moines; (515) 283-0000

Other Resources
Iowa Welcome Center, 11121 Hickman Road, Des Moines; (515) 334-9625
The Bookstore, 606 Locust Street, Des Moines; (515) 288-7267

Des Moines Audubon; www.iowabirds.org/birdingiowa/dmaud.asp
An Illustrated Guide to Iowa Prairie Plants by Paul Christiansen and Mark Muller (University of Iowa Press)
Restoring the Tallgrass Prairie: An Illustrated Manual for Iowa and the Upper Midwest by Shirley Shirley (University of Iowa Press)
Wildflowers of the Tallgrass Prairie by Sylvan T. Runkel and Dean M. Roosa (Iowa State University Press)
A Sand County Almanac, with Essays on Conservation from Round River by Aldo Leopold (Oxford University Press, Inc)
A Tallgrass Prairie Alphabet by Claudia McGehee, (Bur Oak Books Series, University of Iowa Press) (children's book)

29 Hickory Hills Park–Casey's Paha State Preserve

Geologically, biologicallly, and recreationally, Hickory Hills Park is an island in a sea of intense agricultural cultivation. A 665-acre area in Tama County, the park's major feature is Casey's Paha, a ridge formed by glacial till, clay soils, and loess. Mature forests and Casey Lake supply important stopover points for migrating warblers and waterfowl in search of food and rest. Trails wind up and over the paha and around the lake, providing access to some of the only noncultivated land in the surrounding countryside.

Distance: 4.5-mile loop
Approximate hiking time: 2 to 3 hours
Total elevation gain: 516 feet
Trail surface: Forested footpaths
Seasons: Year-round
Trail users: Hikers, cross-country skiers, hunters
Canine compatability: Dogs permitted on leash
Hazards: Poison ivy, ticks
Land status: State preserve, owned and managed by Black Hawk County Conservation Board

Nearest towns: Cedar Falls/Waterloo, Tama/Toledo
Fees and permits: No fees or permits required unless you are camping
Schedule: Open year-round during daylight hours
Map: USGS quad: Eagle Center
Trail contact: Black Hawk County Conservation Board, 2410 West Lone Tree Road, Cedar Falls; (319) 342-3350, www.co.black-hawk.ia.us/depts/conservation

Autumn forest cover on Casey's Paha is amazing.

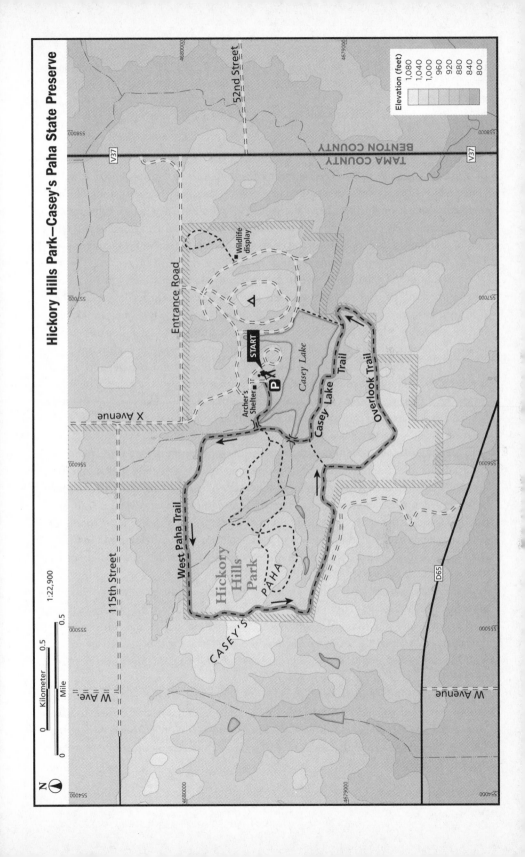

Hickory Hills Park—Casey's Paha State Preserve

N

1:22,900

Kilometer 0   0.5

Mile   0   0.5

Elevation (feet)
1,080
1,040
1,000
960
920
880
840
800

52nd Street

V37

BENTON COUNTY
TAMA COUNTY

Entrance Road

Wildlife display

START

P

Archer's Shelter

Casey Lake

X Avenue

Casey Lake Trail

Overlook Trail

West Paha Trail

Hickory Hills Park

CASEY'S PAHA

115th Street

W Ave.

W Avenue

D65

V37

Finding the trailhead: From the junction of U.S. Highways 218 and 20 southeast of Waterloo, drive south on US 218, immediately turning right (south) onto County Road V37. Drive nearly 12 miles, until you see the sign for Hickory Hills on the right (west) side of the road. Follow the signs on the entrance road to Archer's Shelter. *DeLorme: Iowa Atlas and Gazetteer:* Page 42 A3

The Hike

In 1891 geologist W. J. McGee described the hills of east north-central Iowa as "higher but shorter swells, gracefully curved as the bending backs of dolphins." At the time McGee might have been staring at the silhouette of Casey's Paha, for his text illustrates the beauty of this subtle, ridgelike Iowa landform. Though the illusion of dolphin backs best captures the essence of the landform, McGee named them "paha," the Dakota Sioux word for "ridge" or "hill."

Several hundred paha can be found in east-central Iowa, each of them a window into a time long past. They are composed of the remnants of glacial deposits from the Pre-Illinoian ice sheet, left behind half a million years ago.. Between 16,000 and 21,000 years ago, the glaciers had retreated for a short time from Iowa, but the weather was indicative of their proximity to the north. Tundralike conditions covered this area of the state, and the climate was severe. High winds, freezes and thaws, and very cold temperatures leveled the land, erasing much of the relief. For some reason, be it their vegetative covering or their alignment along drainages and divides, the paha held fast, accumulating loess and sand deposits. Now they stand in stark relief on a landscape that's been smoothed over.

Three trails totaling 5.8 miles exist within the park, and the best place to access either of them is from the Archer's Shelter parking lot. Walk past the shelter and follow the West Paha Trail across the inlet of the lake, where ducks are sure to be flushed or a painted turtle caught sunning. The trail heads north, past several ponds and through some of the only grassland in the park. Heavy runoff from the surrounding cultivated fields has yielded high levels of nitrates and an unusually high pH in Casey Lake. The siltation ponds to its north were created to draw the silt and chemical loads away from the lake.

From the overlook platform, look for ring-necked pheasants scuttling into the grass for food and cover. The trail ascends the paha and skirts the boundary of the state preserve and public hunting ground in a loop, dropping in and out of several drainages. Even after the snow has melted, the ravines are still blanketed in white, with blooms of bloodroot, snow trillium, false rue and rue anemone, spring cress, and toothwort coming up in early April.

Several huge bur and red oak trees, 150 to 200 years old, live to the south and west of Casey Lake. Called "witness trees," they are among the few organisms to have observed the settlement of Iowa by Euro-Americans still with us today. Notice the density of shrubs in the understory around the witness trees; you probably won't see many oak saplings.

Historically, wildfire was the mechanism used to create openings in which oak seedlings could gain a foothold, and when fires were suppressed postsettlement, intensive cattle and goat grazing held back the brushy growth. After the Black Hawk County Conservation Board bought the park in 1969, grazing was halted, and the shrubs have responded with explosive growth. Removal of this excessive woody debris is critical to maintaining healthy wildlife populations, as many depend on oak trees for food and shelter.

Miles and Directions

0.0 Start at the parking area next to Archer's Shelter. Walk west, past the shelter and over the bridge; arrive at intersection of Casey Lake and West Paha Trails, and turn (right) north immediately onto the West Paha Trail.

0.5 Walk past several siltation ponds and wetland areas.

0.65 Turn left (west) and follow the perimeter of the public hunting area and state preserve. (FYI: You're on the paha, its "summit" sits outside the park boundary, at 1,050 feet.)

2.4 At the fork turn right (south) onto the Overlook Trail. **Bailout:** Turn left (north) to return to the trailhead.

3.5 At the fork turn left (west) onto the Casey Lake Trail.

4.1 Cross the bridge and continue straight (north).

4.3 Back at intersection of Casey Lake Trail and West Paha Trail, turn right (east) and walk over the bridge to the trailhead.

4.5 Arrive back at the trailhead.

Hike Information

Local Information

Cedar Falls Tourism and Visitors Bureau; (800) 845-1955, www.cedarfalls.tourism.org

Waterloo Convention and Visitors Bureau; (800) 728-8431, www.waterloocvb.org

Events/Attractions

Cedar Valley Nature Trail (to Cedar Rapids, 52 miles)

Meskwaki Powwow, usually held the second weekend in August, Tama; (641) 484-4678

Tama Farmers' Market, Tama Civic Center, Tama; (641) 484-2177; June through September, Tuesday 5:00 to 6:00 P.M.

Accommodations

House by the Side of the Road, 6804 Ranchers Road, Cedar Falls; (319) 988-3691

Restaurants

Blue Moon Cafe, 2223 College Street, Cedar Falls; (319) 266-6512

The Cellar, 320 East Fourth Street, Waterloo; (219) 274-8889

Montage, 222 Main Street, Cedar Falls; (319) 268-7222

Pablo's Mexican Grill, 310 Main Street, Cedar Falls; (319) 277-8226

Other Resources

Savereide Books, 2227 Greenwood, Cedar Falls; (319) 277-5084

Landforms of Iowa by Jean Prior (University of Iowa Press)

The Guide to Iowa's State Preserves by Ruth Herzberg and John Pearson (Bur Oaks Books Series, University of Iowa Press)

30 Hayden Prairie State Preserve

The state's largest virgin prairie tract outside the Loess Hills, Hayden Prairie is named for an early Iowa botanist and pioneer in prairie preservation, Dr. Ada Hayden. Its 240 acres provide exceptional habitat for prairie and grassland flora and fauna—and a sobering reminder of Iowa's lost past. The grass and wildflower displays in mid- to late summer are unparalleled in their beauty. Listen for the grasshopper sparrow's buzz, the northern harrier's shriek, and the meadowlark's song echoing metallically from a distant fencepost. Here you'll get a taste of the incredibly diverse prairies that once covered the state.

Distance: Perimeter walk, 3.0-mile loop; up to 2.0 miles of exploring within the boundary
Approximate hiking time: 2 to 3 hours
Total elevation gain: 103 feet
Trail surface: Mowed firebreaks, perimeter walk on county roads
Seasons: Summer wildflower bloom, at its height July through September
Trail users: Hikers only
Canine compatability: Dogs not permitted because of the sensitive nature of the preserve

Hazards: Ticks, sunburn
Land status: State preserve and national natural landmark
Nearest town: Cresco
Fees and permits: No fees or permits required
Schedule: Open year-round, 4:00 A.M. to 10:30 P.M.
Map: USGS quad: Lime Springs NW
Trail contact: IDNR Upper Iowa Wildlife Unit; (563) 382–4895, www.state.ia.us/dnr/organiza/ppd/hayden.htm

Finding the trailhead: From Cresco drive west on Highway 9 for 13 miles. Turn north (right) onto County Road V26 (Jade Avenue) and drive 5 miles. At the T-intersection, turn west (left) onto Fiftieth Street and drive 0.25 mile to the preserve parking area on the south side of the road. Beside a small kiosk, a plaque on a rock notes the preserve's status as a national natural landmark. *DeLlorme: Iowa Atlas and Gazetteer:* Page 21 B8

The Hike

The saying, "Is this heaven? No, it's Iowa," made famous in the film *Field of Dreams,* seems to have been written with Hayden Prairie State Preserve in mind. The state's largest remaining tract of black soil prairie is relatively small (140 acres of upland prairie and 100 acres of wet and mesic prairie). However, the preserve provides an exquisite example of Iowa's prairie wilderness of times past.

The preserve's rolling terrain is typical of the Iowan Surface, last grazed by Pre-Illinoian glaciation some 500,000 years ago. During the Late Wisconsinan period, between 16,500 and 21,000 years ago, periglacial weathering took its toll on the topographic features of the Iowan Surface. The close proximity of the Wisconsin ice sheet to the north yielded freeze–thaw action, intense wind erosion, loosening of the

The tallgrass prairie preserved at Hayden Prairie is one part earth, one part sky.

slopes, and, ultimately, smoothing of the existing relief. The result is a subtly billow-ing landscape with undeveloped drainage systems. Lowland swales, wet to mesic prairie, and drier uplands lack distinct edges and expand and retract according to the changes in precipitation from year to year.

The best way to experience Hayden Prairie is to proceed at a very slow pace. Several firebreaks serve as meager trails through the preserve, although by midsum-mer many are overgrown and just as clumsily navigated as the surrounding prairie jungle. Walking slowly is not only likely to keep you from breaking an ankle on the uneven terrain, it also will allow you to take in the grandeur of this seemingly sub-tle landscape. Try nestling down into the tallgrass so that you can't see any of the sur-rounding silos or barns and listening to the prairie.

The blooming of the prairie reaches its apex during July and August. Compass plants and big bluestem will tower above you; both can grow more than 10 feet tall. Midsummer forbs you will encounter include rattlesnake master, bastard toadflax, prairie blazing star, wild rose, leadplant, and Michigan lily. With its great diversity of wildflowers, this small remnant of prairie is home to more than twenty species of

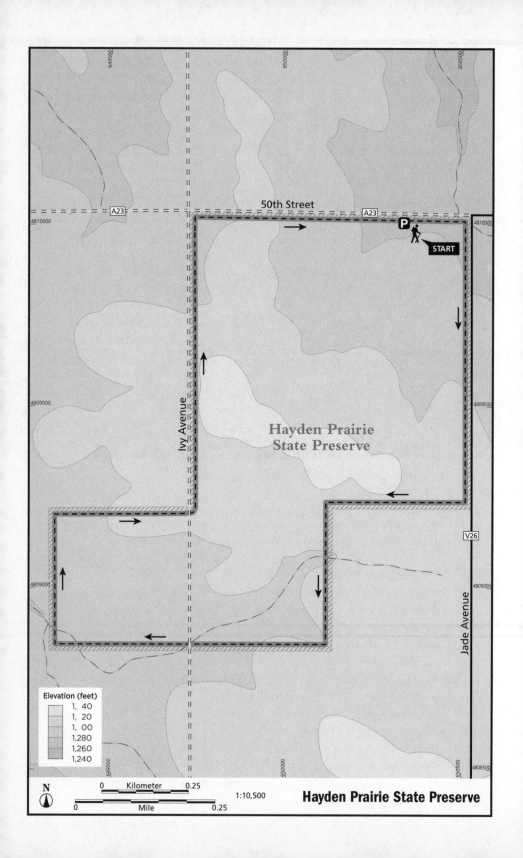

Hayden Prairie
State Preserve

Elevation (feet)
1,340
1,320
1,300
1,280
1,260
1,240

N

0   Kilometer   0.25

0   Mile   0.25

1:10,500

Hayden Prairie State Preserve

50th Street

Ivy Avenue

Jade Avenue

A23

V26

P

START

butterflies, including eastern-tailed blue, pearl cresecent, regal fritillary, and wild indigo duskywing. Look for typical prairie birds: bobolink, dickcissel, northern harrier, meadowlark, and upland sandpiper. Henslow's sparrow, the rarest of Iowa's nesting sparrows, lives here in the sedge-dominated lowlands.

The preserve's namesake, Ada Hayden, was born in 1884 on a farm near Ames. She received her bachelor's degree in 1908 from Iowa State College (now Iowa State University), where she studied with and became the protégé of botany professor and intrepid conservationist Louis Pammel. After earning a master's degree in botany from the University of Washington in St. Louis, Hayden returned home as a botany instructor and doctoral student at Iowa State. In 1918, having completed her dissertation on the ecology of prairie plants in central Iowa, she became the first woman to receive a Ph.D. from that university, following which she held a faculty position for thirty-two years.

Hayden was also one of the first Iowans to call for prairie preservation in the state. She submitted a piece to the report published by the Board of Conservation in 1919: *Iowa Parks: Conservation of Iowa Historic, Scientific and Scenic Areas.* In "Conservation of the Prairie," Hayden urged that a small parcel of native prairie be protected in each county, with larger preserves situated near the three state universities and on railroad rights-of-way. She traversed the state in the early 1940s, surveying the prairie remnants that she believed should be top priorities to preserve and protect.

With help from other conservationists, Hayden's dream of prairie preservation was finally actualized in 1945, five years before her death and long after she and others had first championed the idea. The Iowa Conservation Commission purchased this 240-acre tract in Howard County, creating the state's first prairie preserve, and named it for Hayden posthumously in 1950. In 1966 it was recognized as a national natural landmark and in 1966 received status as a biological state preserve.

Miles and Directions

Because the firebreaks are not always mowed, it is hard to give an exact route for this preserve. For intrepid and interested naturalists, I would recommend a long, slow walk through the tangle of tallgrass. For those who want to avoid the tangle, a walk around the perimeter of the preserve on the county roads will still yield a great look and insight into the Hayden Prairie.

Hike Information

Local Information
Howard County; www.howard-county.com

Events/Attractions
Howard County Log Cabin Museum, 324 Fourth Avenue West, Cresco; (563) 547-3434, www.crescoia.com

Lidtke Mill Historical Site, Mill Street, Lime Springs; (563) 566-2828

Nordic Fest, July, Decorah; (800) 382-3378, www.nordicfest.com

Decorah Time Trials (end of April, May), Decorah; (563) 382-4158, www.decoraharea.com

Cresco Farmers' Market, Second Street and First Avenue, Cresco; (563) 238-8531; May through October, Tuesday and Friday 2:00 to 5:30 P.M.

Accommodations

Lake Hendricks Campground, Howard County Conservation Board; (563) 547-3634

Corner Inn Bed & Breakfast, 129 Sixth Avenue East, Cresco; (563) 547-5234, www.cornerinnbb.com

Restaurants

Jimmy's Bar & Grill, 106 West Main Street, Lime Springs; (563) 566-4443

The Pitt Stop, 107 Second Avenue SE, Cresco; (563) 547-3434

Mabe's Pizza, 119 North Elm Street, Cresco; (563) 547-5707

Other Resources

Iowa Prairie Network; www.iowaprairienetwork.org

An Illustrated Guide to Iowa Prairie Plants by Paul Christiansen and Mark Muller (University of Iowa Press)

The Vascular Plants of Iowa: An Annotated Checklist and Natural History by Lawrence J. Eilers and Dean M. Roosa (Bur Oak Books Series, University of Iowa Press)

The Iowa Breeding Bird Atlas by Laura Spess Jackson, Carol A. Thompson, and James J. Dinsmore (Bur Oak Books Series, University of Iowa Press)

The Guide to Iowa's State Preserves by Ruth Herzberg and John Pearson (Bur Oaks Books Series, University of Iowa Press)

Where the Sky Began: Land of the Tallgrass Prairie by John Madson (Houghton Mifflin Company)

Places of Quiet Beauty: Parks, Preserves, and Environmentalism by Rebecca Conard (University of Iowa Press)

Wildflowers of the Tallgrass Prairie by Sylvan T. Runkel and Dean M. Roosa (Iowa State University Press)

31 Fossil and Prairie Park

A visit to Fossil and Prairie Park will give you an expansive look into north-central Iowa's past, as well as the chance to take a little piece of it home with you. Outside Rockford at the bottom of an old quarry-turned-park, a 350-million-year cross section of Iowa is visible. On the knob next to the quarry, a virgin prairie tract is home to several rare species. Juniper Hill, to the north, is the only recorded site in Iowa for creeping juniper, a species more commonly found in Minnesota and Canada. A rail-to-trail leads from the town of Rockford into the park, where paths are mowed through the prairie and around several ponds and a wetland, leading to access points into the belly of the fossil-rich quarry.

Distance: 4.6 miles round-trip
Approximate hiking time: 2 to 5 hours, depending on your fossil viewing or collecting time
Total elevation gain: 363 feet
Trail surface: Converted rail-to-trail, mowed paths through prairie
Seasons: Year-round; summer wildflowers best June through September
Trail users: Hikers only
Canine compatability: Dogs permitted on leash
Hazards: Steep-sided quarry
Land status: Floyd County Conservation Board park

Nearest towns: Rockford, Mason City, Charles City
Fees and permits: No fees or permits required
Schedule: Open year-round during daylight hours; Fossil & Prairie Center open 1:00 to 4:00 P.M. daily Memorial Day through Labor Day and on weekends in May, September, and October
Map: USGS quad: Rockford
Trail contact: Fossil & Prairie Center, 1227 215th Street, Rockford, IA 50468; (641) 756-3490, e-mail: fpcenter@omnitelcom.com

Finding the trailhead: From the intersection of County Road T24 and Highway 147 in Rockford, drive west on Highway 147 (also called Main Avenue). Look for the FOSSIL & PRAIRIE PARK sign on the north side of the highway.

To walk to the park on the Fossil and Prairie Rail-to-Trail, when Highway 147 turns south, continue west on West Main Avenue, also called Winnebago Street. After 1 block, at the intersection with Ninth Street look for the FLOYD COUNTY CONSERVATION BOARD sign on the south side of the road. *DeLorme: Iowa Atlas and Gazetteer:* Page 20 H2

The Hike

When settlers began crossing the waterlogged marshland of north-central Iowa in the 1800s, stories of wagons becoming stuck in the nearly continuous swath of muck were common. Thinking the marshy land of little value, many settlers waited until the winter freeze and hurried west. However, farmers soon found the soil

A compass plant looks over one of the quarry pits at Fossil and Prairie Park.

beneath the wetlands to be highly fertile and began draining it to plant crops. At first they dug ditches and installed wooden pipes, replacing these with clay tiles in the late 1800s. By 1900, 381 companies in Iowa were producing bricks and drainage tile. When Rockford Brick and Tile Co. began mining the clay deposits in Floyd County in 1910, the rush to drain north-central Iowa's wetlands had already taken an immense toll. Between 1780 and 1980 the state lost an estimated 89 percent of its wetlands.

Rockford Brick and Tile mined the quarry until 1976, all the while exposing Devonian fossils. In 1989 word spread that the quarry might become a dump site for a local foundry. Conservationists lobbied for protection, and in 1990 the Floyd County Conservation Board received the state's first REAP (Resource Enhancement and Protection) grant, which funded the purchase of the 109-acre Rockford Brick and Tile property and an adjoining 47 acres of virgin prairie. In 1991 a nature center was opened and trails installed. Community members and conservationists formed the Fossil and Prairie Center Foundation and raised money for educational exhibits, which are well worth your attention.

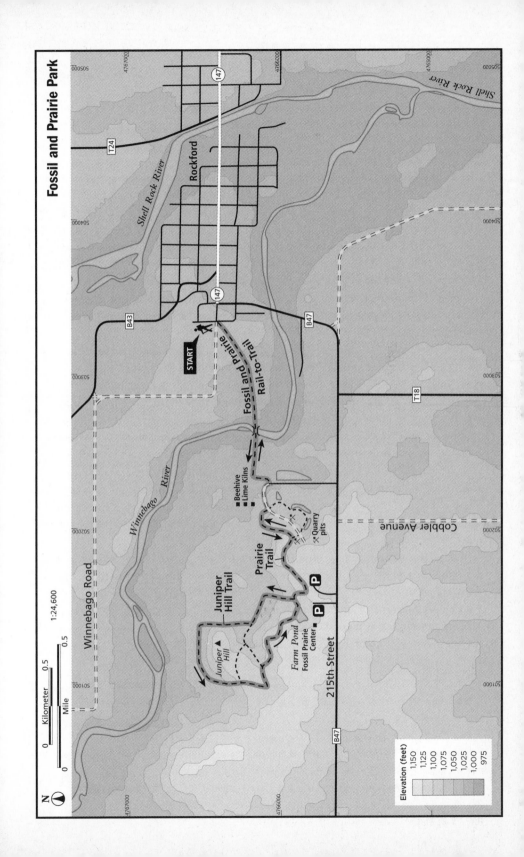

Fossil and Prairie Park

N

1:24,600

Kilometer 0   0.5
Mile   0   0.5

Shell Rock River

T24

Rockford

147

Shell Rock River

B43

147

B47

START

Fossil and Prairie
Rail-to-Trail

Winnebago River

Beehive
Lime Kilns

T18

Cobbler Avenue

Quarry
pits

Prairie
Trail

Juniper
Hill Trail

Juniper
Hill

Winnebago Road

Farm Pond
Fossil Prairie
Center

P

P

215th Street

B47

Elevation (feet)
1,150
1,125
1,100
1,075
1,050
1,025
1,000
975

The best way to access Fossil and Prairie Park is to start from the town of Rockford, where a railroad right-of-way leads to the park. At 0.5 mile an old bridge crosses the Winnebago River just before its confluence with the Shell Rock River. On the east edge of the park, at 0.9 mile, you'll encounter abandoned beehive kilns in which millions of bricks and tiles were fired during the 1900s.

As you approach the quarry pits, at 1.1 miles, your eyes may focus on the crystalline aqua water instead of the excavated cavities. However, as you descend into the belly of the old quarry, you'll delve almost 400 million years into the past. Even great blue heron tracks in the clay shores begin to look prehistoric, and the rattling call of a belted kingfisher fits right into the ancient scene before you.

Be prepared to hop around on the rocks and eroding slopes of the pits, and watch out for sludgy clay at the bottom. A closer look at the side slopes will fill you with awe as fossils seem almost to pop out: solitary and colonial corals, sea lilies, many species of brachiopods and mollusks, and, if you're lucky, the teeth of Ptyctodus, a primeval fish. Modest fossil collection is allowed, but only for personal use, not commercial sale.

After you've spent sufficient time exploring the fossil bonanza, walk north past the pit toilets. Turn west at 1.2 miles onto the Juniper Hill–Prairie Trail. The three main prairie types in Iowa—wet, dry, and mesic—occur here in unlikely places. Because of the soil's high clay content, groundwater and seepage accumulate and spit out in springlike fashion in the middle of the hills, creating wet prairies on hillsides.

You'll pass an old farm pond that now drains into a wetland, where Canada geese and blue-winged teals spend much of the summer. Look for monarch butterflies sipping nectar from the bright fuchsia flowers of swamp milkweed nestled among sedges and cattails. A Department of Transportation wetland mitigation project straddles the dike and the Winnebago River, which you can see to the north. As a result, water entering the river from the park goes through several filtration stages before entering the river.

Cross over the dike and walk up to where the trail passes below Juniper Hill at 2.3 miles. This is the only place in Iowa you'll find the prostrate matted evergreen shrub, normally found thriving on open dunes in northern Minnesota and Michigan.

The visitor center is open most afternoons, so be sure to stop in. Exhibits cover the history of the site, natural history of the prairie, geology and paleontology, and the Euro-American settlement of Iowa and its effects.

Miles and Directions

0.0 Start at the Fossil and Prairie trailhead at the corner of West Main Avenue and Ninth Street.

0.5 Cross the bridge over the Winnebago River.

0.95 Arrive at the beehive kilns. Continue following the wide trail up to the open ridge.

1.3 Arrive at parking lot and pit toilets, where the best access to the quarry is. Explore the quarry on your own, and be modest in your collection of fossils. The following mileage does not consider explorations of the pits. You will also find the trailhead for the Juniper Hill-Prairie Trail at the north end of the parking lot.

1.5 At fork turn right (north). You'll pass the pond on the north side of the Fossil and Prairie Center.

1.7 Arrive at the wetland, where there is a blind hidden in the willow thicket. It is somewhat unstable, so ask park staff before you enter it.

2.0 Juniper Hill rises to the west. There used to be a trail going up and over the top, but because of the extremely sensitive nature of the area, please do not venture off the main trail.

2.5 At the gate turn left (east) to return to the parking area.

3.0 Arrive at the main trail just east of the Fossil and Prairie Center. Check out the great exhibits inside, or stop at the pits again. Backtrack the way you came to return to the trailhead.

4.6 Arrive back at the trailhead.

Hike Information

Local Information
Mason City Convention and Visitors Bureau, Mason City; (800) 423–5724, www .masoncitytourism.com

Events/Attractions
Charles H. MacNider Museum, 303 Second Street SE, Mason City; (641) 421–3666, www.macniderart.org

Prairie Heritage Days and Frontier Market, Fossil and Prairie Run-Walk, Fossil & Prairie Park, Rockford; (641) 756–3490

Charles City Farmers' Market, Theisens parking lot, Charles City; (641) 228–1453; May through October, Wednesday 3:30 to 5:30 P.M., Saturday 9:00 A.M. to noon

Mason City Farmers' Market, 100 South Federal, Mason City; (641) 926–5741; June through October, Tuesday and Friday 4:00 to 6:00 P.M.

Accommodations
The Decker House B&B and Sour Grapes Bistro, 119 Second Street SE, Mason City; (641) 423–4700

Ackley Creek Park (modern campground) and West Idlewild (primitive campsites), Floyd County Conservation Board; www.floydcoia .org/departments/conservationboard/ camping.asp

Restaurants
LDs Filling Station Bar & Grill, 616 Twelfth Street NE; (641) 494–2313

Deja Brew, 10 South Federal, Mason City; (641) 423–0377

The Back Door, 510 Hildreth Street, Charles City; (641) 228–6263

Other Resources
The Bookery, 15 South Delaware Avenue, Mason City

North Iowa Nature Club; www.iowabirds .org/birdingiowa/clubs.asp

The Vascular Plants of Iowa: An Annotated Checklist and Natural History by Lawrence J. Eilers and Dean M. Roosa (Bur Oak Books Series, University of Iowa Press)

An Illustrated Guide to Iowa Prairie Plants by Paul Christiansen and Mark Muller (Bur Oak Books Series, University of Iowa Press)

Iowa's Geological Past: 3 Billion Years of Change by Wayne I. Anderson (Bur Oak Books Series, University of Iowa Press)

Wildflowers and Other Plants of Iowa Wetlands by Sylvan T. Runkel and Dean M. Roosa (Iowa State University Press)

32 Pilot Knob State Park

As settlers heading west crossed the expansive, undulating prairies and wetlands of north-central Iowa in the 1800s, they used Pilot Knob, at 1,450 feet the second highest point in the state, as an indelible beacon. The park contains a fen, home to many rare plants as well as a floating mat of sphagnum moss. Trails wind through beautifully mature forests, around Dead Man's and Pilot Knob Lakes, and through an area dominated by wetlands. On a clear day, you'll be able to see 30-plus miles from the observation tower built atop Pilot Knob by the Civilian Conservation Corps (CCC).

Distance: 7.9-mile loop
Approximate hiking time: 3 to 4 hours
Total elevation gain: 865 feet
Trail surface: Forested footpath (some multi-use), mowed section through grassland
Seasons: Year-round; good cross-country skiing in winter, with warming shelter
Trail users: Hikers, bikers, equestrians, hunters, cross-country skiers
Canine compatability: Dogs permitted on leash

Hazards: Poison ivy, ticks
Land status: State park, state preserve, and state recreation area
Nearest town: Forest City
Fees and permits: No fees or permits required unless you are camping
Schedule: Open year-round, 4:00 A.M. to 10:30 P.M.
Trail contact: 2148 340th Street, Forest City, IA 50436; (641) 581–4835, www.iowadnr .com/parks/state_park_list/pilot_knob.html

Finding the trailhead: From the junction of U.S. Highway 69 and Highway 9 in Forest City, drive east on Highway 9. Turn south onto County Road 332 (205th Street), which will lead you down to the park. Follow the signs to the park office, bypassing the campground. Park in the lot next to the northwest side of Pilot Knob Lake and the warming shelter. *DeLorme: Iowa Atlas and Gazetteer:* Page 19 E78

The Hike

Pilot Knob is a classic glacial kame—a landform associated with retreating glaciers, in this case the Des Moines Lobe around 12,000 to 14,000 years ago. Meltwater poured off the edge or into crevices and chambers in the deteriorating ice sheet, leaving behind large deposits of sand and gravel that now appear as isolated, fairly conical hills.

There are several trailheads in the park from which to choose, but the parking area just south of the office is easy to access and will maximize your ability to make a long loop out of the trails. Start by walking past the warming house and up the hill south toward Dead Man's Lake.

At 0.25 mile, take the 0.5-mile trail around botanically phenomenal Dead Man's Lake. A number of legends, many with headless horsemen and drowning victims, describe the origin of the lake's name. However, the accepted explanation dates to when the Winnebago tribe inhabited the region. Winnebago means "people of the

On a clear day, the view from the Pilot Knob Observation Tower goes on forever.

stinking water" and possibly refers to the attributes of nearby wetlands, where large amounts of decomposing organic matter release fumes. The story tells of a Winnebago member who was excommunicated from the tribe, and thus considered dead, who came to live near the lake.

Dead Man's Lake, better classified as a "nutrient-poor fen," is one of two such fens in Iowa. Earlier the lake was an entire floating mat of sphagnum moss, but excessive harvest of peat in the 1920s left only a remnant. This fen is the only home in the state to several rare northern plants, including cordroot sedge and the carnivorous sundew. Three species of water lilies live in the lake; one of them, commonly known as watershield, is known only from this site in Iowa.

Because of the area's incredibly sensitive nature and exceptional plant community, do NOT walk off the trail surrounding the lake—plus it's illegal.

The park owes its creation to local preservation efforts. More than 150 residents of nearby Forest City campaigned and raised funds to purchase the land surrounding Pilot Knob, including Dead Man's Lake. The land was purchased in 1921 with a matching grant from the state and in 1924 was dedicated as a state park.

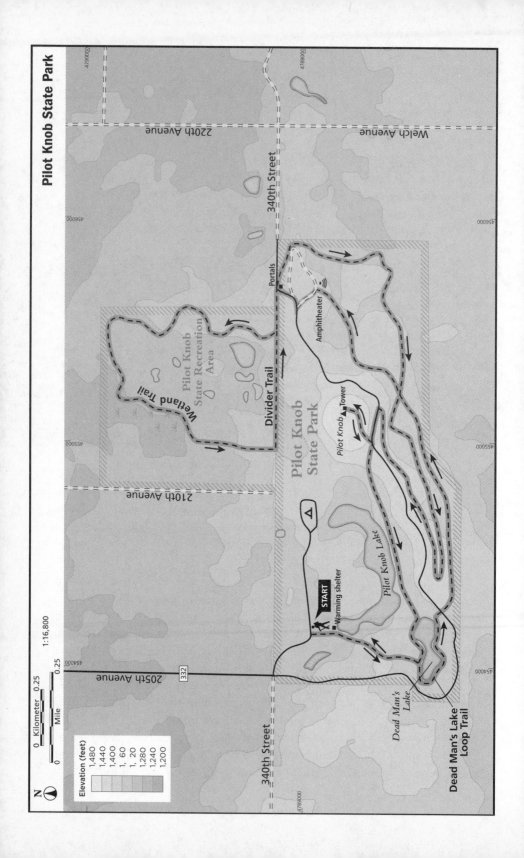

In 1934 a CCC group spent four months developing Pilot Knob's recreational facilities. Glacial erratics, large metamorphic and igneous boulders from Minnesota, were collected and used to build several structures now on the National Register of Historic Places—the amphitheater, observation tower, picnic shelter, and portals at the entrance of the park. In 1968 nearly half the park was dedicated as a biological state preserve. In 1979 land north of the park was sold to the state to create Pilot Knob Recreation Area, where hunting is allowed.

The forests that cover Pilot Knob are dominated by bur, northern pin, and red oaks, elm, ironwood, and hazelnut and serve as a haven for migratory birds during spring, with many species staying to nest. Look for various flycatchers and warblers, veery, scarlet tanager, and the black-billed cuckoo. Hidden among the trees are small, marshy depressions dominated by sedges and rushes, but you'll also find arrowhead, smartweed, marsh fern, monkey flower, swamp milkweed, and blue flag iris.

During winter months, this is one of the best places to cross-country ski in Iowa. The trails are gently sloped and well maintained, and the warming house is a nice incentive to spend some time in the cold.

Miles and Directions

0.0 Start at the parking area; walk over the dike and past the warming shelter.

0.1 Follow the right fork toward Dead Man's Lake.

0.3 Arrive at Dead Man's Lake Loop Trail. Take a right (west) and walk around the southwest rim of the lake until you arrive at the fork. **(Do not go off trail here to explore Dead Man's Lake; you must have a permit to do so.)**

0.65 At the fork turn right (south).

1.9 Walk past the amphitheater and onto the loop road. Take a left (west) onto the road and then a quick right (northeast) onto the road that will take you out of the park through the "portals," (stone pillars). Immediately after walking through the portals, turn left (west) onto the trail (which divides Pilot Knob State Park and Pilot Knob Recreation Area) to explore the recreation area.

2.1 At the fork turn right (north) to take the wetland loop.

3.7 Arrive back at the divider trail and take a left (east). This will take you back to the portals.

4.2 Arrive at the portals to the park's northeast entrance. Continue straight on the road until you see a small trail to the right (south). Turn onto this trail to walk toward the Pilot Knob Observation Tower. **Bailout:** Backtrack past the amphitheater and around Dead Man's Lake to return to the trailhead.

5.2 At the junction of four trails, continue straight ahead (northwest). (FYI: Along this trail, look for the marshy forest openings—little hidden depressions rife with wetland plants!)

6.4 Arrive at the road; take a left (west) onto it for 0.1 mile of road-hiking.

6.5 Arrive at the parking area for the Pilot Knob Observation Tower. The trail leaves from the east side of the parking lot and heads east; you'll see the signs.

6.7 Arrive at the Pilot Knob Observation Tower, and ascend the ninety-nine stairs to 1,450 feet above sea level. Backtrack down the trail to the parking area.

6.8 On the west side of the parking area, the trail goes directly past the restrooms and leads to the west, toward Dead Man's Lake.

7.4 Arrive at the Dead Man's Lake Loop Trail. Turn right (north) and follow the trail to the first fork.

7.6 At the fork turn right (north) to return to the trailhead.

7.9 Arrive back at the trailhead.

Hike Information

Local Information

Forest City Chamber of Commerce; (641) 585-2092, www.forestcityia.com

Clear Lake Area Chamber of Commerce; (800) 285-5338, www.clearlakeiowa.com

Events/Attractions

National Hobo Convention, August, Britt; www.hobo.com/

Pilot Knob Trail Race (15k), May, Pilot Knob State Park; www.pilotknobtrailrace.com

Heritage Park of North Iowa; (641) 585-4332, www.heritageparkofnorthiowa.com

Buddy Holly, the Big Bopper, and Ritchie Valens 1959 crash site; located between Clear Lake and Hanlotown; www.clearlakeiowa.com

Forest City Farmers' Market, 200 block of US 69 South, Forest City; (515) 368-1549; May through October, Thursday 2:30 to 6:00 P.M.

Accommodations

Pilot Knob State Park Campground; (641) 581-4835

Crystal Lake Campground (Hancock County Conservation Board); (641) 923-2720, www.hancockcountyia.org

Thorpe Recreation Area, Forest City; (641) 923-2720, www.hancockcountyia.org/ConservationPage.htm#1

Elderberry Inn Bed and Breakfast, 19024 345th Street, Forest City; (641) 581-2012

Restaurants

The Lodge, Highway 69 South; (641) 585-5060

Cabin Coffee Company, 303 Main Avenue, Clear Lake; (641) 357-6500, www.cabincoffeecompany.com

McKenna's Blues, Booze & BBQ, 444 North Shore Drive, Clear Lake; (641) 357-1443, www.mckennasbbb.com

Other Resources

Enchanted Forest (bookstore), 136 North Clark Street, Forest City

The Guide to Iowa's State Preserves by Ruth Herzberg and John Pearson (Bur Oaks Books Series, University of Iowa Press)

Wildflowers of Iowa Woodlands by Sylvan T. Runkel and Alvin F. Bull (Iowa State University Press)

Wildflowers and Other Plants of Iowa Wetlands by Sylvan T. Runkel and Dean M. Roosa (Iowa State University Press)

The Vascular Plants of Iowa: An Annotated Checklist and Natural History by Lawrence J. Eilers and Dean M. Roosa (Bur Oak Books Series, University of Iowa Press)

Honorable Mentions

W. Kettleson Hogsback Wildlife Management Area

Located on the west side of Spirit Lake, just south of the Minnesota state line, you'll find a wetland-dominated area. The "hogsback" for which the wildlife management area is named is a narrow ridge extending between Hottes and Marble Lakes. As the Des Moines Lobe melted, two large blocks of ice separated and formed the two lakes, or "kettles," while glacial till and gravel were pushed together, forming the ridge. The trail loops around Marble Lake and past Sunken Lake, another kettle and home to large amounts of waterfowl during the spring and fall migrations. From the merging of Highway 9 and U.S. Highway 71 west of Spirit Lake, take Highway 71/9 east, turning (left) north onto County Road M56. Turn left (west) onto Highway 276 and follow this around the southern tip of Spirit Lake. Turn left (west) onto 125th Street and look for signs on the north side of the road for the west entrance, or drive past 125th and take the next left (west) into a parking area. For information: Big Sioux Wildlife Management Unit, 2248 125th Street, Spirit Lake; (712) 336–1485.

X. Cayler Prairie State Preserve

Bought in 1958 by the Iowa Conservation Commission (now Iowa Department of Natural Resources) and designated as a national natural landmark in 1966 and a state preserve in 1971, this tract of land has long been known as a prairie gem. Upland sandpipers and prairie skinks make their homes here amid 225 different plant species. The preserve's marshy areas, eskers, and potholes are reminders of the area's recent glacial history. Wear tall boots to wander around. From the junction of Highways 9 and 86 west of Spirit Lake, take Highway 9 west. Turn left (south) onto County Road M38 (170th Street), you'll see a brown sign pointing the way. Drive 2.5 miles to a parking area on the east side of the road. For information: (515) 281–8524, www.iowadnr.com/preserves/.

Y. Horseshoe Bend Park

This 180-acre park is bisected by the Little Sioux River, with about 3.5 miles of hiking trails on the north and south sides of the river. Several footbridges connect the various loops. This is the place to get away from the highly developed areas around Okoboji and Spirit Lakes. Explore the upland forests, or follow along the oxbow ponds surrounded by floodplain forests to look for migratory songbirds. Cross-country skiers can escape the cold in the warming shelter with a view. From the junction of U.S. Highway 71 and County Road A34 in Milford, take US 71 south. Turn right (west) onto County Road A48 (240th Street), for 3 miles. Turn right (north) onto County Road M38 (190th Street); you'll quickly see the parking area. For information: Dickinson County Conservation Board; (712) 338–4786.

Z. Shell Rock Greenbelt

A gravel road not often traveled by cars spans the 7.5 miles between Nora Springs and Rock Falls along the Shell Rock River. Access the trail from Wilkinson Pioneer Park on the south side of Rock Falls or off Highway 22 on the west end of Nora Springs. Primitive campsites are located about 2.5 miles north of Nora Springs. The riparian forests, pine plantings, and marshy areas along the greenbelt are a haven for migratory songbirds, owls, woodpeckers, and hawks. North of 290th Street, hunting is permitted; the area is used heavily. For information: Cerro Gordo County Conservation Board; (641) 423–5309, www.limecreeknature.org.

AA. Lime Creek Nature Center

Eight miles of trails will take you to an old brewery built in 1873; a bird blind that looks out over the wetland area, a stopover point for many migrating waterfowl; floodplain forests along the Winnebago River; an old quarry-turned-lake; and several prairie restorations. The 0.6-mile Easy Access Trail is paved; the rest of the trails are mowed footpaths. Two "hike-in" campsites cost $1.00 per night to use. From the junction of Highway 122 and U.S. Highway 65 in Mason City, take US 65 north and turn right (east) onto Lime Creek Road, which will lead you to the parking area and nature center. For information: Cerro Gordo County Conservation Board; (641) 423–5309, www.limecreeknature.org.

In Addition

1800s: The Big Change

After emerging from the dense forests of the east, the Iowan landscape encountered by the earliest European explorers must have been a glimpse of heaven. Tallgrass prairie blanketed the hills as far as one could see and resembled the ocean, rolling as waves in the wind. Creeks, streams, and two of the biggest rivers in the country lay within the region and flowed with clean water full of fish and mollusks. Diverse deciduous forests lined these waterways, while the lone sentinels of the prairie, bur oak trees, stood atop upland hills.

Joseph Street, an Indian agent, traveled through northeast Iowa in 1833 and wrote of his trip: "I had never rode through a country so full of game." Bison, elk, antelope, and deer wandered through big bluestem that grew over their heads. Mountain lions, gray wolves, and black bears were common, and earlier settlers wrote often of their fear of the wild animals of the prairie. Extraordinary amounts of waterfowl occupied the north-central lobe of the state during the summers, including whooping cranes, ducks, geese, pelicans, and shorebirds. Prairie chickens, swallow-tailed kites, northern harriers, and Henslow's, vespers, grasshopper, and song sparrows inhabited the drier grasslands.

Iowa was opened up to non-Indian settlement in 1833 and achieved statehood in 1846. Within four years of statehood, Iowa's population doubled to nearly 200,000, and by 1870 it had grown to more than one million. Osceola County, in the northwest corner, was the last to be settled, in 1871. The rapid influx of hungry settlers, the sale of the first steel plow (invented by John Deere) in 1848, and the use of clay tiles to drain wetlands almost immediately took their toll on the land and its creatures. First to go were the mountain lions, the last of which was killed in 1867. From 1870 to 1871 the elk and bison vanished. Black bears were gone within several years. The last gray wolf was killed by a farmer in the winter of 1884–85. Populations of smaller fur-bearing mammals—the muskrat, river otter, beaver, and mink—were devastated by trappers. Hunters killed the ducks, geese, and cranes, as well as the now-extinct passenger pigeon, as if their sources were never ending.

All the while, the most fertile soil on the continent was being plowed; the vast marshes were being drained, rivers channelized, and extensive forests cut down. The grass diversity of the tallgrass prairie did a veritable nosedive, from several hundred to corn and wheat. The turn of the twentieth century was a sad time for many, and the devastation brought about a conservation movement that inspires us still today.

Sadly, that movement lost steam somewhere along the way, for Iowa falls very close to the bottom of the list with regards to percentage of public lands. And although large tracts of state and county land are undergoing restoration and reconstruction programs, the fragmented habitat they offer isn't enough. Surrounding us are hordes of nonhuman organisms that each make our everyday experiences so much more rich, exciting, meaningful, and, most importantly, possible. They are increasingly not finding the resources they need to continue living here. The footsteps of the mountain lion and bison are being followed by the piping plover, massasauga rattler, blue-spotted salamander, and Mead's milkweed. It has long been time for people to join together in a massive effort to aid the health of the land. Unfortunately not everyone hears the call. But you only have to be in the upper reaches of a small creek, standing atop a river bluff, in the midst of the dense forest, or wide open prairie to first learn to listen. And to get to all of these places, you must walk.

The Great Northwest

As you're driving north from Sioux City along the Big Sioux River, the world opens up. Deposits of loess become shallower the farther from the Missouri River you travel, and a gently tilting land is revealed. Unlike the deeply wrinkled deposits of the southern hills, the northwest plains wear the loess as a smooth blanket.

To some it is surprising that Iowa's highest point is found in the topographically challenged northwest plains. The lowest point in the state, at 480 feet, is found in extreme southeast Iowa at the confluence of the Des Moines and Mississippi Rivers, near Keokuk. Hawkeye Point, 1,670 feet, is located on a ridge pushed into place by the outer margins of the Des Moines Lobe ice sheet, in Osceola County near the Minnesota border.

The two corners of the state are also diametrically opposed with regard to the amounts of annual precipitation and forested areas. Comparatively, the northwest corner is overwhelmingly lacking, receiving less than 25 inches of yearly precipitation and marked only by trees growing along creeks or in windbreaks planted by settlers. Historically, the Big Sioux, Rock, Floyd, Ocheyedan, and Little Sioux Rivers were the forested bands winding through a mixed-grass prairie wonderland.

In the extreme northwest corner of Gitchie Manitou State Preserve, the state's oldest exposed rock, Sioux quartzite, lies in outcrops along the Big Sioux River. Just above the Sioux quartzite lie deposits of the state's youngest rocks, Cretaceous-age shales and limestones. The gap in the rock sequence between the quartzite and the limestones spans just over 1.5 billion years!

South of Cherokee sits Pilot Rock, one of the state's largest glacial erratics. The Sioux quartzite boulder measures nearly 180 feet around and 14 feet tall. Standing atop the ancient boulder yields a view of the Little Sioux River Valley.

One of the most incredible places in the region is located at the confluence of Blood Run Creek and the Big Sioux River. A village straddling the Big Sioux River in both Iowa and South Dakota was probably one of the largest trade centers in the region. Pipestone quarries to the north were a source of the malleable red mudstone, used to make sacred figurines, ornaments, and pipes. Pottery resembling that of the Oneota culture of northeast Iowa and the Des Moines River Valley has been uncovered at Blood Run, and more than 250 burial mounds surround the site.

This region is far removed from the major cities in Iowa and is not as popular a tourist center as the neighboring Great Lakes of Iowa. For those of you who like quiet days and nights, interesting landforms and plants, and skies full of stars, this is the place.

33 Ocheyedan Mound State Preserve

In Iowa's topographically disadvantaged northwest corner, even the small rise of Ocheyedan Mound is dramatic. Ocheyedan Mound was long a beacon for travelers and, in later times, a popular hill for sledding. A classic glacial kame, it was long thought to be the state's highest point—until 1970, when the U.S. Geological Survey discovered the mistake. A short jaunt to the summit today will put you 170 feet above the gently tilted landscape, yielding a subtly fantastic view of the surrounding floodplain.

Distance: 0.45 mile up and back
Approximate hiking time: 30 minutes
Total elevation gain: 66 feet
Trail surface: Small footpath
Seasons: Year-round
Trail users: Hikers only
Canine compatability: Dogs permitted on leash
Hazards: None
Land status: State preserve

Nearest town: Ocheyedan
Fees and permits: No fees or permits required
Schedule: Open year-round during daylight hours
Map: USGS quad: Ocheyedan
Trail contact: Osceola County Conservation Board, 5945 Highway 9, P.O. Box 369, Ocheyedan, IA 51354; (712) 758-3709

Finding the trailhead: From the junction of Highways 9 and 60 north of Sibley, drive east on Highway 9. Turn south onto County Road L58 and drive through Ocheyedan. At the T-intersection south of town, turn left (east) onto County Road A22. You'll see the sign on the north side of the road. *DeLorme: Iowa Atlas and Gazetteer:* Page 16 C1

The Hike

When French explorer Jean Nicollet mapped the Ocheyedan River in the early 1800s, he learned that Ocheyedan was the anglicized form of two Dakota Sioux words. "Acheya" and "akicheya," both meaning "the spot where they cry," explained a tradition in which native peoples would ascend a hill from which to mourn the passage of others.

In the mid-1800s, railroad crews surveying the northwest corner of the state estimated the height of Ocheyedan Mound to be 1,655 feet above sea level. They used a barometric altimeter to estimate elevations, and because it relies on the fact that an increase in elevation will produce a decrease in pressure, measurements were variable to changing weather conditions. Knoll-like Ocheyedan Mound, the only significant rise in elevation amid the gently tilted landscape, was written up as the highest point at the state.

Almost a century later, in 1970, U.S. Geological Survey engineers were working on new maps for the area. They discovered that the accepted elevation of Ocheyedan

Mound was wrong and that the summit was 62 feet lower than previously thought. Thus began three years of controversy, called by some observers the "Iowa High-point Crisis." From 1970 to 1974 it was not known where the highest point in Iowa actually was.

Apparently the USGS didn't have the funding or time to conduct the labor-intensive surveys right away. It took three years to determine that Iowa's actual highest point, 1,669 feet above sea level, sat only 10 miles northwest of Ocheyedan Mound, in a privately owned feedlot. In 1998 the Iowa General Assembly passed House Joint Resolution 2004, officially naming the site on Donna and Merrel Sterler's farm "Hawkeye Point." The Sterlers have graciously opened their land to the public, although most people who visit are "highpointers"—peak baggers who seek to stand atop the highest point in each of the fifty states.

Both Ocheyedan Mound and Hawkeye Point are positioned along a ridge of high ground formed when the Des Moines Lobe was surging over north-central Iowa 16,000 to 12,000 years ago. The ice sheet advanced and retreated several times during its tenure in the state, carrying with it large amounts of glacial till and depositing the loads in glacial moraines, or ridges, on the margins of its advances. During the melting of the ice sheet, crevices and holes in the ice were drainage outlets for sediment-laden meltwater, which deposited sand and gravel in conical mounds, now known as kames. Today this noticeably hummocky terrain composed of ridges and mounds is a reminder of the very recent glacial history of the area.

Ocheyedan Mound is a classic glacial kame composed of pebbles, sand, and rocks made of granite, Sioux quartzite, and limestone. About ⅓-mile long, twenty-four acres of the mound were donated to the Iowa Natural Heritage Foundation in 1983. In 1984 Ocheyedan Mound was dedicated as a state preserve, and ownership was transferred to the Osceola County Conservation Board.

Today the summit of the mound is transitioning back to native prairie, and among the invasive species, you'll find sideoats grama and little bluestem along with death camas, butterfly milkweed, purple prairie clover, and blazing star. From the parking lot, a small path leads to the summit, where on a clear day you can see cornfields extending to the horizon. Ocheyedan Mound defines the beauty of Iowa's subtlety. It isn't a high peak, but the short climb yields a big view, and a little investigation exposes the natural and cultural history of the area.

Miles and Directions

This is a short jaunt up to the mound and back—a good leg-stretcher.

A short trail leads to the top of Ocheyedan Mound.

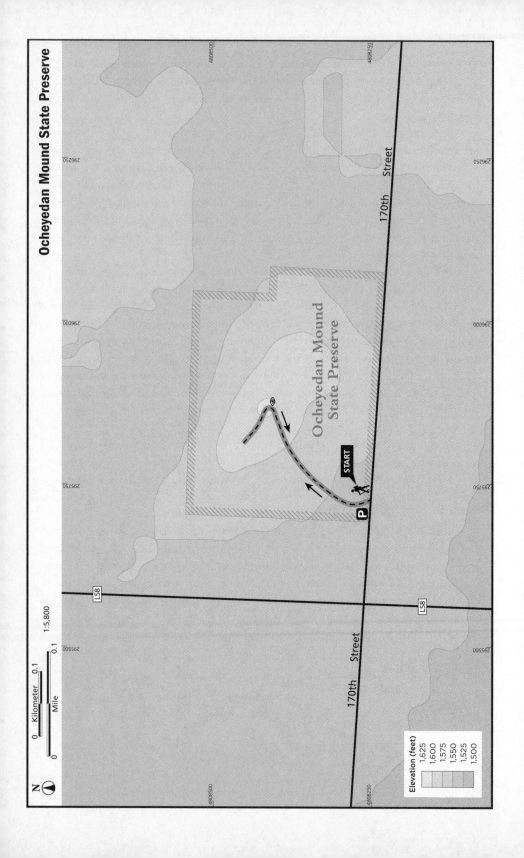

Ocheyedan Mound State Preserve

Hike Information

Local Information

Osceola County; www.osceolacountyia.com
Ocheyedan; www.osceolacounty.com/ocheyedan
Okoboji; www.okoboji.com

Events/Attractions

Abbie Gardner Cabin, Arnold's Park; (712) 332-7248
Spirit Lake Fish Hatchery, Spirit Lake; (712) 336-1840
Dickinson County Trail, 21-mile multiuse trail from Milford to Spirit Lake (Dickinson County Conservation Board); (712) 338-4786
Lakes Art Center, 2201 Highway 71, Okoboji; www.lakesart.org
Iowa Rock 'n' Roll Music Museum, 91 Lake Street, Okoboji; (712) 332-6540, www.iowarocknroll.com
University of Okoboji Winter Games, January, Okoboji; (800) 270-2574
Iowa Northwestern Railroad, Spirit Lake; (866) 621-9600, www.ianwrr.com
Lakes Area Farmers' Market, Dickinson County Fairgrounds, Spirit Lake; (712) 336-4430; June through October, Wednesday and Saturday, 7:30 A.M. to noon

Accommodations

The Wild Rose Inn of Okoboji, 2329 170th Street, Okoboji; (712) 332-9986
Lakeside Bed & Breakfast, 555 Hill Avenue, Spirit Lake; (712) 336-3414, www.nwiowabb.com/lakeside.htm

Restaurants

Sibley Cafe, 326 Ninth Street, Sibley; (712) 754-3136
Cobblestone Restaurant, 1015 Second Avenue, Sibley; (712) 754-2320
Rebel's Family Pub, 15484 Percival Drive, Spirit Lake; (712) 336-9956

Other Resources

Northern Iowa Prairie Audubon; www.iowabirds.org/birdingiowa/clubs.asp
Landforms of Iowa by Jean C. Prior (Bur Oak Books Series, University of Iowa Press)
Take the Next Exit: New Views of the Iowa Landscape edited by Robert Sayre (Iowa State University Press)
The Guide to Iowa's State Preserves by Ruth Herzberg and John Pearson (Bur Oaks Books Series, University of Iowa Press)

34 Gitchie Manitou State Preserve

The preserve contains outcrops of Sioux quartzite, the oldest bedrock in Iowa. Designated a state preserve in 1969, Gitchie Manitou is bordered on the north by the South Dakota–Iowa state line and on the west and south by the Big Sioux River. A visit offers a day filled with birding along the river and rock-hopping on the exposures. Hikers are treated to beds of Sioux quartzite that abound with western flowers, mosses, and lichens.

Distance: 2.0-mile lollipop
Approximate hiking time: 1 to 2 hours
Total elevation gain: 97 feet
Trail surface: Old gravel road
Seasons: Spring through fall, during winter, snow-covered rocks
Trail users: Hikers only
Canine compatability: Dogs permitted on leash
Hazards: Spines of prickly pear cacti
Land status: State preserve

Nearest towns: Sioux Falls, South Dakota; Granite, Iowa
Fees and permits: No fees or permits required
Schedule: Open year-round, 4:00 A.M. to 10:30 P.M.
Map: USGS quad: Klondike
Trail contact: IDNR Big Sioux Wildlife Unit, 2408 Seventeenth Street, Spirit Lake, IA 51360; (712) 336–3524, www.state.ia.us/dnr/organiza/ppd/gitchie.htm

Finding the trailhead: From the junction of Highway 9 and U.S. Highway 75 west of Rock Rapids, take Highway 9 west, and then north, through Lester. Just before you enter the town of Larchwood, turn left (west) onto County Road A18. Drive 6.5 miles and turn north onto County Road K10; go through the town of Granite, following the curves. After 3 miles, in between the big curve in the road to the north and the state line, look for a sign and small parking area to west of the road. *DeLorme: Iowa Atlas and Gazetteer:* Page 14 AB12

The Hike

In the extreme northwest corner of Iowa, a small preserve contains a big look at the geologic history of the state in its 1.7-million-year-old rock. The exposures of Sioux quartzite were created by sand deposits on the braided stream channels and tidal estuaries along a Precambrian marine shoreline. Composed of tightly bound quartz grains interlocked with silicon dioxide, the hard rock's red and pink tones resulted from iron-oxide staining.

Gitchie Manitou comes from the Sioux words for Great Spirit. The Native American reverence for Sioux quartzite is evidenced 45 miles north in Minnesota's Pipestone National Monument, where beds of the rock contain deposits of pipestone, also known as catlinite. Great Plains tribes considered the soft red clay sacred

Little prickly pear cactus is right at home in
Gitchie Manitou State Preserve.

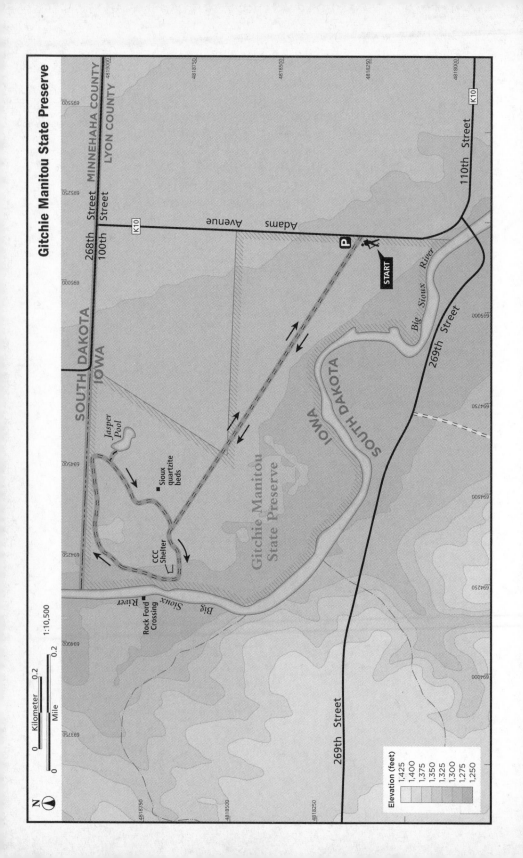

Gitchie Manitou State Preserve

and used it to make ceremonial pipes and beautiful figurines that became valuable trading goods throughout the West.

To enter the preserve, you'll need to walk 0.5 mile on an old access road from the parking area along County Road K10. The access road runs parallel to the Big Sioux River and is fringed by a previously cultivated brome/bluegrass field slowly being overtaken by sumac and dogwood. As you near the Sioux quartzite outcrops, an almost sudden transition to native prairie occurs.

The diverse plant and animal life in this small preserve reflects a remarkable variety of habitats. Tallgrass representatives, such as big and little bluestem and Indian grass, live within feet of western short-grass prairie obligates like blue grama, buffalo grass, and tumblegrass. During June you'll find one of the state's largest populations of little prickly pear cactus, blooming a startling sulphur yellow. Prairie fameflower, another rare, typically western species, can be found growing among the cacti; look for its delicate pink flowers during midsummer. Diverse populations of moss grow on the rocks, as do crustose lichen species, several of which form gray-green bull's-eye patterns on the pinkish quartzite. Rock spikemoss, a member of the club moss family, and Oregon cliff fern, both western plants, also make their homes in cracks in the Sioux quartzite.

Once you've walked past the Civilian Conservation Corps (CCC) shelter built from Sioux quartzite in the 1930s, the road curves north and passes the site of Lyon County's first post office. During the 1880s a small town called Gibraltar stood here next to Rock Ford Crossing, where wagons en route to the Dakota Territory and stagecoaches headed for Sioux Falls negotiated a shallow area in the Big Sioux River.

Continuing north you'll find Jasper Pool, a reminder of the quarrying that took place from 1890 to 1920. Bur oak and cottonwood trees hang over the pool, which is surrounded by small wetlands. Hairy water clover (*Marsilea vestita*), found only in vernal pools adjacent to Sioux quartzite rocks, grows in the shallow water.

Archaeological digs and explorations at Gitchie Manitou have uncovered several groups of low conical mounds, the most extensive containing seventeen mounds. Rim shards, fire-cracked Sioux quartzite, and animal bones have been unearthed as well. The connection between habitation sites here and at Blood Run National Historic Landmark downstream at the confluence of Blood Run Creek and Big Sioux River is unknown. Extensive archaeological research at Blood Run has uncovered several hundred conical mounds, pitted boulders, and catlinite objects thought to have been made by Omaha, Ponca, and possibly Ioway peoples, who mixed hunting-gathering with the cultivation of corn and beans.

Miles and Directions

0.0 Start from the parking area off County Road K10; go through the gate and follow the access road northwest into the preserve.

0.5 Just before you enter the riparian woodland, you will begin to see the pinkish rock exposures north of the CCC-built shelter.

0.6 Just after the CCC shelter, turn right (north) onto the loop road that follows along the Big Sioux River toward Jasper Pool.

0.7 Walking along the river, look down to see Sioux quartzite exposures, which form Rock Ford Crossing. (FYI: Here once stood the somewhat aptly named town of Gibraltar.)

1.0 Arrive at Jasper Pool; loop back around southward. (Note: Check out the hairy water clover growing in the water.)

1.5 Arrive back at the CCC shelter and turn left (east) back onto the access road toward the trailhead.

2.0 Arrive back at parking area.

Hike Information

Local Information
Sioux Falls, South Dakota; www.siouxfalls.com

Events/Attractions
Center for Western Studies, Augustana College, Sioux Falls, South Dakota; (605) 274-4007, www.augie.edu/cws

Sioux Falls Jazzfest, July, Sioux Falls, South Dakota; (605) 335-6101, http://jazzfestsiouxfalls.com

Country Apple Orchard, Minnesota Avenue (5 miles south of Sioux Falls, South Dakota); (605) 743-2424

The Outdoor Campus (South Dakota Game, Fish, and Parks), 4500 South Oxbow Avenue, Sioux Falls, South Dakota; (605) 362-2777, www.sdgfp.info/Wildlife/Education/OutdoorCampus/index.htm

Rock Rapids Farmers' Market, Jubilee Store parking lot, Rock Rapids; (712) 472-3456; June through September, Saturday 8:00 A.M. to noon

Sibley Farmers' Market, 400 block of Ninth Street, Sibley; (712) 754-3212; May through October, Saturday 8:00 A.M. to 3:00 P.M.

Accommodations
Lake Pahoja Recreation Area (Lyon County Conservation Board); (712) 472-2217

Aunt Reba's Bed & Breakfast, 2124 Highway 9, Larchwood; (712) 478-4042

Steever House Bed and Breakfast, 46850 276th Street, Lennox, South Dakota; (605) 647-5055, www.steeverhouse.com

Rose Stone Inn, 504 East Fourth Street, Dell Rapids, South Dakota; (605) 428-3698

Restaurants
Hibachi Japanese Steakhouse and Sushi Bar, 2520 South Louise Avenue, Sioux Falls, South Dakota; (605) 361-8200

Qdoba Mexican Grill, 1900 West Forty-first Street, Sioux Falls, South Dakota; (605) 331-5700

Other Resources
Iowa's Geological Past: 3 Billion Years of Change by Wayne I. Anderson (Bur Oak Books Series, University of Iowa Press)

Landforms of Iowa by Jean C. Prior (Bur Oak Books Series, University of Iowa Press)

An Illustrated Guide to Iowa Prairie Plants by Paul Christiansen and Mark Muller (Bur Oak Books Series, University of Iowa Press)

The Guide to Iowa's State Preserves by Ruth Herzberg and John Pearson (Bur Oaks Books Series, University of Iowa Press)

The Vascular Plants of Iowa: An Annotated Checklist and Natural History by Lawrence J. Eilers and Dean M. Roosa (Bur Oak Books Series, University of Iowa Press)

Honorable Mentions

BB. Hannibal Waterman Wildlife Area

From the junction of U.S. Highway 71 and Highway 10 west of Peterson, take Highway 10 west through Peterson. Three miles west of town, turn right (north) onto Yellow Avenue, which will lead you to the parking area. The tablet near the parking lot tells you that Hannibal H. Waterman, his wife, and child were the first white settlers in O'Brien County. The first fort, town, and county seat, Old O'Brien, was located on his homestead. During the 1940s botanist Ada Hayden recommended that the prairie-covered land at the confluence of Waterman Creek and the Little Sioux River be protected. Explore this park, along with adjacent tracts owned by The Nature Conservancy and Iowa Department of Natural Resources, to learn why Hayden thought this place was so important. For information: O'Brien County Conservation; (712) 448–2254, www.obriencounty.com/government/conservation.htm.

CC. Hidden Bridge–Petersen Prairie Wildlife Area

The prairie-covered hills of this area don't have a real network of trails, but these two parks, situated along the Big Sioux River, are very much worth the energy spent finding your way. An old access road leads from the parking area down to the river terrace, where waves of raptors can be seen migrating south in the fall. Although rarely seen in Iowa, black-billed magpies are rumored to hang out here from time to time. From the junction of County Road A18 and Highway 9 in Larchwood, drive west on CR A18. Turn left (south) onto Apple Avenue and drive 1.5 miles. For information: Lyon County Conservation Board; (712) 472–2214.

DD. Big Sioux River Wildlife Management Area–Kroger Tract

From the junction of U.S. Highway 75 and Highway 9 in Rock Rapids, head south on US 75 for 2 miles. Turn right (west) onto County Road A26 for 13 miles and then turn left (south) onto Highway 182. At the south side of Inwood, turn right (west) onto U.S. Highway 18 for 3 miles before turning left (south) onto Able Boulevard. If you cross the Big Sioux River into South Dakota, you've missed it. Stop at the first parking area you encounter, near the top of the hill. The old access road will take you through the forest down to the river, but you'll have to bushwhack to explore any farther. For Information: Lyon County Conservation Board; (712) 472–2214.

EE. Big Sioux and Oak Grove Parks

Together, Oak Grove and Big Sioux Parks make up a 379-acre tract of densely forested bluffs along the Big Sioux River in Sioux County. From the junction of U.S. Highway 75 and County Road B40 on the north side of Sioux Center, take CR B40 west. Turn left (south) onto County Road K18 (Cherry Avenue); after 1.5 miles turn right (west) at the brown OAK GROVE PARK sign. Trails connect the two outcrops of Sioux quartzite in the southwest corner of the park, a mound of slag, and an ancient coal bed. Sunset views over the Big Sioux River from the ridgetop are the perfect way to end a day of hiking. Camping is available. For information: Sioux County Conservation Board; (712) 552–1047.

FF. Blood Run National Historic Landmark

One of the largest known sites of occupation by American Indians and their ancestors in Iowa, Blood Run is now designated a national historic landmark. The inhabitation site straddles the Big Sioux River (in Iowa and South Dakota), extending more than 650 acres, and is believed to have been occupied for the past 8,000 years—at one time possibly housing upwards of 10,000 people. Most recently, the Oneota—who made shell-tempered pottery and grew corn, squash, and beans—were primary inhabitants, possibly with Ioway and Omaha peoples visiting or living there as well. The interpretive trail from the parking area leads through the burial mound groups and crosses Blood Run Creek (red from iron ore deposits in the creekbed, but stories tell of a battle in the vicinity where the blood of the dead ran in the creek) to the Big Sioux River floodplain. Call for an appointment to visit the site. For information: Lyon County Conservation Board, 311 First Avenue East, Rock Rapids; (712) 472–2217.

Loess Hills

A long the Missouri River floodplain, a ribbon of mysteriously wrinkled hills forms a narrow north-south band nearly 200 miles in length. Known as the Loess Hills, they are some of the most interesting and engaging of Iowa's landforms. To some they are the ridge where the western plains begin. Connie Mutel, author of *Fragile Giants: Natural History of the Loess Hills,* declared that she never felt like she was at home in Iowa until she first encountered the Loess Hills. Aside from being the deepest deposition of loess in the Western Hemisphere and thus some of the most dramatic topographic relief in the state, the Loess Hills harbor incredibly varied ecological communities. They act as an arm of western habitat extended into the Upper Midwest, rich with short-grass prairie and desert plants and animals. The ability for western species to thrive in the Loess Hills is due mainly to the characteristics of the yellow, silty matter that composes them.

Iowa's Loess Hills were formed by three major processes: They were ground by ice and deposited by wind, and are today still being sculpted by water. The name comes from the German word for loose ("löss," rhymes with truss), first given to massive silt deposits along the Rhine River. Originally hailing from Minnesota, the Dakotas, and Canada, the fine loess was created as continental ice sheets scoured the north, effectively grinding the bedrock into flour. During periods of warming, glacial meltwater carted this rock flour away and deposited it along the banks of the major drainages. Winters brought with them colder temperatures and greatly reduced the torrents of meltwater. When the water was low, powerful drafts swirled over the floodplains, lifting the loess and depositing it in huge hummocks and hills on either side of the major river valleys. Loess can be found almost everywhere in Iowa, but nowhere to such depths as along the Missouri River. Only in China, along the Yellow River, named so for its loess, are the deposits deeper. The vulnerability of loess is demonstrated in China, where some of the highest erosion rates in the world occur. Able to stand at 90-degree angles when cut, loess is incredibly solid when undisturbed. However, loess loses its cohesive capabilities as soon as it becomes saturated or shifted.

The Loess Hills' fragility is their very essence. Because of the variance in slope gradient, aspect, and moisture content, the Loess Hills were historically less disturbed by agriculture and development. However, fire-suppression and grazing has, for now, determined the tumultuous relationship of prairie and forest on the once-bald hills. Forest cover has risen exponentially since the area's settlement in the 1840s and merited the creation of Loess Hills State Forest in 1986. The push to preserve tracts of land within the Loess Hills has been spurred by recognition of their exceptional and distinctive traits and communities. Today the Broken Kettle Grassland, Iowa's biggest prairie preserve, lies in the northern reaches. In 1986 the National Park Service designated nearly 10,000 acres in the north-central Loess Hills a national natural landmark.

Hiking the Loess Hills is the best way to experience their grandeur, and the bulk of the trails traverse prairie-covered ridgetops or cool, dark hollows. The native peoples who once lived here believed that by standing atop a ridge at dusk, one's soul would be transmitted to the ever after via the rays of the setting sun. After a long day spent walking the magnificent hills, it's hard to imagine otherwise.

35 Five-Ridge Prairie

Named for the five ridges that dissect the preserve, this mixture of prairie and woodland in the far northern reaches of the Loess Hills is a gem. Old farm roads and mowed firebreaks provide ample space for wandering in a location where the land opens up to the great Northwest. An eastern outpost for many western species, it features plant and animal diversity that ranges from short- and tallgrass prairie plants to forest-loving neotropical migrants.

Distance: 8.3 miles of several loops
Approximate hiking time: 3 to 5 hours
Total elevation gain: 1,476 feet
Trail surface: Old gravel roads and mowed firebreaks
Seasons: Year-round
Trail users: Hikers, cross-country skiers, hunters
Canine compatability: Dogs permitted
Hazards: Ticks, poison ivy, sunburn on exposed ridges
Land status: State preserve, owned and managed by Plymouth County Conservation Board
Nearest town: Sioux City
Fees and permits: No fees or permits required
Schedule: Year-round; open to hunters during Department of Natural Resources regulated seasons
Map: USGS quad: Elk Point NE
Trail contact: Plymouth County Conservation Board; (712) 568-2596, http://remseniowa.net/Plymouth_County_Conservation/PCCA_450im.html

Finding the trailhead: From Interstate 29 take exit 151 (Highway 12 to Riverside) and drive north on Highway 12 through Riverside. Pass Stone State Park. Turn right (east) onto County Road K18 North (be sure not to turn onto County Road K18 South, which is just before CR K18 North). Drive 3 miles and turn left (west) onto 260th Avenue. This will lead you all the way to the parking area and gate. *DeLorme: Iowa Atlas and Gazetteer:* Page 24 D2

The Hike

NOTE: Steep climbs could make this hike difficult for some.

As you drive north on Highway 12 toward Five-Ridge Prairie, the world seems to open up. Loess deposits become shallower and the hills smaller, as they gradually begin smoothing into the northwest Iowa plains. The thin deposits of loess, aided by the carving action of the Big Sioux River, have left Cretaceous-age bedrock exposed underneath. You'll find it on the east side of the Big Sioux River floodplain from Sioux City north. Outcrops along the highway expose the Dakota Formation's eighty- to ninety-million-year-old shale, limestone, and sandstone.

With assistance from The Nature Conservancy, the Plymouth County Conservation Board bought Five-Ridge Prairie in 1981; it was dedicated as a state preserve five years later. Wild turkey reintroduction began in 1981, and now the preserve is open for most of the scheduled hunting seasons, although during spring it's open for hunting only until noon.

Forested ravines dissect prairie-covered ridges at Five-Ridge Prairie in the north Loess Hills.

The preserve takes its name from the five prairie-covered ridges that lie between its borders, each of them parted by the deep fissures of forested valleys. The trails, either old farm roads or mowed firebreaks, traverse four-fifths of the ridges in the park and dip into three of the valleys. From the parking lot on the east end of the preserve, pick your loop or walk the entire trail system, well worth the energy and time. Be sure to take ample water with you; the hiking is hard and on the ridges, and you'll be exposed to full sun.

Low precipitation and extreme weather in the northern hills give the prairies an edge over the invading woodlands, as shrubby growth is stunted by the harsh climate. However, you'll notice on the forest edge that large thickets of dogwood and sumac seem to be gaining ground on the prairie. The shrub creep is still a problem, but prescribed burns on the preserve have helped maintain large tracts of prairie. Several areas close to the parking area were cultivated at one time and now are riddled with invasive plants easily differentiated from the native prairie.

The south- and west-facing ridgetops are dominated by a mix of tall- and mixed-grass prairies. Little bluestem, sideoats grama, Indian grass, purple locoweed,

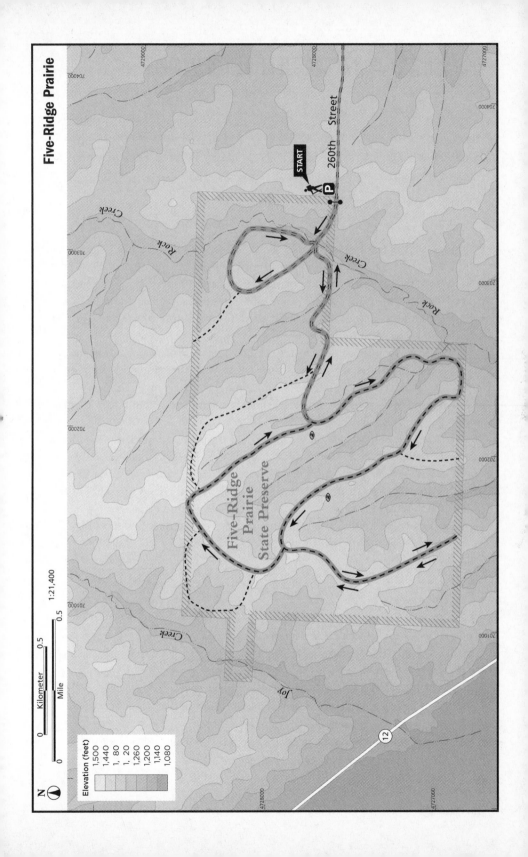

Five-Ridge Prairie

BIRD CONSERVATION AT BROKEN KETTLE GRASSLANDS In 2003 Five-Ridge
Prairie, The Nature Conservancy's Broken Kettle Grasslands, and neighboring private land were designated a Bird Conservation Area by the Iowa Department of Natural Resources. Encompassing nearly 24,500 acres of northern Loess Hills prairie and woodland, the area provides homes and nesting habitat for rare birds, as well as the state's remnant population of prairie rattlesnakes. The designation commits the site, along with two others in Iowa, to the conservation and creation of habitat for diverse wildlife populations.

New Jersey tea, skeleton weed, prairie violet, silky aster, and rough blazing star can be found blooming through the summer. Here in the high and dry northern Loess Hills, twenty-five typically western organisms are at the very edge of their eastern range. Cut-leaf iron plant, yucca, plains muhly, blue grama, plains pocket mouse, northern grasshopper mouse, western kingbird, and blue grosbeak are a few of these species better known in the West.

Prairie makes up only half the preserve, and the bur oak woodlands in the valleys are just as impressive as the ridges they divide. Wide-stretching bur oaks towering above spring wildflower displays are a stunning sight. During summer look for such woodland birds as yellow- and black-billed cuckoos, indigo bunting, scarlet tanager, Bell's vireo, and ovenbird.

The Nature Conservancy's efforts to preserve tracts of land in the Loess Hills are extremely noticeable here, where from most of the ridges you can see only conserved land. Regal fritillary butterflies, obligates of prairie violets, have slowly been making a comeback in many preserved areas of the Loess Hills. On a tract of land close to Five-Ridge, hundreds of such butterflies were found in one survey, reflecting their population growth as efforts intensify to preserve their habitat.

Miles and Directions

0.0 Start at the parking area at the end of 260th Avenue; walk through the gate onto the access road.

0.3 At the first fork take the left (south) road.

1.0 At the fork, turn left; you'll be walking directly south.

2.0 Walk north, climbing onto the finger ridge.

3.0 At the fork turn left (southwest). **Bailout:** Take the right fork and loop back to the parking lot without checking out the southwest corner of the preserve.

4.0 Reach the southern boundary of the preserve and backtrack to the last fork.

4.8 Arrive back at the fork and take a left (north).

5.5 Arrive at the northern boundary of the preserve; turn right (south) onto the ridge.

6.2 At the fork (back at the main access road), turn left (east).

6.9 At the fork turn left (north) to explore the easternmost ridge in the park. **Bailout:** turn right to continue back to the parking lot.

7.3 At the fork turn right (east) to complete the loop back down to the access road.

8.0 Arrive at main access road; turn left (east) for a jaunt up the hill to the parking area.

8.3 Arrive back at the trailhead.

Hike Information

Local Information

LeMars; www.lemarsiowa.com

Siouxland Chamber of Commerce, Sioux City; (712) 255-7903, www.siouxlandchamber.com

Sioux City; www.downtownsiouxcity.com/

Events/Attractions

Ice Cream Capital of the World Visitor Center, 16 Fifth Avenue NW, LeMars; (712) 546-4090, www.bluebunny.com

LeMars Area Farmers' Market, Bomgaars parking lot, U.S. Highway 75 South, LeMars; (712) 546-8821; July through September, Saturday 8:00 A.M. to noon

Accommodations

Oak Grove Park and Big Sioux Park (Sioux County Conservation Board), 7 miles north of Hawarden; (712) 552-1047

Rose Hill B&B, 1602 Douglas Street, Sioux City; (712) 258-8678

English Mansion B&B, 1525 Douglas Street, Sioux City; (712) 277-1386

Stone State Park Campground; (712) 255-4698

Hillview Recreation Area (Plymouth County Conservation Board), 1 mile west of Hinton; (712) 947-4270

Restaurants

Lally's Eastside Cafe, 125 Plymouth Street, LeMars; (712) 546-4406

Mr. P's Pizza, 122 Plymouth Street, LeMars; (712) 546-8777

Other Resources

Broken Kettle Nature Center, The Nature Conservancy; www.nature.org

Golden Hills Resource Conservation and Development; www.goldenhillsrcd.org

Loess Hills Audubon Society; www.lhas.org

Fragile Giants: A Natural History of the Loess Hills by Cornelia Mutel (Bur Oak Books Series, University of Iowa Press)

Land of the Fragile Giants: Landscapes, Environments, and Peoples of the Loess Hills edited by Cornelia Mutel and Mary Swander (Bur Oak Books Series, University of Iowa Press)

A Tallgrass Prairie Alphabet children's book by Claudia McGehee (Bur Oak Books Series, University of Iowa Press)

The Iowa Breeding Bird Atlas by Laura Spess Jackson, Carol A. Thompson, and James J. Dinsmore (Bur Oak Books Series, University of Iowa Press)

The Guide to Iowa's State Preserves by Ruth Herzberg and John Pearson (Bur Oaks Books Series, University of Iowa Press)

An Illustrated Guide to Iowa Prairie Plants by Paul Christiansen and Mark Muller (Bur Oak Books Series, University of Iowa Press)

36 Stone State Park

Designated as an "urban wildlife sanctuary," Stone State Park seems so removed from the city that once you're hiking up Mount Lucia, you won't believe you're within Sioux City limits. A 9.2-mile loop around the park leads up dark, forested hollows to prairie-covered hilltops overlooking the Missouri and Big Sioux Rivers. The Dorothy Pecaut Nature Center, located in the southwest corner of the park, houses natural history exhibits and another 2.0 miles of trails.

Distance: 9.2-mile round-trip or much shorter loops
Approximate hiking time: 3 to 5 hours
Total elevation gain: 1,278 feet
Trail surface: Mowed paths, small footpaths
Seasons: Year-round
Trail users: Hikers, mountain bikers, equestrians
Canine compatability: Dogs permitted on leash
Hazards: Poison ivy, ticks
Land status: State park

Nearest town: Sioux City
Fees and permits: No fees or permits required
Schedule: Open year-round, 4:00 A.M. to 10:30 P.M.
Map: USGS quad: Sioux City North
Trail contact: Stone State Park, 5001 Talbot Road, Sioux City; (712) 255-4698, www .state.ia.us/dnr/organiza/ppd/stone.htm; Dorothy Pecaut Nature Center, (712) 258-0838

Finding the trailhead: From Interstate 29, take exit 151 (toward Riverside) and head north on Highway 12 through Riverside. Three miles north of town you'll see a sign for Dorothy Pecaut Nature Center; turn right (east) here to explore the nature center first, or continue 0.1 mile and turn right (east) onto Stone State Park Road, which bisects the park. *DeLorme: Iowa Atlas and Gazetteer:* Page 24 F3

The Hike

Beginning in the 1880s, Daniel Talbot, a lawyer and amateur naturalist in Sioux City, acquired 7,500 acres along the Big Sioux River in Woodbury and Plymouth Counties. He grew crops and grazed livestock and raised a plethora of exotic animals. When Talbot ran into financial problems, Sioux City banker Thomas Stone, assumed Talbot's debt and the land. Stone's family deeded the land to the city in 1912, but it was transferred to the state soon after and became a state park in 1935. In 1989 ninety acres on the north side of the property were designated a state preserve for its diverse prairie ridgetops and butterfly species.

Historical accounts of Stone State Park and adjacent Mount Talbot State Preserve from the 1800s describe the hills as being almost treeless, covered in billowing prairies. Today the endless prairies have been whittled down to south- and west-facing ridgetops. Although the prairie is diminished in size, you'll still find incredible diversity within the remnants. During May and June look for large-

Eastern tiger swallowtails are frequent visitors to Stone State Park.

flowered beardtongue, prairie larkspur, and prairie turnip. Both big and little bluestem serve as caterpillar hosts for crossline, dusted, and Ottoe skippers, aptly named for their bouncing flight.

Along Highway 12, between the turnoffs for the Dorothy Pecaut Nature Center and Stone State Park, you'll find some of the few exposures of bedrock in the Loess Hills. The Missouri River southward bend cut deeply into the hills on the east side of the floodplain. In the ninety-million-year-old Cretaceous bedrock you'll see dark bands of lignite and iron oxide staining amid limestone, sandstone, and shale. Fossils of both marine and land-dwelling organisms have been found here, testament to the shifting shoreline of a shallow sea that once covered the Midwest.

The Dorothy Pecaut Nature Center is located in the extreme southwest corner of the state park and can be hiked to from Mount Lucia. You'll find stellar natural history exhibits and another 2.0 miles of trails. The nature center is the perfect place to bring a troop of kids on a summer afternoon. They'll delight in the indoor beehive and walk-under prairie and expend their energy on the short but satisfying trails.

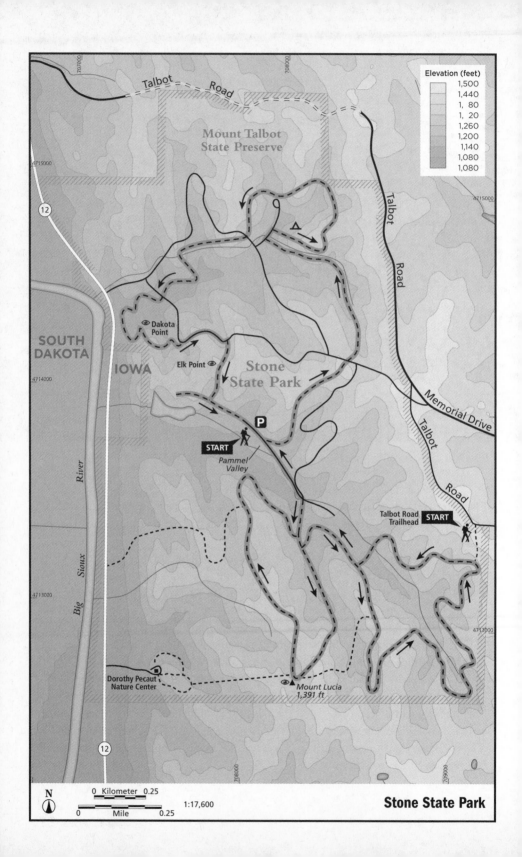

Elevation (feet)
1,500
1,440
1, 80
1, 20
1,260
1,200
1,140
1,080
1,080

Talbot — Road

Mount Talbot State Preserve

Talbot Road

12

SOUTH DAKOTA

IOWA

Dakota Point

Elk Point

Stone State Park

Memorial Drive

Talbot Road

P

START

Pammel Valley

Talbot Road Trailhead **START**

River

Big Sioux

Dorothy Pecaut Nature Center

Mount Lucia 1,391 ft

12

N

Kilometer
0   0.25

1:17,600

Mile
0   0.25

Stone State Park

A 9.2-mile loop around the entire park can be made by starting at the shelter at Pammel Valley. Follow the trail northeast, cross the road, and continue past the park office toward the campground. Continue on the trail leading to the Carolyn Benne Nature Trail, named for the local environmental educator who started the Loess Hills Prairie Seminar. This trail connects with the path that leads past Stone Lodge (built of Sioux quartzite from Gitchie Manitou State Preserve) and through Dakota Valley up to Dakota Point. From this overlook you can look west to Nebraska and South Dakota and see the Missouri and Big Sioux Rivers as well. Here you'll have to road-hike for a short jaunt up to Elk Point, another scenic lookout. A small trail heads south, back down to Pammel Valley, passing a small lake along the way. Follow the road up to just before the shelter, where a trail heads south toward Mount Lucia. You can follow it directly up to the summit or take an out-and-back trail to Highway 12 to view the Cretaceous bedrock. Continue back and follow the Mount Lucia ridge over to Ruth's Ridge and toward the Talbot Road parking area. Instead of going up the hill to the parking area, take a left (west) to head back to the main trail. You'll end up back at the Mount Lucia trailhead, where you can walk west down the road to end up back at the Pammel Valley parking lot.

Miles and Directions

0.0   Start at the Pammell Valley Shelter.

0.5   Cross the road; walk past the park office, and continue north on the trail.

1.0   Arrive at campground; walk north up the ridge to connect with the Carolyn Benne Nature Trail.

1.8   Cross the road; continue down into Dakota Valley.

2.7   Arrive at Dakota Point; road-hike eastward to Elk Point.

3.0   Arrive at Elk Point; look for the trail heading directly south down the ridge toward the lake.

3.4   Arrive at lake and shelter; the trailhead lies directly east of here.

3.6   Arrive back at the Pammel Valley trailhead. **Bailout:** Stop here or continue on the southern trails by walking east up the road to the Mount Lucia trailhead.

4.0   Before you get to the shelter, turn right (south) onto Mount Lucia trail.

4.6   You're atop Mount Lucia, 1,391 feet.

5.4   At the fork turn right (north). **Option:** Take a 1.4-mile out-and-back hike out to the Cretaceous bedrock exposures overlooking the Big Sioux River on the west side of the park.

5.8   Cross the Mount Lucia Trail. **Option:** Turning left (north) here will take you back to the trailhead. Continue on the right (east) to add 3.5 miles to your total, climbing up and over Ruth's Ridge and passing the Tabor Road trailhead before returning to Pammel Valley.

8.6   Arrive back at Mount Lucia Trail; turn right (north) to reach the trailhead. At the road turn left (west) for a quick walk back to the Pammel Valley parking area.

9.2   Arrive back at trailhead.

Hike Information

Local Information

Siouxland Chamber of Commerce, Sioux City; (712) 255-7903, www.siouxlandchamber.com
Sioux City; www.downtownsiouxcity.com/

Events/Attractions

Lewis and Clark Interpretive Center, 900 Larsen Park Road; (712) 224-5242, www.siouxlandchamber.com/lewis_clark/interpretive_center.cfm
Awesome Harley Nights, weekend in June, Fourth Street, Sioux City; (712) 224-2759, www.awesomeharleynights.com
Orpheum Theatre, 528 Pierce Street, Sioux City; (712) 258-9164
Siouxland Farmers' Market, Corner of Fourth and Floyd Streets, Sioux City; (712) 252-0014; May through October, daily 8:00 A.M. to noon

Accommodations

Rose Hill B&B, 1602 Douglas Street, Sioux City; (712) 258-8678
English Mansion B&B, 1525 Douglas Street, Sioux City; (712) 277-1386
Stone State Park Campground; (712) 255-4698

Hillview Recreation Area (Plymouth County Conservation Board), 1 mile west of Hinton; (712) 947-4270

Restaurants

Daily Grind, 511 Fifth Street, Sioux City; (712) 277-2020
Buffalo Alice, 1022 Fourth Street, Sioux City; (712) 255-4822
Marty's Tavern, 1306 Court Street, Sioux City; (712) 277-9568

Other Resources

The Book People, 2901 Hamilton Boulevard, Sioux City
Loess Hills Audubon Society; www.lhas.org
Fragile Giants: A Natural History of the Loess Hills by Cornelia Mutel (Bur Oak Books Series, University of Iowa Press)
Land of the Fragile Giants: Landscapes, Environments, and Peoples of the Loess Hills edited by Cornelia Mutel and Mary Swander (Bur Oak Books Series, University of Iowa Press)

37 Loess Hills Wildlife Management Area– Sylvan Runkel State Preserve

There's good reason this is home to the Loess Hills Prairie Seminar: These two preserved areas encompass some of the most incredible terrain for hiking and naturalizing in western Iowa. From your ridgetop perch, billowing bunchgrasses and prairie wildflowers of every hue encircle you. Dramatic, forest-covered hills extend to the south and east. To the west the wrinkled hills plummet down to a patchwork quilt of agricultural fields in the Little Sioux and Missouri floodplains.

Distance: 12.4 miles round-trip or shorter loops
Approximate hiking time: 4 to 6 hours
Total elevation gain: 1,172 feet
Trail surface: Mowed forest trails, small ridgeline footpaths
Seasons: Year-round; July through September best for prairie watching
Trail users: Hikers, hunters
Canine compatability: Dogs permitted
Hazards: Poison ivy, ticks, sunburn on exposed ridges

Land status: State preserve within a wildlife management area
Nearest town: Onawa
Fees and permits: No fees or permits required
Schedule: Open year-round
Map: USGS quad: Castana
Trail contact: Iowa Department of Natural Resources, Missouri River Wildlife Unit, RR 2, Box 15A, Onawa, IA 51040; (712) 423-2426

Finding the trailhead: From Interstate 29 take exit 112 (Onawa and Lewis and Clark State Park), and drive east on Highway 175 through Onawa. To reach the 205th Street parking area, continue on Highway 175 to Turin and turn left (north) onto Larpenteur Memorial Road. Turn right (northeast) onto 205th Street, and look for a small parking area on the north side of the road.

To reach the 178th Street and Oak Avenue parking areas, just as you drive out of town on Highway 175, turn left (north) onto County Road L12. Turn right (northeast) onto Nutmeg Avenue and cross over the Little Sioux River, taking an immediate right (south) onto 178th Street. Follow this to the parking areas at the corner of 178th Street and Oak Avenue. *DeLorme: Iowa Atlas and Gazetteer:* Page 36 C2

The Hike

Originally acquired by the state in 1973, the 3,000-acre Loess Hills Wildlife Area was selected by the National Park System to be part of a 10,420-acre national natural landmark in 1985. In 1996 a 330-acre parcel of high-quality prairie in the area's northwestern corner was designated as the Sylvan Runkel State Preserve, commemorating one of the most respected naturalists to ever walk the Loess Hills. Sylvan Runkel's reverence for natural communities and ability to captivate audiences

Looking south from the Sylvan Runkel State Preserve to the Loess Hills Wildlife Management Area.

with his natural history teachings inspired the masses he connected with. Along with his many modes of conservation-oriented work, he was a cherished presenter at the Loess Hills Prairie Seminar until his death in 1995.

The one trail within the preserve follows the narrow, branching ridgeline covered with tall- and mixed-grass prairie. From atop a high point along the ridge, notice that woodlands thrive on the moist north- and east-facing slopes. Though the preserve is dominated by prairie, colonizing shrubs such as eastern red cedar, rough-leaved dogwood, and sumac climb up the ravines, which are soon invaded by woodlands.

Looking at the hills on private land to the north of the preserve, note the terraced "catsteps," virtual staircases leading down the hills. These were created by loess's tendency toward slipping and slumping and were probably exacerbated by grazing cattle.

If you've visited native prairies throughout spring and summer, you know that the height of prairie plants usually depends on when they bloom. In early spring, when aboveground vegetation hasn't had much of a chance to grow, blooming flowers don't need to be very tall to collect sunlight or be pollinated. The opposite occurs in autumn, when bunchgrasses and goldenrod are head-high, competing for sunlight and pollinators.

Pasqueflower is the first wildflower you'll see blooming, dotting the hillsides with shades of violet soon after the snow has melted. Take this time to look for the small soil lichens, hidden by tall vegetation during summer. Get down on your hands and knees to peer closely at the ground. Small, multicolored discs start coming into view. Spend a short time looking, and you'll begin to find the interlocking patterns of lichens colonizing the interface between earth and sky.

By May a very tiny fern named prairie moonwort (*Boytrichium campestre*) shoots up its fragile 2 -to 3- inch-tall fiddleheads, which sporulate and disappear by early June. First discovered by Loess Hills Prairie Seminar attendees in 1982, prairie moonwort has since been found in several other Loess Hills locales, as well as in Minnesota and Nebraska.

To the south and east of Sylvan Runkel State Preserve, you'll find the more extensively forested Loess Hills Wildlife Area. Wide-spreading bur oaks intermingle with Kentucky coffee trees, American and slippery elms, white ash, and bitternut hickory. Two trails leave the parking lot: One leads to the west to explore a cool hollow; the other heads directly south onto a ridge loop.

To explore the preserve and wildlife area in one big loop, park at the southernmost access point, north of 205th Street. The trail will take you onto a ridge that leads to the main ridge loop trail in the wildlife area. Follow this down to the parking area, and turn right (northeast) onto 178th Avenue, which immediately intersects with Oak Avenue. You'll see a parking area on the east side of Oak Avenue and a brown state preserve sign on the west side. The ridge you want to get onto lies directly behind (north of) the sign, and a small trail leads up to it. Follow the ridges to the northwesternmost point in the preserve and turn back, taking the opposite side of the main ridge loop trail on your way back through the wildlife area.

LOESS HILLS PRAIRIE SEMINAR Attending the Loess Hills Prairie Seminar, held annually for thirty years, is the best way to acquaint yourself with the natural communities of the region and the people who understand and appreciate them most. For three days in early June, participants camp out in Loess Hills Wildlife Area and attend workshops and nature hikes on archaeology, biology, ecology, conservation, geology, and a variety of related topics. The seminar is open to people of all ages and interests, and it's entirely worth the trip. Western Hills Area Education Agency: (712) 274-6000, www.aea12.k12.ia.us/services/loesshillsseminar/welcome.html.

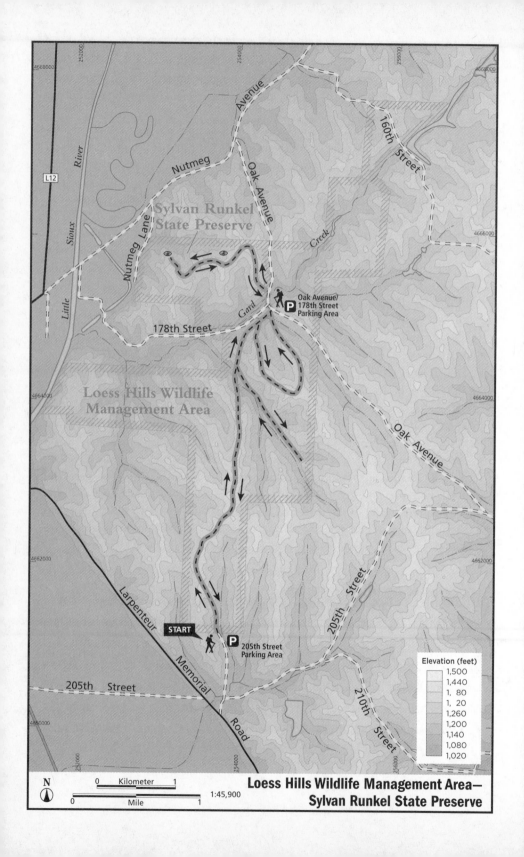

L12

Sioux

River

Little

Nutmeg

Nutmeg Lane

Avenue

Oak Avenue

Creek

160th Street

Sylvan Runkel
State Preserve

Oak Avenue/
178th Street
Parking Area

P

178th Street

Gard

Loess Hills Wildlife
Management Area

4668000

4666000

4664000

4662000

4660000

Oak Avenue

205th Street

Larpenteur

START

P

205th Street
Parking Area

Memorial

Road

210th Street

205th Street

Elevation (feet)
1,500
1,440
1, 80
1, 20
1,260
1,200
1,140
1,080
1,020

N

0   Kilometer   1

0   Mile   1

1:45,900

**Loess Hills Wildlife Management Area—
Sylvan Runkel State Preserve**

Miles and Directions

0.0 Start at the trailhead off 205th Street. Walk north on the trail, climbing to the ridge.

2.2 The trail forks; take a right (southeast) to explore the hollow.

3.1 Arrive at the southeast boundary of the wildlife management area; backtrack to the fork.

4.0 Back at the fork, turn right (north).

4.9 As you near the 178th Street parking lot, a finger ridge to the south of the parking lot will take you up for the ridge loop.

6.5 Arrive back on the main trail west of the parking area; continue northeast to the 178th Street parking area.

6.7 At 178th Street walk east toward the junction with Oak Avenue, where you'll take a left (north). You'll see another parking lot on the east side of the road. Directly across (west) the road from the parking area is a brown SYLVAN RUNKEL STATE PRESERVE sign. Hop off the road and walk past the sign to the small trail that leads up the finger ridge directly north of the sign.

8.2 Arrive at the summit of the westernmost ridge in Sylvan Runkel State Preserve. Backtrack along the ridges all the way back to the 178th Street parking lot.

9.6 Arrive back at the 178th Street parking lot. Walk west on the trail, taking the right fork (the left would take you back up the hollow) up to the ridgeline and back to the 205th Street parking lot.

12.4 Arrive back at the trailhead.

Hike Information

Local Information
Onawa; www.onawa.com/index1.htm

Events/Attractions
Battle Hills Museum of Natural History, Highway 175 East, Battle Creek; (712) 365-4414

Monona County Arboretum, 318 East Iowa Avenue, Moorhead; (712) 423-2400

Loess Hills Prairie Seminar, Western Hills Area Education Agency; (712) 274-6000, www .aea12.k12.ia.us/services/loesshillsseminar/ welcome.html

Onabike, bike ride through the Loess Hills, August, Onawa; (712) 423-1801, www .onawa.com/index1.htm

Accommodations
The Country Homestead B&B, 22133 Larpenteur Road, Turin; (712) 353-6772

Dormitory Inn, 130 Fourth Street, Castana; (712) 353-6797

Loess Hills Wildlife Management Area; primitive camping allowed on-site

Preparation Canyon State Park; primitive backpack campsites; (712) 423-2829, www .iowadnr.com/parks/state_park_list/ preparation_canyon.html

Restaurants
Onawa Cafe, 811 Iowa Avenue, Onawa; (712) 423-3233

O'Neill's Tavern, 1034 Eighth Street, Onawa; (712) 423-1043

Other Resources
Loess Hills Prairie Seminar (Western Hills Area Education Agency–Sioux City); www.aea12 .k12.ia.us/services/loesshillsseminar/ welcome.html

Loess Hills Audubon Society; www.lhas.org

Sylvan T. Runkel, Citizen of the Natural World by Larry Stone and Jon Stravers (Turkey River Environmental Expressions)

Fragile Giants: A Natural History of the Loess Hills by Cornelia Mutel (Bur Oak Books Series, University of Iowa Press)
Land of the Fragile Giants: Landscapes, Environments, and Peoples of the Loess Hills, edited by Cornelia Mutel and Mary Swander (Bur Oak Books Series, University of Iowa Press)
A Tallgrass Prairie Alphabet, children's book by Claudia McGehee (Bur Oak Books Series, University of Iowa Press)

The Vascular Plants of Iowa: An Annotated Checklist and Natural History by Lawrence J. Eilers and Dean M. Roosa (Bur Oak Books Series, University of Iowa Press)
An Illustrated Guide to Iowa Prairie Plants by Paul Christiansen and Mark Muller (Bur Oak Books Series, University of Iowa Press)

38 Loess Hills State Forest

If you wish to explore the latest addition to Iowa's state forest system, you'll have to drive a little and walk a little—there are two trails with different trailheads. It's worth the short time spent in the car, however, for the loop trails you'll find follow ridgelines that abound with prairie remnants and then drop into valleys being replanted to forest, prairie, and food plots for wildlife. Nestled in the Loess Hills between the Soldier and Missouri Rivers, a large piece of important preserved habitat waits for your explorations.

Distance: Overlook Trail: 0.8-mile loop; Two-Ridges Trail: 4.8-mile loop
Approximate hiking time: 4 to 5 hours
Total elevation gain: Overlook Trail: 220 feet; Two-Ridges Trail: 775 feet
Trail surface: Dirt road, gravel road, worn footpath
Seasons: Year-round
Trail users: Hikers, equestrians
Canine compatability: Dogs permitted
Hazards: Poison ivy, ticks, sunburn on exposed ridges

Land status: State forest
Nearest towns: Pisgah, Moorhead
Fees and permits: No fees or permits required
Schedule: Year-round, 4:00 A.M. to 10:30 P.M.
Map: USGS quad: Moorhead NW
Trail contact: Loess Hills State Forest Visitors Center, 206 Polk Street, Pisgah; (712) 456-2924, www.iowadnr.com/forestry/loesshills.htm

Finding the trailhead: From Pisgah drive north on Highway 183 to 314th Street. Turn right (west) and follow the state forest signs to the overlook for the Overlook Trail. Turn left (south) onto County Road E60 to get to the Two-Ridges trailhead. *DeLorme: Iowa Atlas and Gazetteer:* Page 36 F2

Loess Hills Overlook is the best jumping-off point for exploring Loess Hills State Forest.

The Hike

In 1986 the National Park Service studied whether to establish a Loess Hills National Park, but because 95 percent of the hills are privately owned, it wasn't feasible. Instead, the Park Service designated two areas in Harrison and Monona Counties as national natural landmarks.

State and county agencies were left with the major responsibility of protecting and managing the future of this uniquely Iowan treasure. When state lottery monies became available through REAP grants in the late 1980s, the Department of Natural Resources began acquiring land and established this state forest. One day, it is hoped, the parcel will encompass 20,000 acres of Loess Hills land. Thus far the forest includes 10,600 acres purchased by the DNR. Six hundred acres have replanted to red and white oaks, green and white ashes, and black walnut; and 250 acres have been replanted to native prairie. Eight hundred acres are burned annually, and invasive woodlands are cut down.

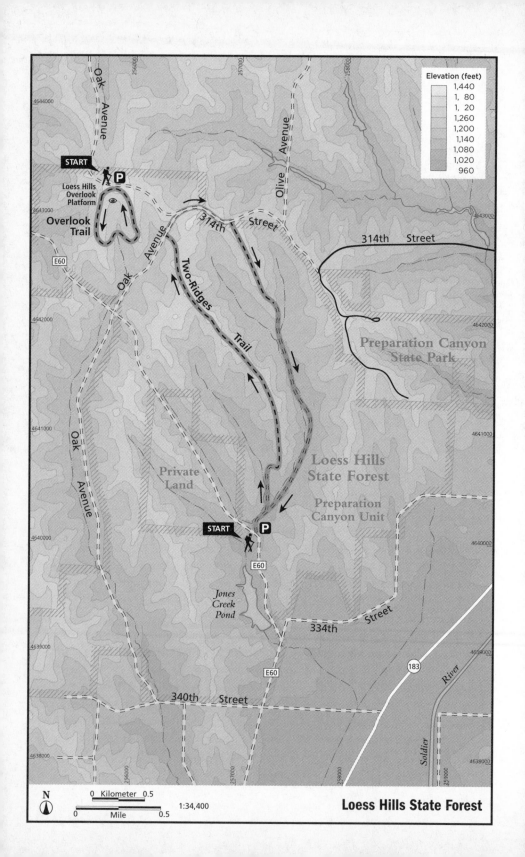

Elevation (feet)

	1,440
	1, 80
	1, 20
	1,260
	1,200
	1,140
	1,080
	1,020
	960

START

Loess Hills
Overlook
Platform

**Overlook
Trail**

E60

Oak Avenue

Two-Ridges

Trail

314th   Street

Olive   Avenue

314th   Street

Preparation Canyon
State Park

Private
Land

Loess Hills
State Forest

Preparation
Canyon Unit

START

P

E60

*Jones
Creek
Pond*

334th   Street

Oak   Avenue

340th   Street

E60

183

Soldier   *River*

N

0	Kilometer	0.5

| 0 | Mile | 0.5 |

1:34,400

Loess Hills State Forest

Start your tour of the forest with a visit to the overlook, located just off 314th Street at the north end of the Preparation Canyon Unit. The overlook is perched atop a prairie-covered finger ridge that extends southward toward the panorama of valleys and hilltops that make up the unit. A 0.75-mile loop trail follows the ridge south and drops down into a valley where attempts at prairie restoration are under way. Ascend the next ridge to the east, where the trail turns north, bringing you back up to the overlook. On either side of the ridges during summer, a spectrum of wild-flowers draws hundreds of nectar-seeking butterflies.

The second hike in the Preparation Canyon Unit is similar to the Overlook Trail. You'll head north on one ridge, road-hike east to the next, and follow it south back to the parking area.

From the overlook drive back down 314th Street and turn right (south) onto Oak Avenue. Then left (southeast) onto County Road E60; the parking area you're looking for is on the northeast side of the road, just across the road from the north side of Jones Creek Pond. Walk past the gate onto the gravel road that quickly splits into two dirt roads. Take the left fork that leads toward the west side of the ridge directly in front of you, which you'll quickly ascend and follow north.

The trail traverses the top of the ridge, which is dominated by prairie being encroached upon by bur oak woodlands from the east and groves of eastern red cedar from the west. At 1.0 mile you'll encounter roadcut in the ridge, leaving a gaping chasm between where you stand on the south side and where you want to get on the north. Follow a small gully on the east side of the trail down to the roadcut, and scramble up the other side.

When you reach the second roadcut, follow it left (west) and quickly turn right (north) onto a trail that will take you up to Oak Avenue. Turn right (north) onto Oak Avenue and follow to its intersection with 314th Street; turn right (east), road-hiking for another 0.4 mile.

You'll see the ridge you want to hop onto from the road, and there's an opening in the barbed-wire fence that leads up to the trail you'll follow south. After following the ridge for 1.5 miles, this trail will taper out at a steep gully where the ridge

WHAT ABOUT THE PRAIRIE?
When the idea to acquire land for Loess Hills State Forest was proposed, many responded with cynicism. The idea of a state forest in an area where prairies are being invaded by woodlands does seem somewhat ironic. In fact, there was a good deal of controversy over the establishment of the state forest because of the dueling principles of preserving forest and prairie in the Loess Hills. However, the management regime of Loess Hills State Forest reflects the need not only to plant and harvest trees but also to preserve the prairie remnants that remain and reconstruct more. There are 1,300 acres of native prairie (of the 10,600 acres) within the forest, managed by burns and some plantings.

seems to end. Just below you to the east is a dirt road between corn and soybean plantings and a line of cottonwood trees. You won't be able to see this road until you navigate the tangle of sumac downslope and emerge onto it. Walk south 0.5 mile back to the parking area.

A maze of mowed firebreaks and ridgetop trails in the Modamin Unit can be explored with intrepid motivation and the aid of a compass. Keep in mind that you're never far from a road; as long as you keep to the ridgetops, the vistas in every direction will help guide your movements.

Miles and Directions

0.0 Start at the parking area on the east side of CR E60, across from the northern tip of Jones Creek Pond. Walk through the gate and follow the dirt road to the northeast.

0.4 At the fork turn left (northwest). This trail will immediately switchback, ascending to the ridgetop.

1.0 Arrive at steep drop down to the roadcut. Descend in a gully on the right (east) side of the ridge and ascend the other side to continue the ridgetop walk.

1.9 Arrive at the second roadcut; turn left (west) onto the road and follow it down the west slope of the ridge.

2.0 At the fork turn right onto a small trail that will take you up to Oak Avenue.

2.1 Arrive at Oak Avenue; turn right (north) onto the road.

2.2 At the junction of Oak Avenue and 314th Street, turn right (east) onto 314th Street. As you walk, look to the south to examine the valley separating the two ridges you're exploring.

2.6 Be on the lookout for an opening in the barbed-wire fence as you approach the second ridge. If you miss the opening, keep focused on the idea that you need to get to the ridgetop—you'll find your way to the trail.

3.1 As the ridge tapers, walk down the east side of it to the dirt road that heads south along the base of the ridge. On your way back to the trailhead, you'll walk along the base of the first ridge you walked on as well.

4.3 At the fork turn left (south) back onto a small dirt road that will bring you back to the gate and trailhead.

4.8 Arrive back at the trailhead.

Hike Information

Local Information
Loess Hills State Forest Visitor Center, 206 Polk Street, Pisgah; (712) 456-2924

Events/Attractions
Small's Fruit Farm, 3 miles east of Mondamin; (712) 646-2723

Accommodations
Loess Hills Hideaway Cabins & Campground, 33774 Plum Avenue, Moorhead; (712) 886-5003
Preparation Canyon State Park; primitive backpack campsites; (712) 423-2829, www .iowadnr.com/parks/state_park_list/ preparation_canyon.html

Restaurants

Old Home Fill'er Up and Keep on Truckin' Cafe, Main Street, Pisgah; (712) 456–2727
Teri's Watering Hole, 101 Railroad Street, Moorhead; (712) 886–5111

Other Resources

Loess Hills Hospitality Association, 119 Oak Street, Moorhead; (712) 886–5441 or (800) 886–5441 (motor tour available)
Moorhead Cultural Center, 109 Oak Street, Moorhead; (712) 886–5284

Loess Hills Audubon Society; www.lhas.org
Fragile Giants: A Natural History of the Loess Hills by Cornelia Mutel (Bur Oak Books Series, University of Iowa Press)
Land of the Fragile Giants: Landscapes, Environments, and Peoples of the Loess Hills, edited by Cornelia Mutel and Mary Swander (Bur Oak Books Series, University of Iowa Press)

39 Preparation Canyon State Park

During the 1850s this valley was home to a group of Mormon settlers, who described it as their "school of preparation for the life beyond." Today it can be hiked in preparation for longer, steeper, more exhausting hikes in the neighboring Loess Hills State Forest and Loess Hills Wildlife Management Area. Trails that total 4.5 miles lead through cool hollows and ascend steep ridges that overlook the 3,000-acre tract of public land to the south and west. Eight hike-in campsites provide a welcome respite from state park camping often dominated by recreational vehicles.

Distance: 4.4 miles round-trip
Approximate hiking time: 1 to 2 hours for a loop around the park, but best as an overnight backpacking trip
Total elevation gain: 1,166 feet
Trail surface: Well-worn footpaths, mowed paths
Seasons: Year-round
Trail users: Hikers and cross-country skiers
Canine compatability: Dogs permitted on leash
Hazards: Poison ivy, ticks

Land status: State park
Nearest towns: Moorehead to the north, Pisgah to the south
Fees and permits: No fees or permits required
Schedule: Open year-round
Map: USGS quad: Moorhead NW
Trail contact: Preparation Canyon State Park, c/o Lewis & Clark State Park, 21914 Park Loop, Onawa, IA 51040; (712) 423–2829, www.iowadnr.com/parks/state_park_list/preparation_canyon.html

Finding the trailhead: From Interstate 29, take exit 95 (River Sioux and Little Sioux) and drive east on County Road F20. At Pisgah turn north onto Highway 183. To get to the backpacker's parking area, drive 5 miles north of Pisgah; you'll see a small turnoff with a state park sign. To get to the day-use area, drive past the backpacker's parking area and turn left (west) onto 314th Street. At the fork in the road, turn right (east) and follow the signs to parking area. *DeLorme: Iowa Atlas and Gazetteer:* Page 36 F2

The Hike

Though it may not be apparent at first, the current site of Preparation Canyon State Park was once a small town. As Mormon wagon trains crossed Iowa in 1853 toward Utah, a small group led by Charles B. Thompson broke off, settled in the present-day park, and named their town Preparation.

Later the local newspaper, which Thompson owned and published, ran a message from a spirit he called "Beneemy," who told townspeople to hand over their assets to Thompson, the self-proclaimed "Father Ephraim." After several years of Thompson's greed and poor leadership, the townspeople recognized the scam and threatened to hang him. Thompson narrowly escaped his disillusioned followers and fled the state. Most of the residents of Preparation continued on to settle in Utah, and in 1856 the Iowa Supreme Court divided the land among the remaining families. The town of Preparation slowly faded away, but several of the families remained, and the land for the park was donated by descendents of some of the original Mormon settlers.

All that's left of the town are the remnants of two houses and the successional grassland east of the creek, now choked with invasive plants because of previous cultivation. Here you'll find eastern kingbirds, eastern bluebirds, and northern rough-winged swallows flying and foraging, while turkey vultures swirl in the skies overhead. Bell's vireos can be found in the scrubby, brushy edges; listen for their *tweedle-deedle-dum? tweedle-deedle-dee!* From the highest hill in the northeast corner of the park, look south and east for a sweeping view of the Soldier River Valley.

As you descend westward to the creek, you'll pass through a grove of gnarled bur oaks with many branches and broad canopies. The spacing and wide canopies of the trees and the understory of grasses, sedges, and shrubs suggest that at one time this may have been an oak-savanna. Historically, frequent prairie fires would have nourished the savanna by holding shrub growth in check and stimulating the bur oaks to vigorously resprout. Suppression of fire has drastically altered much of the Loess Hills oak savannas by allowing the shrubs to take over. Today you can look for a hint of times past in the overarching branches of our state tree.

Follow the trail over the small creek and up into the forested hills that cover the western three-quarters of the park. The steep grade of the hills may tire you—as soon as you've climbed to a ridgetop, the trail immediately plunges into another hollow. You'll run into fox squirrels munching acorns or pumping their tails and squeaking defensively at your presence. Look for other common forest-dwelling mammals such as woodchuck, white-tailed deer, and red fox. During summer, rose-breasted grosbeaks, scarlet tanagers, and northern orioles can be seen flitting among the trees.

◀ *Gnarly bur oaks hang over the steep trails of Preparation Canyon.*

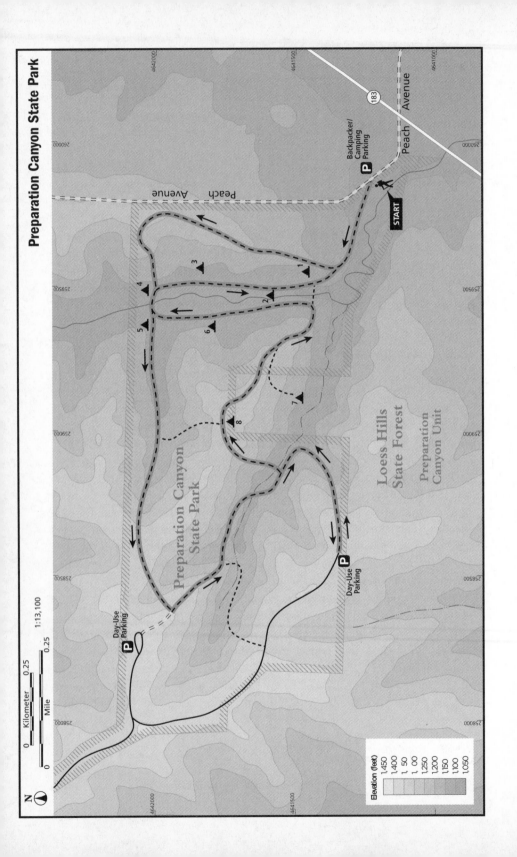

Preparation Canyon State Park

Elevation (feet)
- 1,450
- 1,400
- 1,350
- 1,300
- 1,250
- 1,200
- 1,150
- 1,100
- 1,050

N

1:13,100

Kilometer 0 0.25
Mile 0 0.25

Peach Avenue

Backpacker/
Camping
Parking

183

START

Preparation Canyon
State Park

Loess Hills
State Forest

Preparation
Canyon Unit

Day-Use
Parking

Day-Use
Parking

Eight hike-in campsites (noted by numbers on the map) are nestled along the creek and on ridgetops, each with a fire pit and picnic table. Of the two parking areas in the park, the westernmost is for day-use only; the easternmost is for campers. The Preparation Canyon Unit of Loess Hills State Forest borders the state park on the south and west sides and can be explored by using one of the campsites as a base camp.

Miles and Directions

0.0 Start at the trailhead off Highway 183 (Peach Avenue), and start walking up the creek on the main trail.

0.2 At the fork take the right trail, which climbs up the ridge in the northeast corner of the park.

0.9 After you've descended from the ridge, cross the creek and continue directly west up the hollow.

1.6 Arrive at one of the day-use areas; continue on the trail that leads to the southeast.

1.8 At the fork take the left (east) trail.

2.1 At the fork take right (south) trail.

2.5 Arrive at the second day-use area and backtrack to the fork.

2.9 At the fork take the right (east) trail.

3.5 Arrive back at the creek and take the left (north) fork.

3.9 Cross the creek and turn right (south) onto the trail that follows the creek along its east side.

4.4 Arrive back at the main trail, just west of the trailhead and parking area. You've completed the circuit and can take another loop or find a campsite.

Hike Information

Local Information
Loess Hills State Forest Visitors Center, 206 Polk Street, Pisgah; (712) 456-2924

Events/Attractions
Small's Fruit Farm, 3 miles east of Mondamin; (712) 646-2723

Accommodations
Loess Hills Hideaway Cabins & Campground, 33774 Plum Avenue, Moorhead; (712) 886-5003
Preparation Canyon State Park; free on-site camping

Restaurants
Old Home Fill'er Up and Keep on Truckin' Cafe, Main Street, Pisgah; (712) 456-2727
Teri's Watering Hole, 101 Railroad Street, Moorhead; (712) 886-5111

Other Resources
Loess Hills Hospitality Association, 119 Oak Street, Moorhead; (712) 886-5441 or (800) 886-5441 (motor tour available)
Moorehead Cultural Center, 109 Oak Street, Moorhead; (712) 886-5284
Loess Hills Audubon Society; www.lhas.org
Fragile Giants: A Natural History of the Loess Hills by Cornelia Mutel (Bur Oak Books Series, University of Iowa Press)
Land of the Fragile Giants: Landscapes, Environments, and Peoples of the Loess Hills, edited by Cornelia Mutel and Mary Swander (Bur Oak Books Series, University of Iowa Press)

MIGRATION ALONG THE MISSOURI As the snow goose flies, DeSoto National Wildlife Refuge lies only 30 miles to the southwest of Preparation Canyon State Park—and fly they do. During fall an estimated half million snow geese, along with upwards of 75,000 ducks, stop at DeSoto on migration from their summer breeding grounds in the north to Gulf Coast wintering areas. DeSoto National Wildlife Refuge, located on an oxbow of the Missouri River, is best visited during spring or fall for migration viewing.

40 Hitchcock Nature Area

Just twenty minutes northeast of the Council Bluffs–Omaha area, this new park will enchant you. Trails wind through restored prairie and dark hollows, then climb steep loess bluffs to the ridgelines for a fabulous view. Each fall, Hawkwatch International holds a count from the lodge, from which thousands of raptors can be seen. Summer wildflowers on the ridgetop prairies are especially pretty, and two hike-in campsites make the area a perfect overnight destination.

Distance: 6.4 miles round-trip
Approximate hiking time: 3 to 4 hours, but best as an overnight trip
Total elevation gain: 1,075 feet
Trail surface: Brush-cut paths through forest, mowed swaths through prairie, small ridgeline footpaths; 0.25-mile-long wooden boardwalk ends in a huge observation deck with picnic tables
Seasons: Year-round; ridgetop prairies bloom during midsummer; the Hitchcock Hawkwatch is September through December
Trail users: Hikers

Canine compatability: Dogs permitted on leash
Hazards: Poison ivy, ticks, sunburn on exposed ridges
Land status: Pottawattamie County Conservation Board park
Nearest towns: Crescent (gas only), Council Bluffs (more amenities)
Fees and permits: $2.00 per vehicle per day; $10.00 annual permit
Schedule: Open year-round, 6:00 A.M. to 10:00 P.M.
Map: USGS quad: Honey Creek
Trail contact: Hitchcock Nature Area; (712) 545-3283, www.pottcounty.com/html/departments7a.shtml#Hitchcock

Finding the trailhead: From Interstate 29 take exit 61 (Crescent) and drive east on Highway 988 to the town of Crescent. In Crescent turn north onto Old Lincoln Highway (Highway 183). Turn left (west) onto Page Lane, and then make a quick right (north) onto Ski Hill Loop. Follow the nature center signs to the trailhead parking. *DeLorme: Iowa Atlas and Gazetteer:* Page 46 D3

Bur oak and sunset from the Hitchcock's Westridge Trail.

The Hike

A twenty-minute drive from downtown Omaha, Hitchcock Nature Area lies directly beneath the flight path of the city's airport and within earshot of trains thundering down the tracks at the park's western edge. With these urban reminders screaming at you from every direction, it might seem hard to believe that a hike in Hitchcock could be anything close to a wilderness experience. Before making up your mind, spend one night at either Cottonwood or High Point campsite. As the sun fades into the western horizon, ridgetop prairie grasses shine a brilliant amber in the light, a bobcat screams, the barred owl calls, and it's as though the nearby city didn't even exist.

To truly appreciate the vista from your campsite, you should first wear yourself out as much as possible. Walk the innumerable trails to fully understand how steep the slope gradients of these central Loess Hills can be. The Dozer Cut Trail takes you into two valleys being replanted to prairie and native woodlands after having been bulldozed by previous landowners. Many of the southwest-facing ridges in the 806-

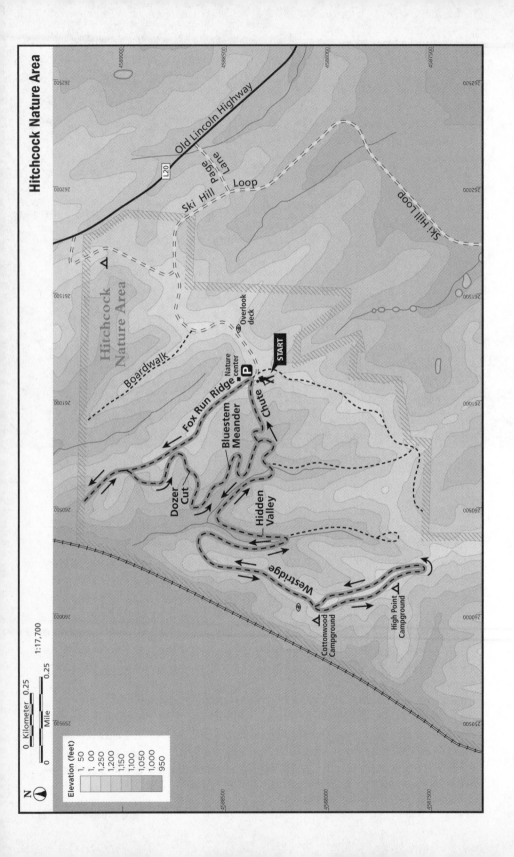

acre preserve are covered in native prairie plants, such as purple prairie clover, lead-plant, skeleton plant, whorled milkweed, and ground plum. Follow Bluestem Mean-der over to Hidden Valley Trail, which has been taken over by invasive garlic mustard. You'll find a number of sulphur and swallowtail butterflies there in the hollow before you make the final haul up to Westridge Trail and Hitchcock's two campsites. Each campsite—Cottonwood to the north and High Point to the south—has a fire pit and a spectacular view.

From above, you'll notice the encroachment of "woodland creep" on the hilltop prairies. Below, forests in the drainages are dominated by bur oak, hackberry, green ash, and red oak, with sumac and dogwood pushing out the edge onto the prairie. Reintroduction of fire into the preserve has slowed the shrub creep and has been a saving grace for many plants and prairie-dependent animals. In recent decades it has become evident that the Loess Hills' unique ecosystems are imperiled. Restoration projects at Hitchcock, such as prescribed burns and plantings, are critical to the con-tinuation of this incomparable landform. Equally important is the preservation of large tracts of land; fragmentation of the hills has contributed to the loss of habitat and species.

The Missouri River floodplain has always served as a migrational corridor for thousands of ducks and geese that arrive in spring on their way north. From mid-September to mid-December, cold fronts and winter weather in northern breeding grounds push the birds south in large groups. This southward movement, viewed from the Hitchcock Lodge, can be just as impressive as the springtime migration.

In the preserve you may see birds rarely observed in Iowa, including prairie fal-con, merlin, black vulture, northern goshawk, and ferruginous hawk. Hitchcock Hawkwatch, associated with the Hawk Migration Association of North America, is held each fall to monitor the vast numbers of raptors that travel the Missouri River Valley "hawk highway." Around twenty species of raptors/vultures are seen every year, with the 2004 total surpassing 11,000 birds.

In 1990 a landfill proposal on the site of the present-day Hitchcock Nature Area prompted a local citizens' group to take action to preserve the area. With help from the Iowa Natural Heritage Foundation and a Resource Enhancement and Protec-tion (REAP) grant from the state, the Pottawattamie County Conservation Board assumed ownership of the area in 1991. Thank goodness for those folks!

Miles and Directions

0.0 Start from next to the kiosk and the lodge. Walk down Fox Run Ridge Trail (this becomes the Dozer Cut North for a short while as it navigates to the northwest corner of the pre-serve).

0.9 Once you've reached the property line (gate) backtrack to the last fork.

1.0 At the fork turn right (southwest) onto Dozer Cut South.

1.6 At the fork turn left (southeast) onto the Bluestem Meander, following the zigzags.

2.5 Arrive at T-intersection with Hidden Valley Trail. Turn right (northeast) to ascend to the Westridge campsites. **Option:** Turn left (south) to connect to the Badger Run Ridge Trail to return to the trailhead, or add 1.0 mile out and back via the group campsite.

3.0 Take the right fork onto Westridge Trail for a longer, steeper climb to the campsites. **Option:** Take the left fork to connect to the Shortcut Trail.

3.8 Taking the longer route, climb up the steep hills to Westridge and arrive at Cottonwood campsite.

4.1 Arrive at the High Point campsite.

4.3 Arrive at the southern boundary of the park and loop back around; the trail loops around and leads you north, just east and downslope of Westridge Trail.

4.7 Arrive back at Westridge Trail, just north of Cottonwood campsite. Set up camp if you're staying over, or backtrack down to Hidden Valley to return to the trailhead. (FYI: The sunset from the Westridge campsites is something all Iowans should experience).

6.1 Arrive at a fork; turn left (north) onto Bluestem Meander.

6.3 At the fork take a right (east) onto the "Chute," which will take you back up to the trailhead.

6.4 Arrive back at the trailhead.

Hike Information

Local Information

Council Bluffs Conventions and Visitors Bureau; (800) 228-6878, www .councilbluffsiowa.com

Events/Attractions

DeSoto National Wildlife Refuge; (712) 642-4121, http://midwest.fws.gov/desoto/dsotobro.html

Acorn Supply, Saturday afternoon music, 329 Sixteenth Street, Council Bluffs; (712) 325-9282

Union Pacific Railroad Museum, 200 Pearl Street, Council Bluffs; (712) 329-8307

Western Historic Trails Center, 3434 Richard Downing Avenue, Council Bluffs; (712) 366-4900, www.iowahistory.org/sites/western_trails/western_trails.html

Mount Crescent Ski Area; (712) 545-3850

Wabash Trace Nature Trail—longest rail-to-trail in Iowa, 63 miles to the Missouri border; http://wabashtrace.connections.net/; information at Endless Trail Bike Shop, 506 South Main, Council Bluffs; (712) 322-9760

River City Farmers' Market, Omni Center loading dock area, Council Bluffs; (712) 545-3680; June through October, Saturday 8:00 A.M. to 1:00 P.M.

Accommodations

Apple Orchard Inn, RR 3, Missouri Valley; (712) 642-2418

Wilson Island State Recreation Area Campground; (712) 642-2069

Lion's Den Bed & Breakfast, 136 South Seventh Street, Council Bluffs; (712) 322-7162

Restaurants

Duncan's Cafe, 501 South Main, Council Bluffs; (712) 328-3360

Upstream Brewing Company, 514 South Eleventh Street, Omaha, Nebraska; (402) 344-0200

Other Resources

Loess Hills Audubon Society; www.lhas.org

Audubon Society of Omaha; http://audubon-omaha.org

Fragile Giants: A Natural History of the Loess Hills by Cornelia Mutel (Bur Oak Books Series, University of Iowa Press)

Land of the Fragile Giants: Landscapes, Environments, and Peoples of the Loess Hills, edited by Cornelia Mutel and Mary Swander (Bur Oak Books Series, University of Iowa Press)

41 Waubonsie State Park

The southernmost protected area in Iowa's Loess Hills, Waubonsie actually serves as a refuge. To be found here are typical southern and western plants, butterflies, birds, mammals, and reptiles, many of which are listed in Iowa as rare, threatened, or endangered species. Seven miles of trails in the hiking unit and 8.0 miles in the equestrian unit wind up steep ridges, through mature woodlands, and onto ridgetop prairie remnants. They can be enjoyed in an intense hike or a mellow stroll. For naturalists who visit Waubonsie, binoculars and the appropriate field guides are absolute necessities.

Distance: 5.6 miles round-trip
Approximate hiking time: 3 to 4 hours
Total elevation gain: 1,064 feet
Trail surface: Brush-cut swaths through forest, ridgeline footpaths
Seasons: Year-round
Trail users: Hikers only
Canine compatability: Dogs permitted on leash
Hazards: Poison ivy, ticks

Land status: State park
Nearest towns: Hamburg and Sidney, Iowa; Nebraska City, Nebraska
Fees and permits: No fees or permits required unless you're camping here
Schedule: Year-round, 4:00 A.M. to 10:30 P.M.
Map: USGS quad: Sidney
Trail contact: Waubonsie State Park; (712) 382-2786, www.state.ia.us/dnr/organiza/ppd/waubonsi.htm

Finding the trailhead: From the junction of U.S. Highway 275 and Highway 2 in Sidney, take US 275/Highway 2 south, turning west onto Highway 2 when the road forks. Turn left (south) onto Highway 239, and follow the signs for the overlook. *DeLorme: Iowa Atlas and Gazetteer:* Page 56 E4

The Hike

In July 1804, while explorers Meriwether Lewis and William Clark camped near the Missouri River west of present-day Waubonsie State Park, Clark described in his journal a scene far different from that of today: "A large prairie . . . which we called Baldpated prairie . . . a ridge of naked hills which bound it, running parallel with the river as far as we could see."

Woody invasion of the southern Loess Hills would parallel Euro–American settlement, and the prairie and oak savanna that once dominated the rugged hills were replaced by extensive woodlands. The usual suspects: fire suppression, agricultural cultivation, extermination of once-numerous hoofed grazers, and the subsequent overgrazing by domestic cattle. All of these factors permanently altered the landscape seen by Lewis and Clark two centuries ago. Today west-facing ridgetop prairie remnants and woodland openings offer only scattered reminders of Iowa's once "bald hills."

"Waubonsie" comes from the name of an honored chief of the Potowatomi tribe (pronounced Wah-*bon*-sey, meaning "Break of Day"), who originally came from the

Dense forests have replaced the once "bald-pated hills" of Waubonsie State Park.

Great Lakes region. During the early 1800s waves of white settlement forced tribe members to abandon their homes in Michigan. From 1837 to 1848 up to 2,000 Potowatomi occupied a reserve in southwest Iowa. Wahbonsey traveled to Washington, D.C., to meet with presidents Andrew Jackson and James Polk to assure peace between his tribe and settlers. However, Iowa statehood in 1846 resulted in federal seizure of Potowatomi lands, and the tribe was pushed into Kansas. It's said that Wahbonsey died in 1848 as the last of his people left Iowa and that he's buried in a hidden grave somewhere north of the park.

The main overlook is a relatively safe spot for watching dramatic midsummer thunderstorms approach from the west, but on clear days a jaunt down the sunset ridge trail is a must. From the westernmost ridge in the park, your eyes will strain to

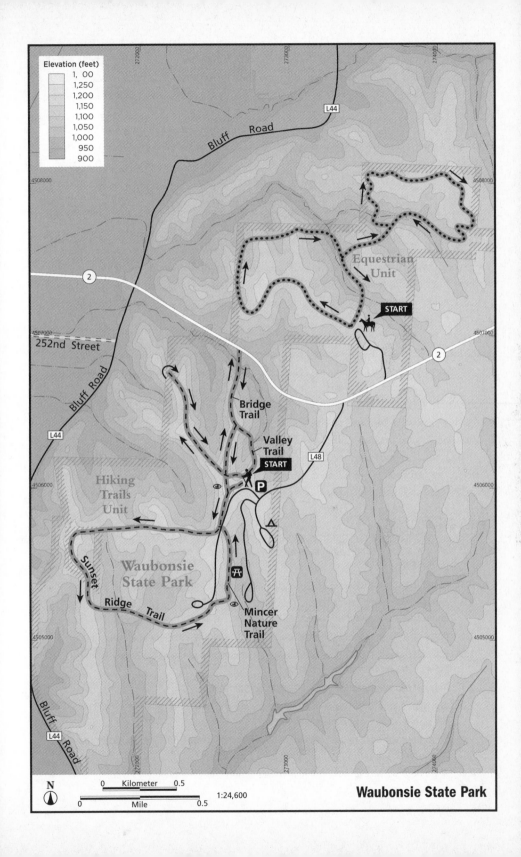

Elevation (feet)
1,⎕00
1,250
1,200
1,150
1,100
1,050
1,000
950
900

Bluff   Road

L44

2

Equestrian
Unit

START

252nd Street

Bluff Road

L44

2

Bridge
Trail

Valley
Trail

START

L48

Hiking
Trails
Unit

P

Waubonsie
State Park

Sunset   Ridge   Trail

Mincer
Nature
Trail

Bluff
Road

L44

N

0   Kilometer   0.5
0   Mile   0.5
1:24,600

Waubonsie State Park

push the horizon beyond the Missouri River floodplain into infinity. Here you'll find a ridgetop prairie dense with big and little bluestem, Indian grass, sideoats grama, pale purple coneflower, lead plant, fringed puccoon, and the endangered biscuit root.

Many woodland animals, such as the summer tanager, chuck-will's-widow, Keen's myotis, and woodland vole, are expanding their typically more southern range into the northward-expanding forests. The pawpaw tree serves as a host to the stunning zebra swallowtail, the most abundant of North American "kite swallowtails," named for their triangular wings and long, sharp tails. The savanna-like openings are refuge for other rare butterflies, including the Olympia marblewing, hoary edge, white-M hairstreak, and Henry's elfin.

To make the most of the park's lengthy hiking-only trails, a figure-eight pattern is recommended. Start at the overlook parking lot, and follow the sunset ridge interpretive trail down the finger ridge. From here a smaller footpath leads south and east into a valley, where you'll find a dug-out cave probably made by settlers for safekeeping food.

Climb up the ridge to the southernmost picnic area, and follow the trail parallel to the road or the Mincer Nature Trail north back up to the main overlook. Complete the top loop by following the Bridge Trail north through well-developed forests dominated by the gnarled and fissured bodies of bur oaks. Connect with the valley trail, where cross sections of underground root systems are visible in the trail cuts that lead you back up to the parking area.

If you want a grueling hike and a long day, continue walking the equestrian trails on the north side of Highway 2. They'll wear you out with their steepness but won't offer as picturesque a view, and they are seriously eroded from excessive horse traffic. No matter what, bring binoculars—you'll need them.

Miles and Directions

0.0 Start from the main overlook parking area. Turn left (south) onto the Sunset Ridge Interpretive Trail.

0.3 At the fork turn right (west) to explore the westernmost ridge in the park.

0.8 Emerge onto a west-facing ridgetop covered in prairie. (FYI: You're looking at Iowa, Kansas, Missouri, and Nebraska, the "four corners" of the Midwest—well, kind of.)

1.5 Angle east down the ridge. The trail cuts steeply down into the lowland forests.

1.55 Look for a dug-out cave once used to store potatoes or hide from tornadoes. From here the trail ascends yet another ridge up to the road.

2.1 Arrive at the lower picnic area; walk north on the road.

2.2 Turn right onto Mincer Nature Trail. Follow around in a small loop and immediately turn left onto the trail that parallels the road.

2.6 Cross the road back to the beginning of the Sunset Overlook Trail and back up to the main overlook.

2.8 Arrive back at the overlook. Continue straight, toward the Bridge and Valley Trails.

2.85 Just after the small shelter/kiosk, turn left onto the Bridge Trail. This leads down the ridge 0.6 mile to the property boundary.

3.45 Reach the fence with a sign that reads TRAIL END. Turn around and backtrack up to the kiosk. About halfway back there's a bench with a view, the perfect place for lunch or a snack.

4.0 Arrive back at the kiosk; turn left (north) onto the Bridge/Valley Trail.

4.2 At the fork continue straight (north) on the Bridge Trail. You'll wind down a steep ridge into riparian forests.

4.5 Arrive at Highway 2; turn around and backtrack to the last fork.

4.9 At the fork turn left (east) onto the Valley Trail.

5.4 Arrive back at main ridgetop, just north of the overlook.

5.6 Arrive back at the trailhead.

Hike Information

Local Information
Nebraska City; www.nebraskacity.com

Events/Attractions
Todd House, a stop on the Underground Railroad, Park Street, Tabor; (712) 629-2675
River County Nature Center, Nebraska City, Nebraska; (402) 873-3000
Mincer Orchard, fruit stand, entrance to Waubonsie State Park during summer; (712) 382-1484

Accommodations
Waubonsie State Park Campground; (712) 382-2786
Pinky's Glen County Park (Fremont County Conservation Board), very primitive lakeside camping 2 miles west of Tabor on County Road J10; (712) 374-2347
The Victorian Inn, 807 Main Street, Tabor; (712) 629-5605

Restaurants
Stoner Drug (lunch counter), 1105 Main, Tabor; (712) 382-2551

Longhome Coffee Company, 1121 Central Avenue, Nebraska City, Nebraska; (402) 873-3777

Other Resources
Loess Hills Audubon Society; www.lhas.org
Audubon Society of Omaha; http://audubon-omaha.org
Fragile Giants: A Natural History of the Loess Hills by Cornelia Mutel (Bur Oak Books Series, University of Iowa Press)
Land of the Fragile Giants: Landscapes, Environments, and Peoples of the Loess Hills, edited by Cornelia Mutel and Mary Swander (Bur Oak Books Series, University of Iowa Press)
The Iowa Breeding Bird Atlas by Laura Spess Jackson, Carol A. Thompson, and James J. Dinsmore (Bur Oak Books Series, University of Iowa Press)
Bicycle Trails of Iowa, American Bike Trails & Iowa Trails Council

Honorable Mentions

GG. Southwood Conservation Area

This 623-acre park has a campground for use as a base camp to explore the many other Woodbury County parks. The 2.1-mile trail, also used by equestrians, winds through ridgetop prairie remnants and reconstructions as well several brome fields. Adjacent to Southwood is Fowler Forest Preserve, which also contains a small footpath. From the junction of Highways, 141 and 3 in Smithland, head west on Highway 141. Turn left (south) onto Jewell Avenue, then left (east) onto 330th Street. For information: Woodbury County Conservation Board, Southwood Conservation Area Office; (712) 889–2215, www.woodburyparks.com.

HH. Gleason-Hubel Wildlife Area

From the junction of Highway 301 and Eden Avenue (Main Street) in Little Sioux, take Main Street 2 blocks north; turn onto Mulberry Street. At the base of the hills, turn south onto Larpenteur Memorial Road. Pass the Little Sioux Pioneer Cemetery, and look for the GLEASON HUBEL WILDLIFE AREA sign on the east side of the road. From the parking area head directly east on the Hollow Trail. At the second fork take the left trail, which immediately begins climbing the finger ridge to the northeast. Once you've gained all the ground possible, a skinny swath of prairie straddles the ridgeline, and you'll find big and little bluestem, sideoats grama, skeletonweed, large-flowered beardtongue, and blazing star. The view to the east encompasses steep, forested hillsides leading down to the floodplain of the channalized Soldier River just before it enters the Missouri River, which lies to the west. Follow the ridgeline as it swings south to loop around back down to the parking area. For information: Harrison County Conservation Board; (712) 647–2785, www .har risoncountyia.org/hccb/wildlife_areas.htm#gleason-hubel.

II. Sioux City Prairie Preserve

Together, this preserve, Stone State Park, and Riverside Bluffs probably account for the largest amount of prairie within an urban boundary in the country. Adjacent to Briar Cliff College, the 157-acre prairie was rescued from development after serving as a golf course. Look for regal fritillaries dancing over yucca plants and the rare prairie moonworts poking their fiddleheads up in spring. Listen for eastern meadowlarks and grasshopper sparrows or yellow-breasted chats, also sometimes found here. From Interstate 29, take exit 149 (Hamilton Boulevard) north for 2.5 miles. Turn left (northwest) onto Stone Park Boulevard and then left (west) onto West Clifton Avenue. Signs will lead you up to the north entrance of Briar Cliff College, where you can park in the westernmost lot to access the prairie. Footpaths lead over the predominantly prairie-covered hills to the other entrance, off Talbot Road, which borders the west side of the prairie. Regular bird, butterfly, and plant walks are given by local naturalists associated with Friends of the Sioux City Prairie. For information: The Nature Conservancy; (515) 244–5044, http://nature.org/wherewework/northamerica/states/iowa/preserves/art2215.html.

JJ. Murray Hill

Although this may be the shortest hike in the book, it provides one of the most beautiful views in the state. Murray Hill's summit rises almost 300 feet above the Missouri River floodplain, and the short, steep jaunt to the top is a must. Diverse, drought-tolerant plants hold onto the edge of the nearly vertical west-facing slope. To the east a fence separates the diverse native prairie of Murray Hill from heavily grazed adjacent land, and you can compare the relative health of the two sides of the fence. From the junction of County Road F20 and Highway 183 in Pisgah, take CR F20 west. Just before you reach the end of the hills and before you start descending, turn into the small parking lot on the south side of the road. Sweet plants, and an even sweeter view. For information: Harrison County Conservation Board; (712) 647-2785, www.harrisoncountyia.org/hccb/recreation_areas.html.

KK. Willow Lake

A 4.0-mile out-and-back hike takes you around Willow Lake, a man-made lake on the eastern slope of the hills. The lake's two north inlets are fringed with wetland plants, but the park predominantly comprises prairie reconstructions with interspersed woodlands. Food plots planted by the county conservation board draw in many of the game species, and public hunting is permitted on the north side of the lake. Camping is available on-site, as well as in several spacious rental cabins. From the junction of Highway 30 and County Road F20 (Easton Trail) in Woodbine, take CR F20 west 6 miles. Signs on the north side of the highway will direct you to the parking area. For information: Harrison County Conservation Board; (712) 647–2785, www.harrisoncountyia.org.

LL. Broken Kettle Grasslands

Broken Kettle is a place unto its own—the largest tract of prairie remaining in Iowa, the lone remnant population of prairie rattlesnakes, and one of the few bird conservation areas in Iowa. Just about everything that lives there is special: ten-petal blazing star, western kingbird, plains spadefoot, and Ottoe skipper, among countless other rare organisms. Intensive management efforts such as prescribed burns and grazing protect the extensive and diverse prairie from encroaching woodlands. The nature center is the extent of the development—so explore! From Sioux City take

Highway 12 north along the Big Sioux River through Riverside. Four miles north of the turnoff to County Road K18, turn east onto Butcher Road to drive through the preserve. To visit the nature center continue on Highway 12 past Butcher Road 0.5 mile to 24764 Highway 12, where an access road will take you 0.25 mile to the headquarters. For information: The Nature Conservancy; (515) 244–5044, http://nature.org/wherewework/northamerica/states/iowa/preserves/art2210.html.

The Art of Hiking

When standing nose to nose with a mountain lion, you're probably not too concerned with the issue of ethical behavior in the wild. No doubt you're just terrified. But let's be honest. How often are you nose to nose with a mountain lion? For most of us, a hike into the "wild" means loading up the SUV with expensive gear and driving to a toileted trailhead. Sure, you can mourn how civilized we've become—how GPS units have replaced natural instinct and Gore-Tex, true-grit—but the silly gadgets of civilization aside, we have plenty of reason to take pride in how we've matured. With survival now on the back burner, we've begun to reason—and it's about time—that we have a responsibility to protect, no longer just conquer, our wild places: that they, not we, are at risk. So please, do what you can. The following section will help you understand better what it means to "do what you can" while still making the most of your hiking experience. Anyone can take a hike, but hiking safely and well is an art requiring preparation and proper equipment.

Trail Etiquette

Zero impact. Always leave an area just like you found it—if not better than you found it. Avoid camping in fragile, alpine meadows and along the banks of streams and lakes. Use a camp stove versus building a wood fire. Pack up all of your trash and extra food. Bury human waste at least 100 feet from water sources under 6 to 8 inches of topsoil. Don't bathe with soap in a lake or stream—use prepackaged moistened towels to wipe off sweat and dirt, or bathe in the water without soap.

Stay on the trail. It's true, a path anywhere leads nowhere new, but purists will just have to get over it. Paths serve an important purpose; they limit impact on natural areas. Straying from a designated trail may seem innocent, but it can cause damage to sensitive areas—damage that may take years to recover, if it can recover at all. Even simple shortcuts can be destructive. So, please, stay on the trail.

Leave no weeds. Noxious weeds tend to overtake other plants, which in turn affects animals and birds that depend on them for food. To minimize the spread of noxious weeds, hikers should regularly clean their boots, tents, packs, and hiking poles of mud and seeds. Also brush your dog to remove any weed seeds before heading off into a new area.

Keep your dog under control. You can buy a flexi-lead that allows your dog to go exploring along the trail, while allowing you the ability to reel him in should another hiker approach or should he decide to chase a rabbit. Always obey leash laws and be sure to bury your dog's waste or pack it in resealable plastic bags.

Respect other trail users. Often you're not the only one on the trail. With the rise in popularity of multiuse trails, you'll have to learn a new kind of respect, beyond the nod and "hello" approach you may be used to. First investigate whether you're on a multiuse trail, and assume the appropriate precautions. When you encounter motorized vehicles (ATVs, motorcycles, and 4WDs), be alert. Though they should always yield to the hiker, often they're going too fast or are too lost in the buzz of their engine to react to your presence. If you hear activity ahead, step off the trail just to be safe. Note that you're not likely to hear a mountain biker coming, so be prepared and know ahead of time whether you share the trail with them. Cyclists should always yield to hikers, but that's little comfort to the hiker. Be aware. When you approach horses or pack animals on the trail, always step quietly off the trail, preferably on the downhill side, and let them pass. If you're wearing a large backpack, it's often a good idea to sit down. To some animals, a hiker wearing a large backpack might appear threatening. Many national forests allow domesticated grazing, usually for sheep and cattle. Make sure your dog doesn't harass these animals, and respect ranchers' rights while you're enjoying yours.

Getting into Shape

Unless you want to be sore—and possibly have to shorten your trip or vacation—be sure to get in shape before a big hike. If you're terribly out of shape, start a walking program early, preferably eight weeks in advance. Start with a fifteen-minute walk during your lunch hour or after work and gradually increase your walking time to an hour. You should also increase your elevation gain. Walking briskly up hills really strengthens your leg muscles and gets your heart rate up. If you work in a storied office building, take the stairs instead of the elevator. If you prefer going to a gym, walk the treadmill or use a stair machine. You can further increase your strength and endurance by walking with a loaded backpack. Stationary exercises you might consider are squats, leg lifts, sit-ups, and push-ups. Other good ways to get in shape include biking, running, aerobics, and, of course, short hikes. Stretching before and after a hike keeps muscles flexible and helps avoid injuries.

Preparedness

It's been said that failing to plan means planning to fail. So do take the necessary time to plan your trip. Whether going on a short day hike or an extended backpack trip, always prepare for the worst. Simply remembering to pack a copy of the U.S. Army Survival Manual is not preparedness. Although it's not a bad idea if you plan on entering truly wild places, it's merely the tourniquet answer to a problem. You need to do your best to prevent the problem from arising in the first place. In order to survive—and to stay reasonably comfortable—you need to concern yourself with the basics: water, food, and shelter. Don't go on a hike without having these bases covered. And don't go on a hike expecting to find these items in the woods.

Water. Even in frigid conditions, you need at least two quarts of water a day to function efficiently. Add heat and taxing terrain and you can bump that figure up to one gallon. That's simply a base to work from—your metabolism and your level of conditioning can raise or lower that amount. Unless you know your level, assume that you need one gallon of water a day. Now, where do you plan on getting the water?

Preferably not from natural water sources. These sources can be loaded with intestinal disturbers, such as bacteria, viruses, and fertilizers. *Giardia lamblia,* the most common of these disturbers, is a protozoan parasite that lives part of its life cycle as a cyst in water sources. The parasite spreads when mammals defecate in water sources. Once ingested, *Giardia* can induce cramping, diarrhea, vomiting, and fatigue within two days to two weeks after ingestion. Giardiasis is treatable with prescription drugs. If you believe you've contracted giardiasis, see a doctor immediately.

Treating water. The best and easiest solution to avoid polluted water is to carry your water with you. Yet, depending on the nature of your hike and the duration, this may not be an option—one gallon of water weighs eight-and-a-half pounds. In that case, you'll need to look into treating water. Regardless of which method you choose, you should always carry some water with you in case of an emergency. Save this reserve until you absolutely need it.

There are three methods of treating water: boiling, chemical treatment, and filtering. If you boil water, it's recommended that you do so for ten to fifteen minutes. This is often impractical because you're forced to exhaust a great deal of your fuel supply. You can opt for chemical treatment, which will kill *Giardia* but will not take care of other chemical pollutants. Another drawback to chemical treatments is the unpleasant taste of the water after it's treated. You can remedy this by adding powdered drink mix to the water. Filters are the preferred method for treating water. Many filters remove *Giardia,* organic and inorganic contaminants, and don't leave an aftertaste. Water filters are far from perfect as they can easily become clogged or leak if a gasket wears out. It's always a good idea to carry a backup supply of chemical treatment tablets in case your filter decides to quit on you.

Food. If we're talking about survival, you can go days without food, as long as you have water. But we're also talking about comfort. Try to avoid foods that are high in sugar and fat like candy bars and potato chips. These food types are harder to digest and are low in nutritional value. Instead, bring along foods that are easy to pack, nutritious, and high in energy (e.g., bagels, nutrition bars, dehydrated fruit, gorp, and jerky). If you are on an overnight trip, easy-to-fix dinners include rice mixes with dehydrated potatoes, corn, pasta with cheese sauce, and soup mixes. For a tasty breakfast, you can fix hot oatmeal with brown sugar and reconstituted milk powder topped off with banana chips. If you like a hot drink in the morning, bring along herbal tea bags or hot chocolate. If you are a coffee junkie, you can purchase coffee that is packaged like tea bags. You can prepackage all of your meals in heavy-duty resealable plastic bags to keep food from spilling in your pack. These bags can be reused to pack out trash.

Shelter. The type of shelter you choose depends less on the conditions than on your tolerance for discomfort. Shelter comes in many forms—tent, tarp, lean-to, bivy sack, cabin, cave, etc. If you're camping in the desert, a bivy sack may suffice, but if you're above the treeline and a storm is approaching, a better choice is a three- or four-season tent. Tents are the logical and most popular choice for most backpackers as they're lightweight and packable—and you can rest assured that you always have shelter from the elements. Before you leave on your trip, anticipate what the weather and terrain will be like and plan for the type of shelter that will work best for your comfort level (see Equipment later in this section).

Finding a campsite. If there are established campsites, stick to those. If not, start looking for a campsite early—around 3:30 or 4:00 P.M. Stop at the first decent site you see. Depending on the area, it could be a long time before you find another suitable location. Pitch your camp in an area that's level. Make sure the area is at least 200 feet from fragile areas like lakeshores, meadows, and stream banks. And try to avoid areas thick in underbrush, as they can harbor insects and provide cover for approaching animals.

If you are camping in stormy, rainy weather, look for a rock outcrop or a shelter in the trees to keep the wind from blowing your tent all night. Be sure that you don't camp under trees with dead limbs that might break off on top of you. Also, try to find an area that has an absorbent surface, such as sandy soil or forest duff. This, in addition to camping on a surface with a slight angle, will provide better drainage. By all means, don't dig trenches to provide drainage around your tent—remember you're practicing zero-impact camping.

If you're in bear country, steer clear of creekbeds or animal paths. If you see any signs of a bear's presence (i.e., scat, footprints), relocate. You'll need to find a campsite near a tall tree where you can hang your food and other items that may attract bears such as deodorant, toothpaste, or soap. Carry a lightweight nylon rope with which to hang your food. As a rule, you should hang your food at least 20 feet from the ground and 5 feet away from the tree trunk. You can put food and other items in a waterproof stuff sack and tie one end of the rope to the stuff sack. To get the other end of the rope over the tree branch, tie a good-size rock to it, and gently toss the rock over the tree branch. Pull the stuff sack up until it reaches the top of the branch and tie it off securely. Don't hang your food near your tent! If possible, hang your food at least 100 feet away from your campsite. Alternatives to hanging your food are bear-proof plastic tubes and metal bear boxes.

Lastly, think of comfort. Lie down on the ground where you intend to sleep and see if it's a good fit. For morning warmth (and a nice view to wake up to), have your tent face east.

First Aid

I know you're tough, but get 10 miles into the woods and develop a blister and you'll wish you had carried that first-aid kit. Face it, it's just plain good sense. Many companies produce lightweight, compact first-aid kits. Just make sure yours contains at least the following:

- adhesive bandages
- moleskin or duct tape
- various sterile gauze and dressings
- white surgical tape
- an Ace bandage
- an antihistamine
- aspirin
- Betadine solution
- a first-aid book
- antacid tablets

- tweezers
- scissors
- antibacterial wipes
- triple-antibiotic ointment
- plastic gloves
- sterile cotton tip applicators
- syrup of ipecac (to induce vomiting)
- thermometer
- wire splint

Here are a few tips for dealing with and hopefully preventing certain ailments.

Sunburn. Take along sunscreen or sun block, protective clothing, and a wide-brimmed hat. If you do get a sunburn, treat the area with aloe vera gel, and protect the area from further sun exposure. At higher elevations, the sun's radiation can be particularly damaging to skin. Remember that your eyes are vulnerable to this radiation as well. Sunglasses can be a good way to prevent headaches and permanent eye damage from the sun, especially in places where light-colored rock or patches of snow reflect light up in your face.

Blisters. Be prepared to take care of these hike-spoilers by carrying moleskin (a lightly padded adhesive), gauze and tape, or adhesive bandages. An effective way to apply moleskin is to cut out a circle of moleskin and remove the center—like a doughnut—and place it over the blistered area. Cutting the center out will reduce the pressure applied to the sensitive skin. Other products can help you combat blisters. Some are applied to suspicious hot spots before a blister forms to help decrease friction to that area, while others are applied to the blister after it has popped to help prevent further irritation.

Insect bites and stings. You can treat most insect bites and stings by applying hydrocortisone 1 percent cream topically and taking a pain medication such as ibuprofen or acetaminophen to reduce swelling. If you forgot to pack these items, a cold compress or a paste of mud and ashes can sometimes assuage the itching and discomfort. Remove any stingers by using tweezers or scraping the area with your fingernail or a knife blade. Don't pinch the area as you'll only spread the venom.

Some hikers are highly sensitive to bites and stings and may have a serious allergic reaction that can be life threatening. Symptoms of a serious allergic reaction can include wheezing, an asthmatic attack, and shock. The treatment for this severe type of reaction is epinephrine. If you know that you are sensitive to bites and stings, carry a prepackaged kit of epinephrine, which can be obtained only by prescription from your doctor.

Ticks. Ticks can carry diseases such as Rocky Mountain spotted fever and Lyme disease. The best defense is, of course, prevention. If you know you're going to be hiking through an area littered with ticks, wear long pants and a long-sleeved shirt. You can apply a permethrin repellent to your clothing and a Deet repellent to exposed skin. At the end of your hike, do a spot check for ticks (and insects in general). If you do find a tick, coat the insect with petroleum jelly or tree sap to cut off its air supply. The tick should release its hold, but if it doesn't, grab the head of the tick firmly—with a pair of tweezers if you have them—and gently pull it away from the skin with a twisting motion. Sometimes the mouth parts linger, embedded in your skin. If this happens, try to remove them with a disinfected needle. Clean the affected area with an antibacterial cleanser and then apply triple antibiotic ointment. Monitor the area for a few days. If irritation persists or a white spot develops, see a doctor for possible infection.

Poison ivy, oak, and sumac. These skin irritants can be found most anywhere in North America and come in the form of a bush or a vine, having leaflets in groups of three, five, seven, or nine. Learn how to spot the plants. The oil they secrete can cause an allergic reaction in the form of blisters, usually about twelve hours after exposure. The itchy rash can last from ten days to several weeks. The best defense against these irritants is to wear clothing that covers the arms, legs and torso. For summer, zip-off cargo pants come in handy. There are also nonprescription lotions you can apply to exposed skin that guard against the effects of poison ivy/oak/sumac and can be washed off with soap and water. If you think you were in contact with the plants, after hiking (or even on the trail during longer hikes) wash with soap and water. Taking a hot shower with soap after you return home from your hike will also help to remove any lingering oil from your skin. Should you contract a rash from any of these plants, use an antihistamine to reduce the itching. If the rash is localized, create a light bleach/water wash to dry up the area. If the rash has spread, either tough it out or see your doctor about getting a dose of cortisone (available both orally and by injection).

Snakebites. Snakebites are rare in North America. Unless startled or provoked, the majority of snakes will not bite. If you are wise to their habitats and keep a careful eye on the trail, you should be just fine. When stepping over logs, first step on the log, making sure you can see what's on the other side before stepping down. Though your chances of being struck are slim, it's wise to know what to do in the event you are.

If a *nonpoisonous* snake bites you, allow the wound to bleed a small amount and then cleanse the wounded area with a Betadine solution (10 percent povidone iodine). Rinse the wound with clean water (preferably) or fresh urine (it might sound ugly, but it's sterile). Once the area is clean, cover it with triple antibiotic ointment and a clean bandage. Remember, most residual damage from snakebites, poisonous or otherwise, comes from infection, not the snake's venom. Keep the area as clean as possible and get medical attention immediately.

If you are bitten by a poisonous snake, remove the toxin with a suctioning device, found in a snakebite kit. If you do not have such a device, squeeze the wound—DO NOT use your mouth for suction, as the venom will enter your bloodstream through the vessels under the tongue and head straight for your heart. Then, clean the wound just as you would a nonpoisonous bite. Tie a clean band of cloth snuggly around the afflicted appendage, about an inch or so above the bite (or the rim of the swelling). This is NOT a tourniquet—you want to simply slow the blood flow, not cut it off. Loosen the band if numbness ensues. Remove the band for a minute and reapply a little higher every ten minutes.

If it is your friend who's been bitten, treat him or her for shock—make the person comfortable, have him or her lie down, elevate the legs, and keep him or her warm. Avoid applying anything cold to the bite wound. Immobilize the affected area and remove any constricting items such as rings, watches, or restrictive clothing— swelling may occur. Once your friend is stable and relatively calm, hike out to get help. The victim should get treatment within twelve hours, ideally, which usually consists of a tetanus shot, antivenin, and antibiotics.

If you are alone and struck by a poisonous snake, stay calm. Hysteria will only quicken the venom's spread. Follow the procedure above, and do your best to reach help. When hiking out, don't run—you'll only increase the flow of blood throughout your system. Instead, walk calmly.

Dehydration. Have you ever hiked in hot weather and had a roaring headache and felt fatigued after only a few miles? More than likely you were dehydrated. Symptoms of dehydration include fatigue, headache, and decreased coordination and judgment. When you are hiking, your body's rate of fluid loss depends on the outside temperature, humidity, altitude, and your activity level. On average, a hiker walking in warm weather will lose four liters of fluid a day. That fluid loss is easily replaced by normal consumption of liquids and food. However, if a hiker is walking briskly in hot, dry weather and hauling a heavy pack, he or she can lose one to three liters of water an hour. It's important to always carry plenty of water and to stop often and drink fluids regularly, even if you aren't thirsty.

Heat exhaustion is the result of a loss of large amounts of electrolytes and often occurs if a hiker is dehydrated and has been under heavy exertion. Common symptoms of heat exhaustion include cramping, exhaustion, fatigue, lightheadedness, and nausea. You can treat heat exhaustion by getting out of the sun and drinking an electrolyte solution made up of one teaspoon of salt and one tablespoon of sugar dissolved in a liter of water. Drink this solution slowly over a period of one hour.

Drinking plenty of fluids (preferably an electrolyte solution/sports drink) can prevent heat exhaustion. Avoid hiking during the hottest parts of the day, and wear breathable clothing, a wide-brimmed hat, and sunglasses.

Hypothermia is one of the biggest dangers in the backcountry, especially for day hikers in the summertime. That may sound strange, but imagine starting out on a hike in midsummer when it's sunny and 80 degrees out. You're clad in nylon shorts and a cotton T-shirt. About halfway through your hike, the sky begins to cloud up, and in the next hour a light drizzle begins to fall and the wind starts to pick up. Before you know it, you are soaking wet and shivering—the perfect recipe for hypothermia. More advanced signs include decreased coordination, slurred speech, and blurred vision. When a victim's temperature falls below 92 degrees, the blood pressure and pulse plummet, possibly leading to coma and death.

To avoid hypothermia, always bring a windproof/rainproof shell, a fleece jacket, tights made of a breathable, synthetic fiber, gloves, and hat when you are hiking in the mountains. Learn to adjust your clothing layers based on the temperature. If you are climbing uphill at a moderate pace you will stay warm, but when you stop for a break you'll become cold quickly, unless you add more layers of clothing.

If a hiker is showing advanced signs of hypothermia, dress him or her in dry clothes and make sure he or she is wearing a hat and gloves. Place the person in a sleeping bag in a tent or shelter that will protect him or her from the wind and other elements. Give the person warm fluids to drink and keep him awake.

Frostbite. When the mercury dips below 32 degrees, your extremities begin to chill. If a persistent chill attacks a localized area, say, your hands or your toes, the circulatory system reacts by cutting off blood flow to the affected area—the idea being to protect and preserve the body's overall temperature. And so it's death by attrition for the affected area. Ice crystals start to form from the water in the cells of the neglected tissue. Deprived of heat, nourishment, and now water, the tissue literally starves. This is frostbite.

Prevention is your best defense against this situation. Most prone to frostbite are your face, hands, and feet, so protect these areas well. Wool is the material of choice because it provides ample air space for insulation and draws moisture away from the skin. Synthetic fabrics, however, have recently made great strides in the cold weather clothing market. Do your research. A pair of light silk liners under your regular gloves is a good trick for keeping warm. They afford some additional warmth, but more importantly they'll allow you to remove your mitts for tedious work without exposing the skin.

If your feet or hands start to feel cold or numb due to the elements, warm them as quickly as possible. Place cold hands under your armpits or bury them in your crotch. If your feet are cold, change your socks. If there's plenty of room in your boots, add another pair of socks. Do remember, though, that constricting your feet in tight boots can restrict blood flow and actually make your feet colder more quickly. Your socks need to have breathing room if they're going to be effective.

Dead air provides insulation. If your face is cold, place your warm hands over your face, or simply wear a head stocking.

Should your skin go numb and start to appear white and waxy, chances are you've got or are developing frostbite. Don't try to thaw the area unless you can maintain the warmth. In other words, don't stop to warm up your frostbitten feet only to head back on the trail. You'll do more damage than good. Tests have shown that hikers who walked on thawed feet did more harm, and endured more pain, than hikers who left the affected areas alone. Do your best to get out of the cold entirely and seek medical attention—which usually consists of performing a rapid rewarming in water for twenty to thirty minutes.

The overall objective in preventing both hypothermia and frostbite is to keep the body's core warm. Protect key areas where heat escapes, like the top of the head, and maintain the proper nutrition level. Foods that are high in calories aid the body in producing heat. Never smoke or drink when you're in situations where the cold is threatening. By affecting blood flow, these activities ultimately cool the body's core temperature.

Altitude sickness (AMS). High lofty peaks, clear alpine lakes, and vast mountain views beckon hikers to the high country. But those who like to venture high may become victims of altitude sickness (also known as Acute Mountain Sickness— AMS). Altitude sickness is your body's reaction to insufficient oxygen in the blood due to decreased barometric pressure. While some hikers may feel lightheaded, nauseous, and experience shortness of breath at 7,000 feet, others may not experience these symptoms until they reach 10,000 feet or higher.

Slowing your ascent to high places and giving your body a chance to acclimatize to the higher elevations can prevent altitude sickness. For example, if you live at sea level and are planning a weeklong backpacking trip to elevations between 7,000 and 12,000 feet, start by staying below 7,000 feet for one night, then move to between 7,000 and 10,000 feet for another night or two. Avoid strenuous exertion and alcohol to give your body a chance to adjust to the new altitude. It's also important to eat light food and drink plenty of nonalcoholic fluids, preferably water. Loss of appetite at altitude is common, but you must eat!

Most hikers who experience mild to moderate AMS develop a headache and/or nausea, grow lethargic, and have problems sleeping. The treatment for AMS is simple: stop heading uphill. Keep eating and drinking water and take meds for the headache. You actually need to take more breaths at altitude than at sea level, so breathe a little faster without hyperventilating. If symptoms don't improve over twenty-four to forty-eight hours, descend. Once a victim descends about 2,000 to 3,000 feet, his signs will usually begin to diminish.

Severe AMS comes in two forms: High Altitude Pulmonary Edema (HAPE) and High Altitude Cerebral Edema (HACE). HAPE, an accumulation of fluid in the lungs, can occur above 8,000 feet. Symptoms include rapid heart rate, shortness of breath at rest, AMS symptoms, dry cough developing into a wet cough, gurgling sounds, flulike or bronchitis symptoms, and lack of muscle coordination. HAPE is life threatening so descend immediately, at least 2,000 to 4,000 feet. HACE usually occurs above 12,000 feet but sometimes occurs above 10,000 feet. Symptoms are similar to HAPE but also include seizures, hallucinations, paralysis, and vision disturbances. Descend immediately—HACE is also life threatening.

Hantavirus Pulmonary Syndrome (HPS). Deer mice spread the virus that causes HPS, and humans contract it from breathing it in, usually when they've disturbed an area with dust and mice feces from nests or surfaces with mice droppings or urine. Exposure to large numbers of rodents and their feces or urine presents the greatest risk. As hikers, we sometimes enter old buildings, and often deer mice live in these places. We may not be around long enough to be exposed, but do be aware of this disease. About half the people who develop HPS die. Symptoms are flulike and appear about two to three weeks after exposure. After initial symptoms, a dry cough and shortness of breath follow. Breathing is difficult. If you even think you might have HPS, see a doctor immediately!

Natural Hazards

Besides tripping over a rock or tree root on the trail, there are some real hazards to be aware of while hiking. Even if where you're hiking doesn't have the plethora of poisonous snakes and plants, insects, and grizzly bears found in other parts of the United States, there are a few weather conditions and predators you may need to take into account.

Lightning. Thunderstorms build over the mountains almost every day during the summer. Lightning is generated by thunderheads and can strike without warning, even several miles away from the nearest overhead cloud. The best rule of thumb is to start leaving exposed peaks, ridges, and canyon rims by about noon. This time can vary a little depending on storm buildup. Keep an eye on cloud formation and don't underestimate how fast a storm can build. The bigger they get, the more likely a thunderstorm will happen. Lightning takes the path of least resistance, so if you're the high point, it might choose you. Ducking under a rock overhang is dangerous as you form the shortest path between the rock and ground. If you dash below treeline, avoid standing under the only or the tallest tree. If you are caught above treeline, stay away from anything metal you might be carrying. Move down off the ridge slightly to a low, treeless point and squat until the storm passes. If you have an insulating pad, squat on it. Avoid having both your hands and feet touching the ground at once and never lay flat. If you hear a buzzing sound or feel your hair standing on end, move quickly as an electrical charge is building up.

Flash floods. On July 31, 1976, a torrential downpour unleashed by a thunderstorm dumped tons of water into the Big Thompson watershed near Estes Park. Within hours, a wall of water moved down the narrow canyon killing 139 people and causing more than $30 million in property damage. The spooky thing about flash floods, especially in western canyons, is that they can appear out of nowhere from a storm many miles away. While hiking or driving in canyons, keep an eye on the weather. Always climb to safety if danger threatens. Flash floods usually subside quickly, so be patient and don't cross a swollen stream.

Bears. Most of the United States (outside of the Pacific Northwest and parts of the Northern Rockies) does not have a grizzly bear population, although some rumors exist about sightings where there should be none. Black bears are plentiful, however. Here are some tips in case you and a bear scare each other. Most of all, avoid scaring a bear. Watch for bear tracks (five toes) and droppings (sizable with leaves, partly digested berries, seeds, and/or animal fur). Talk or sing where visibility or hearing are limited. Keep a clean camp, hang food, and don't sleep in the clothes you wore while cooking. Be especially careful in spring to avoid getting between a mother and her cubs. In late summer and fall bears are busy eating berries and acorns to fatten up for winter, so be extra careful around berry bushes and oakbrush. If you do encounter a bear, move away slowly while facing the bear, talk softly, and avoid direct eye contact. Give the bear room to escape. Since bears are very curious, it might stand upright to get a better whiff of you, and it may even charge you to try to intimidate you. Try to stay calm. If a bear does attack you, fight back with anything you have handy. Unleashed dogs have been known to come running back to their owners with a bear close behind. Keep your dog on a leash or leave it at home.

Mountain lions. Mountain lions appear to be getting more comfortable around humans as long as deer (their favorite prey) are in an area with adequate cover. Usually elusive and quiet, lions rarely attack people. If you meet a lion, give it a chance to escape. Stay calm and talk firmly to it. Back away slowly while facing the lion. If you run, you'll only encourage the curious cat to chase you. Make yourself look large by opening a jacket, if you have one, or waving your hiking poles. If the lion behaves aggressively, throw stones, sticks, or whatever you can while remaining tall. If a lion does attack, fight for your life with anything you can grab.

Moose. Because moose have very few natural predators, they don't fear humans like other animals. You might find moose in sagebrush and wetter areas of willow, aspen, and pine, or in beaver habitats. Mothers with calves, as well as bulls during mating season, can be particularly aggressive. If a moose threatens you, back away slowly and talk calmly to it. Keep your pets away from moose.

Other considerations. Hunting is a popular sport in the United States, especially during rifle season in October and November. Hiking is still enjoyable in those months in many areas, so just take a few precautions. First, learn when the different hunting seasons start and end in the area in which you'll be hiking. During this time frame, be sure to wear at least a blaze orange hat, and possibly put an orange vest over your pack. Don't be surprised to see hunters in camo outfits carrying bows or muzzleloading rifles around during their season. If you would feel more comfortable without hunters around, hike in national parks and monuments or state and local parks where hunting is not allowed.

Navigation

Whether you are going on a short hike in a familiar area or planning a weeklong backpack trip, you should always be equipped with the proper navigational equipment—at the very least a detailed map and a sturdy compass.

Maps. There are many different types of maps available to help you find your way on the trail. Easiest to find are Forest Service maps and BLM (Bureau of Land Management) maps. These maps tend to cover large areas, so be sure they are detailed enough for your particular trip. You can also obtain National Park maps as well as high-quality maps from private companies and trail groups. These maps can be obtained either from outdoor stores or ranger stations.

U.S. Geological Survey topographic maps are particularly popular with hikers—especially serious backcountry hikers. These maps contain the standard map symbols such as roads, lakes, and rivers, as well as contour lines that show the details of the trail terrain like ridges, valleys, passes, and mountain peaks. The 7.5-minute series (1 inch on the map equals approximately ⅖ mile on the ground) provides the closest inspection available. USGS maps are available by mail (U.S. Geological Survey, Map Distribution Branch, P.O. Box 25286, Denver, CO 80225), or at mapping.usgs.gov/esic/to_order.html.

If you want to check out the high-tech world of maps, you can purchase topographic maps on CD-ROM. These software-mapping programs let you select a route on your computer, print it out, then take it with you on the trail. Some software mapping programs let you insert symbols and labels, download waypoints from a GPS unit, and export the maps to other software programs.

The art of map reading is a skill that you can develop by first practicing in an area you are familiar with. To begin, orient the map so the map is lined up in the correct direction (i.e., north on the map is lined up with true north). Next, familiarize yourself with the map symbols and try to match them up with terrain features around you such as a high ridge, mountain peak, river, or lake. If you are practicing with a USGS map, notice the contour lines. On gentler terrain these contour lines are spaced farther apart, and on steeper terrain they are closer together. Pick a short loop trail, and stop frequently to check your position on the map. As you practice map reading, you'll learn how to anticipate a steep section on the trail or a good place to take a rest break, and so on.

Compasses. First off, the sun is not a substitute for a compass. So, what kind of compass should you have? Here are some characteristics you should look for: a rectangular base with detailed scales, a liquid-filled housing, protective housing, a sighting line on the mirror, luminous alignment and back-bearing arrows, a luminous north-seeking arrow, and a well-defined bezel ring.

You can learn compass basics by reading the detailed instructions included with your compass. If you want to fine-tune your compass skills, sign up for an orienteering class or purchase a book on compass reading. Once you've learned the basic skills of using a compass, remember to practice these skills before you head into the backcountry.

If you are a klutz at using a compass, you may be interested in checking out the technical wizardry of the GPS (Global Positioning System) device. The GPS was developed by the Pentagon and works off twenty-four NAVSTAR satellites, which were designed to guide missiles to their targets. A GPS device is a handheld unit that calculates your latitude and longitude with the easy press of a button. The Department of Defense used to scramble the satellite signals a bit to prevent civilians (and spies!) from getting extremely accurate readings, but that practice was discontinued in May 2000, and GPS units now provide nearly pinpoint accuracy (within 30 to 60 feet).

There are many different types of GPS units available and they range in price from $100 to $400. In general, all GPS units have a display screen and keypad where you input information. In addition to acting as a compass, the unit allows you to plot your route, easily retrace your path, track your travelling speed, find the mileage between waypoints, and calculate the total mileage of your route.

Before you purchase a GPS unit, keep in mind that these devices don't pick up signals indoors, in heavily wooded areas, on mountain peaks, or in deep valleys.

Pedometers. A pedometer is a small, clip-on unit with a digital display that calculates your hiking distance in miles or kilometers based on your walking stride. Some units also calculate the calories you burn and your total hiking time. Pedometers are available at most large outdoor stores and range in price from $20 to $40.

Trip Planning

Planning your hiking adventure begins with letting a friend or relative know your trip itinerary so they can call for help if you don't return at your scheduled time. Your next task is to make sure you are outfitted to experience the risks and rewards of the trail. This section highlights gear and clothing you may want to take with you to get the most out of your hike.

Day Hikes

- camera/film
- compass/GPS unit
- pedometer
- daypack
- first-aid kit
- food
- guidebook
- headlamp/flashlight with extra batteries and bulbs
- hat
- insect repellent
- knife/multipurpose tool
- map
- matches in waterproof container and fire starter
- fleece jacket
- rain gear
- space blanket
- sunglasses
- sunscreen
- swimsuit
- watch
- water
- water bottles/water hydration system

Overnight Trip

- backpack and waterproof rain cover
- backpacker's trowel
- bandanna
- bear repellent spray
- bear bell
- biodegradable soap
- pot scrubber
- collapsible water container (2–3 gallon capacity)
- clothing—extra wool socks, shirt and shorts
- cook set/utensils
- ditty bags to store gear
- extra plastic resealable bags
- gaiters
- garbage bag
- ground cloth
- journal/pen
- nylon rope to hang food
- long underwear
- permit (if required)
- rain jacket and pants
- sandals to wear around camp and to ford streams
- sleeping bag
- waterproof stuff sack
- sleeping pad
- small bath towel
- stove and fuel
- tent
- toiletry items
- water filter
- whistle

Equipment

With the outdoor market currently flooded with products, many of which are pure gimmickry, it seems impossible to both differentiate and choose. Do I really need a tropical-fish-lined collapsible shower? (No, you don't.) The only defense against the maddening quantity of items thrust in your face is to think practically—and to do so before you go shopping. The worst buys are impulsive buys. Since most name brands will differ only slightly in quality, it's best to know what you're looking for in terms of function. Buy only what you need. You will, don't forget, be carrying what you've bought on your back. Here are some things to keep in mind before you go shopping.

Clothes. Clothing is your armor against Mother Nature's little surprises. Hikers should be prepared for any possibility, especially when hiking in mountainous areas. Adequate rain protection and extra layers of clothing are a good idea. In summer, a wide-brimmed hat can help keep the sun at bay. In the winter months the first layer you'll want to wear is a "wicking" layer of long underwear that keeps perspiration away from your skin. Wear long underwear made from synthetic fibers that wick moisture away from the skin and draw it toward the next layer of clothing, where it then evaporates. Avoid wearing long underwear made of cotton as it is slow to dry and keeps moisture next to your skin.

The second layer you'll wear is the "insulating" layer. Aside from keeping you warm, this layer needs to "breathe" so you stay dry while hiking. A fabric that provides insulation and dries quickly is fleece. It's interesting to note that this one-of-a-kind fabric is made out of recycled plastic. Purchasing a zip-up jacket made of this material is highly recommended.

The last line of layering defense is the "shell" layer. You'll need some type of waterproof, windproof, breathable jacket that will fit over all of your other layers. It should have a large hood that fits over a hat. You'll also need a good pair of rain pants made from a similar waterproof, breathable fabric. Some Gore-Tex jackets cost as much as $500, but you should know that there are more affordable fabrics out there that work just as well.

Now that you've learned the basics of layering, you can't forget to protect your hands and face. In cold, windy, or rainy weather you'll need a hat made of wool or fleece and insulated, waterproof gloves that will keep your hands warm and toasty. As mentioned earlier, buying an additional pair of light silk liners to wear under your regular gloves is a good idea.

Footwear. If you have any extra money to spend on your trip, put that money into boots or trail shoes. Poor shoes will bring a hike to a halt faster than anything else. To avoid this annoyance, buy shoes that provide support and are lightweight and flexible. A lightweight hiking boot is better than a heavy, leather mountaineering boot for most day hikes and backpacking. Trail running shoes provide a little extra cushion and are made in a high-top style that many people wear for hiking. These running shoes are lighter, more flexible, and more breathable than hiking boots. If you know you'll be hiking in wet weather often, purchase boots or shoes with a Gore-Tex liner, which will help keep your feet dry.

When buying your boots, be sure to wear the same type of socks you'll be wearing on the trail. If the boots you're buying are for cold weather hiking, try the boots on while wearing two pairs of socks. Speaking of socks, a good cold weather sock combination is to wear a thinner sock made of wool or polypropylene covered by a heavier outer sock made of wool. The inner sock protects the foot from the rubbing effects of the outer sock and prevents blisters. Many outdoor stores have some type of ramp to simulate hiking uphill and downhill. Be sure to take advantage of this test, as toe-jamming boot fronts can be very painful and debilitating on the downhill trek.

Once you've purchased your footwear, be sure to break them in before you hit the trail. New footwear is often stiff and needs to be stretched and molded to your foot.

Hiking poles. Hiking poles help with balance, and more importantly take pressure off your knees. The ones with shock absorbers are easier on your elbows and knees. Some poles even come with a camera attachment to be used as a monopod. And heaven forbid you meet a mountain lion, bear, or unfriendly dog, the poles can make you look a lot bigger.

Backpacks. No matter what type of hiking you do you'll need a pack of some sort to carry the basic trail essentials. There are a variety of backpacks on the market, but let's first discuss what you intend to use it for. Day hikes or overnight trips? If you plan on doing a day hike, a daypack should have some of the following characteristics: a padded hip belt that's at least 2 inches in diameter (avoid packs with only a small nylon piece of webbing for a hip belt); a chest strap (the chest strap helps stabilize the pack against your body); external pockets to carry water and other items that you want easy access to; an internal pocket to hold keys, a knife, a wallet, and other miscellaneous items; an external lashing system to hold a jacket; and a hydration pocket for carrying a hydration system (which consists of a water bladder with an attachable drinking hose).

For short hikes, some hikers like to use a fanny pack to store just a camera, food, a compass, a map, and other trail essentials. Most fanny packs have pockets for two water bottles and a padded hip belt.

If you intend to do an extended, overnight trip, there are multiple considerations. First off, you need to decide what kind of framed pack you want. There are two backpack types for backpacking: the internal frame and the external frame. An internal frame pack rests closer to your body, making it more stable and easier to balance when hiking over rough terrain. An external frame pack is just that, an aluminum frame attached to the exterior of the pack. An external frame pack is better for long backpack trips because it distributes the pack weight better and you can carry heavier loads. It's easier to pack, and your gear is more accessible. It also offers better back ventilation in hot weather.

The most critical measurement for fitting a pack is torso length. The pack needs to rest evenly on your hips without sagging. A good pack will come in two or three sizes and have straps and hip belts that are adjustable according to your body size and characteristics.

When you purchase a backpack, go to an outdoor store with salespeople who are knowledgeable in how to properly fit a pack. Once the pack is fitted for you, load the pack with the amount of weight you plan on taking on the trail. The weight of the pack should be distributed evenly and you should be able to swing your arms and walk briskly without feeling out of balance. Another good technique for evaluating a pack is to walk up and down stairs and make quick turns to the right and to the left to be sure the pack doesn't feel out of balance. Other features that are nice to have on a backpack include a removable day pack or fanny pack, external pockets for extra water, and extra lash points to attach a jacket or other items.

Sleeping bags and pads. Sleeping bags are rated by temperature. You can purchase a bag made of synthetic fiber, or you can buy a goose down bag. Goose down bags are more expensive, but they have a higher insulating capacity by weight and will keep their loft longer. You'll want to purchase a bag with a temperature rating that fits the time of year and conditions you are most likely to camp in. One caveat: The techno-standard for temperature ratings is far from perfect. Ratings vary from manufacturer to manufacturer, so to protect yourself you should purchase a bag rated 10 to 15 degrees below the temperature you expect to be camping in. Synthetic bags are more resistant to water than down bags, but many down bags are now made with a Gore-Tex shell that helps to repel water. Down bags are also more compressible than synthetic bags and take up less room in your pack, which is an important consideration if you are planning a multiday backpack trip. Features to look for in a sleeping bag include a mummy style bag, a hood you can cinch down around your head in cold weather, and draft tubes along the zippers that help keep heat in and drafts out.

You'll also want a sleeping pad to provide insulation and padding from the cold ground. There are different types of sleeping pads available, from the more expensive self-inflating air mattresses to the less expensive closed-cell foam pads. Self-inflating air mattresses are usually heavier than closed-cell foam mattresses and are prone to punctures.

Tents. The tent is your home away from home while on the trail. It provides protection from wind, snow, rain, and insects. A three-season tent is a good choice for backpacking and can range in price from $100 to $500. These lightweight and versatile tents provide protection in all types of weather, except heavy snowstorms or high winds, and range in weight from four to eight pounds. Look for a tent that's easy to set up and will easily fit two people with gear. Dome type tents usually offer more headroom and places to store gear. Other tent designs include a vestibule where you can store wet boots and backpacks. Some nice-to-have items in a tent include interior pockets to store small items and lashing points to hang a clothesline. Most three-season tents also come with stakes so you can secure the tent in high winds. Before you purchase a tent, set it up and take it down a few times to be sure it is easy to handle. Also, sit inside the tent and make sure it has enough room for you and your gear.

Cell phones. Many hikers are carrying their cell phones into the backcountry these days in case of emergency. That's fine and good, but please know that cell phone coverage is often poor to nonexistent in valleys, canyons, and thick forest. More importantly people have started to call for help because they're tired or lost. Let's go back to being prepared. You are responsible for yourself in the backcountry. Use your brain to avoid problems, and if you do encounter one, first use your brain to try to correct the situation. Only use your cell phone, if it works, in true emergencies.

Hiking with Children

Hiking with children isn't a matter of how many miles you can cover or how much elevation gain you make in a day; it's about seeing and experiencing nature through their eyes.

Kids like to explore and have fun. They like to stop and point out bugs and plants, look under rocks, jump in puddles, and throw sticks. If you're taking a toddler or young child on a hike, start with a trail that you're familiar with. Trails that have interesting things for kids, like piles of leaves to play in or a small stream to wade through during the summer, will make the hike much more enjoyable for them and will keep them from getting bored.

You can keep your child's attention if you have a strategy before starting on the trail. Using games is not only an effective way to keep a child's attention, it's also a great way to teach him or her about nature. Play hide and seek, where your child is the mouse and you are the hawk. Quiz children on the names of plants and animals. If your children are old enough, let them carry their own daypack filled with snacks and water. So that you are sure to go at their pace and not yours, let them lead the way. Playing follow the leader works particularly well when you have a group of children. Have each child take a turn at being the leader.

With children, a lot of clothing is key. The only thing predictable about weather is that it will change. Especially in mountainous areas, weather can change dramatically in a very short time. Always bring extra clothing for children, regardless of the season. In the winter, have your children wear wool socks and warm layers such as long underwear, a fleece jacket and hat, wool mittens, and good rain gear. It's not a bad idea to have these along in late fall and early spring as well. Good footwear is also important. A sturdy pair of high-top tennis shoes or lightweight hiking boots are the best bet for little ones. If you're hiking in the summer near a lake or stream, bring along a pair of old sneakers that your child can put on when he wants to go exploring in the water. Remember when you're near any type of water, always watch your child at all times. Also, keep a close eye on teething toddlers who may decide a rock or leaf of poison oak is an interesting item to put in their mouths.

From spring through fall, you'll want your kids to wear a wide-brimmed hat to keep their face, head, and ears protected from the hot sun. Also, make sure your children wear sunscreen at all times. Choose a brand without Paba—children have sensitive skin and may have an allergic reaction to sunscreen that contains Paba. If you are hiking with a child younger than six months, don't use sunscreen or insect repellent. Instead, be sure that their head, face, neck, and ears are protected from the sun with a wide-brimmed hat, and that all other skin exposed to the sun is protected with the appropriate clothing.

Remember that food is fun. Kids like snacks so it's important to bring a lot of munchies for the trail. Stopping often for snack breaks is a fun way to keep the trail interesting. Raisins, apples, granola bars, crackers and cheese, cereal, and trail mix all make great snacks. If your child is old enough to carry her own backpack, fill it with treats before you leave. If your kids don't like drinking water, you can bring boxes of fruit juice.

Avoid poorly designed child-carrying packs—you don't want to break your back carrying your child. Most child-carrying backpacks designed to hold a forty-pound child will contain a large carrying pocket to hold diapers and other items. Some have an optional rain/sun hood.

Hiking with Your Dog

Bringing your furry friend with you is always more fun than leaving him behind. Our canine pals make great trail buddies because they never complain and always make good company. Hiking with your dog can be a rewarding experience, especially if you plan ahead.

Getting your dog in shape. Before you plan outdoor adventures with your dog, make sure he's in shape for the trail. Getting your dog into shape takes the same discipline as getting yourself into shape, but luckily, your dog can get in shape with you. Take your dog with you on your daily runs or walks. If there is a park near your house, hit a tennis ball or play Frisbee with your dog.

Swimming is also an excellent way to get your dog into shape. If there is a lake or river near where you live and your dog likes the water, have him retrieve a tennis ball or stick. Gradually build your dog's stamina up over a two- to three-month period. A good rule of thumb is to assume that your dog will travel twice as far as you will on the trail. If you plan on doing a 5-mile hike, be sure your dog is in shape for a 10-mile hike.

Training your dog for the trail. Before you go on your first hiking adventure with your dog, be sure he has a firm grasp on the basics of canine etiquette and behavior. Make sure he can sit, lie down, stay, and come. One of the most important commands you can teach your canine pal is to "come" under any situation. It's easy for your friend's nose to lead him astray or possibly get lost. Another helpful command is the "get behind" command. When you're on a hiking trail that's narrow, you can have your dog follow behind you when other trail users approach. Nothing is more bothersome than an enthusiastic dog that runs back and forth on the trail and disrupts the peace of the trail for others. When you see other trail users approaching you on the trail, give them the right of way by quietly stepping off the trail and making your dog lie down and stay until they pass.

Equipment. The most critical pieces of equipment you can invest in for your dog are proper identification and a sturdy leash. Flexi-leads work well for hiking because they give your dog more freedom to explore but still leave you in control. Make sure your dog has identification that includes your name and address and a number for your veterinarian. Other forms of identification for your dog include a tattoo or a microchip. You should consult your veterinarian for more information on these last two options.

The next piece of equipment you'll want to consider is a pack for your dog. By no means should you hold all of your dog's essentials in your pack—let him carry his own gear! Dogs that are in good shape can carry 30 to 40 percent of their own weight.

Most packs are fitted by a dog's weight and girth measurement. Companies that make dog packs generally include guidelines to help you pick out the size that's right for your dog. Some characteristics to look for when purchasing a pack for your dog include a harness that contains two padded girth straps, a padded chest strap, leash attachments, removable saddle bags, internal water bladders, and external gear cords.

You can introduce your dog to the pack by first placing the empty pack on his back and letting him wear it around the yard. Keep an eye on him during this first introduction. He may decide to chew through the straps if you aren't watching him closely. Once he learns to treat the pack as an object of fun and not a foreign enemy, fill the pack evenly on both sides with a few ounces of dog food in resealable plastic bags. Have your dog wear his pack on your daily walks for a period of two to three weeks. Each week add a little more weight to the pack until your dog will accept carrying the maximum amount of weight he can carry.

You can also purchase collapsible water and dog food bowls for your dog. These bowls are lightweight and can easily be stashed into your pack or your dog's. If you are hiking on rocky terrain or in the snow, you can purchase footwear for your dog that will protect his feet from cuts and bruises.

Always carry plastic bags to remove feces from the trail. It is a courtesy to other trail users and helps protect local wildlife.

The following is a list of items to bring when you take your dog hiking: collapsible water bowls, a comb, a collar and a leash, dog food, plastic bags for feces, a dog pack, flea/tick powder, paw protection, water, and a first-aid kit that contains eye ointment, tweezers, scissors, stretchy foot wrap, gauze, antibacterial wash, sterile cotton tip applicators, antibiotic ointment, and cotton wrap.

First aid for your dog. Your dog is just as prone—if not more prone—to getting in trouble on the trail as you are, so be prepared. Here's a rundown of the more likely misfortunes that might befall your little friend.

Bees and wasps. If a bee or wasp stings your dog, remove the stinger with a pair of tweezers and place a mudpack or a cloth dipped in cold water over the affected area.

Porcupines. One good reason to keep your dog on a leash is to prevent it from getting a nose full of porcupine quills. You may be able to remove the quills with pliers, but a veterinarian is the best person to do this nasty job because most dogs need to be sedated.

Heat stroke. Avoid hiking with your dog in really hot weather. Dogs with heat stroke will pant excessively, lie down and refuse to get up, and become lethargic and disoriented. If your dog shows any of these signs on the trail, have him lie down in the shade. If you are near a stream, pour cool water over your dog's entire body to help bring his body temperature back to normal.

Heartworm. Dogs get heartworms from mosquitoes which carry the disease in the prime mosquito months of July and August. Giving your dog a monthly pill prescribed by your veterinarian easily prevents this condition.

Plant pitfalls. One of the biggest plant hazards for dogs on the trail are foxtails. Foxtails are pointed grass seed heads that bury themselves in your friend's fur, between his toes, and even get in his ear canal. If left unattended, these nasty seeds can work their way under the skin and cause abscesses and other problems. If you have a long-haired dog, consider trimming the hair between his toes and giving him a summer haircut to help prevent foxtails from attaching to his fur. After every hike, always look over your dog for these seeds—especially between his toes and his ears.

Other plant hazards include burrs, thorns, thistles, and poison oak. If you find any burrs or thistles on your dog, remove them as soon as possible before they become an unmanageable mat. Thorns can pierce a dog's foot and cause a great deal of pain. If you see that your dog is lame, stop and check his feet for thorns. Dogs are immune to poison oak but they can pick up the sticky, oily substance from the plant and transfer it to you.

Protect those paws. Be sure to keep your dog's nails trimmed so he avoids getting soft tissue or joint injuries. If your dog slows and refuses to go on, check to see that his paws aren't torn or worn. You can protect your dog's paws from trail hazards such as sharp gravel, foxtails, lava scree, and thorns by purchasing dog boots.

Sunburn. If your dog has light skin he is an easy target for sunburn on his nose and other exposed skin areas. You can apply a nontoxic sunscreen to exposed skin areas that will help protect him from overexposure to the sun.

Ticks and fleas. Ticks can easily give your dog Lyme disease, as well as other diseases. Before you hit the trail, treat your dog with a flea and tick spray or powder. You can also ask your veterinarian about a once-a-month pour-on treatment that repels fleas and ticks.

Mosquitoes and deer flies. These little flying machines can do a job on your dog's snout and ears. Best bet is to spray your dog with fly repellent for horses to discourage both pests.

Giardia. Dogs can get giardia, which results in diarrhea. It is usually not debilitating, but it's definitely messy. A vaccine against giardia is available.

Mushrooms. Make sure your dog doesn't sample mushrooms along the trail. They could be poisonous to him, but he doesn't know that.

When you are finally ready to hit the trail with your dog, keep in mind that national parks and many wilderness areas do not allow dogs on trails. Your best bet is to hike in national forests, BLM lands, and state parks. Always call ahead to see what the restrictions are.

Appendix A:

Hikes by Interest

Hikes for Backpackers
Stephens State Forest—Woodburn Unit
Yellow River State Forest
Hitchcock Nature Area
Loess Hills Wildlife Management—Sylvan Runkel State Preserve
Clanton Creek Recreation Area
Preparation Canyon State Park

Hikes for Geology Lovers
Backbone State Park
Maquoketa Caves State Park
Mines of Spain State Recreation Area
Palisades Kepler State Park
Starr's Cave Park and Preserve
Geode State Park
Cedar Bluffs State Park
Wildcat Den State Park
Ledges State Park
Hickory Hills Park and Casey's Paha State Preserve
Pilot knob State Park
Loess Hills Landform Parks
Ocheyedan Mound State Preserve
Gitchie Manitou State Preserve

Hikes for River Lovers
Des Moines River Hikes
Rivers Over Bluffs Hikes

Hikes for Bird Lovers
Port Louisa National Wildlife Refuge
Effigy Mounds National Monument
Backbone State Park
Coralville Reservoir—Linder and Squire Points
Lacey-Keosauqua State Park
Shimek State Forest
Neal Smith National Wildlife Refuge

Hayden Prairie
Five-Ridge Prairie
Stone State Park
Loess Hills Wildlife Management Area—Sylvan Runkel State Preserve
Hitchcock Nature Area

Hikes for Plant Lovers
Backbone State Park
Palisades-Kepler State Park
Cedar Bluffs State Natural Area and State Preserve
Ledges State Park
Neal Smith National Wildlife Refuge
Hayden Prairie State Preserve
Pilot Knob State Park
Fossil and Prairie Park
Gitchie Manitou State Preserve

Hikes for Children and Beginning Hikers
Bellevue State Park
Mines of Spain State Park
Maquoketa State Park
Wildcat Den State Park
Starr's Cave Park and Preserve
Lake Ahquabi State Park
Lacey-Keosauqua State Park
Jacob Krumm Prairie
Neal Smith National Wildlife Refuge
Fossil and Prairie Park
Waubonsie State Park

Hikes for Lake Lovers
Lake Ahquabi State Park
Lake of Three Fires State Park
Nine Eagles State Park
Coralville Reservoir—Linder and Squire Points
Geode State Park
Brushy Creek State Recreation Area
Pilot Knob State Park

Hikes for Prairie Lovers
Loess Hills hikes
Neal Smith National Wildlife Refuge

Hayden Prairie State Preserve
Jacob Krumm Prairie
Rock Creek State Park
Fossil and Prairie Park

Hikes for Butterfly Lovers
Neal Smith National Wildlife Refuge
Loess Hills hikes
Hayden Prairie State Preserve

Hikes for Cultural History Buffs
Mines of Spain State Recreation Area
Effigy Mounds National Monument
Maquoketa Caves State Park
Pike's Peak State Park
Backbone State Park
Lacey-Keosauqua State Park
Cedar Bluffs State Natural Area and State Preserve

Appendix B:

Additional Resources

Iowa Department of Natural Resources, *Iowa—Portrait of the Land*

James J. Dinsmore, *A County So Full of Game: The Story of Wildlife in Iowa* (Bur Oak Books Series, University of Iowa Press)

Paul Christiansen and Mark Muller, *An Illustrated Guide to Iowa Prairie Plants* (Bur Oak Books Series, University of Iowa Press)

Jean C. Prior, *Landforms of Iowa* (Bur Oak Books Series, University of Iowa Press)

Greg A. Brick, *Iowa Underground: A Guide to the State's Subterranean Treasures* (Trails Books)

Rebecca Conard, *Places of Quiet Beauty: Parks, Preserves, and Environmentalism* (University of Iowa Press)

Robert Sayre, editor, *Take the Next Exit: New Views of the Iowa Landscape* (Iowa State University Press)

John Madson, *Where the Sky Began: Land of the Tallgrass Prairie* (Houghton Mifflin Company)

Larry Stone and Jon Stravers, *Sylvan T. Runkel, Citizen of the Natural World* (Turkey River Environmental Expressions)

John Madson, *Up on the River: An Upper Mississippi Chronicle* (Nick Lyons Books)

Nate Hoogeveen, *Paddling Iowa* (Trails Books)

Ruth Herzberg and John Pearson, *The Guide to Iowa's State Preserves* (Bur Oaks Books Series, University of Iowa Press)

Wayne I. Anderson, *Iowa's Geological Past: 3 Billion Years of Change* (Bur Oak Books Series, University of Iowa Press)

Carl Kurtz, *Iowa's Wild Places* (Bur Oak Books Series, University of Iowa Press)

Gladys Black, *Iowa Birdlife* (Bur Oak Book Series, University of Iowa Press)

Laura Spess Jackson, Carol A. Thompson, and James J. Dinsmore, *The Iowa Breeding Bird Atlas* (Bur Oak Books Series, University of Iowa Press)

Lynn Marie Alex, *Iowa's Archaeological Past* (Bur Oak Books Series, University of Iowa Press)

Lawrence J. Eilers and Dean M. Roosa, *The Vascular Plants of Iowa: An Annotated Checklist and Natural History* (Bur Oak Books Series, University of Iowa Press)

Gretchen M. Bataille, David M. Gradwohl, and Charles L. P. Silet, editors, *The Worlds between Two Rivers: Perspectives on American Indians in Iowa* (University of Iowa Press)

Paul Garvin, *Iowa's Minerals: Their Occurrence, Origins, Industries, and Lore* (Bur Oak Books Series, University of Iowa Press)

James L. Theler and Robert F. Boszhardt, *Twelve Millennia: Archaeology of the Upper Mississippi River Valley* (Bur Oak Books Series, University of Iowa Press)

Michael J. Lannoo, *Okoboji Wetlands: A Lesson in Natural History* (Bur Oak Books Series, University of Iowa Press)

Claudia McGehee, *A Tallgrass Prairie Alphabet* (Bur Oak Books Series, University of Iowa Press)

James L. Christiansen and Reeve M. Bailey, *The Lizards and Turtles of Iowa* (Nongame Technical Series No. 3; Iowa Department of Natural Resources)

James L. Christiansen and Reeve M. Bailey, *The Snakes of Iowa* (Nongame Technical Series No. 1; Iowa Department of Natural Resources, Des Moines)

James L. Christiansen and Reeve M. Bailey, *The Salamanders and Frogs of Iowa* (Nongame Technical Series No. 3; Iowa Department of Natural Resources, Des Moines)

Stephen J. Dinsmore, Laura S. Jackson, Bruce L. Ehresman, and James J. Dinsmore, *Iowa Wildlife Viewing Guide* (Falcon Press Publishing, Inc.)

J. R. Harlan, E. V. Speaker, and J. Mayhew, *Iowa Fish and Fishing* (Iowa Department of Natural Resources)

Tom C. Cooper, editor, *Iowa's Natural Heritage* (Iowa Natural Heritage Foundation & the Iowa Academy of Science)

American Bike Trails and Iowa Trails Council, *Bicycle Trails of Iowa*

Thomas H. Kent and James J. Dinsmore, *Birds in Iowa* (published by the authors, Iowa City and Ames)

Christyna M. Laubach, John B. Bowles, and René Laubach, *A Guide to the Bats of Iowa* (Nongame Technical Series No. 2; Iowa Department of Natural Resources, Des Moines)

Aldo Leopold, *A Sand County Almanac, with Essays on Conservation from Round River* (Oxford University Press, Inc.)

Sylvan T. Runkel and Dean M. Roosa, *Wildflowers of the Tallgrass Prairie* (Iowa State University Press)

Sylvan T. Runkel and Dean M. Roosa, *Wildflowers and Other Plants of Iowa Wetlands* (Iowa State University Press)

Sylvan T. Runkel and Alvin F. Bull, *Wildflowers of Iowa Woodlands* (Iowa State University Press)

Shirley Shirley, *Restoring the Tallgrass Prairie: An Illustrated Manual for Iowa and the Upper Midwest* (University of Iowa Press)

Larry Stone, *Listen to the Land* (Mid-Prairie Books)

Janette R. Thompson, *Prairies, Forests, and Wetlands: The Restoration of Natural Landscape Communities in Iowa,* (University of Iowa Press)

Peter J. Van der Linden and Donald R. Farrar, *Forest and Shade Trees of Iowa* (Iowa State University Press)

Iowa State University Extension has a published a number of valuable natural history booklets and guides, which you can find at local libraries. Order by calling (515) 294–6222 or visiting www.extension.iastate.edu/pubs/wi.htm.

Index of Place Names